"No one has done more than Raymond
sion of UFO abductions in a scientific
pose of human life, evil and death—in short, the nature and destiny of man."

Dr. Barry H. Downing
Northminster Presbyterian Church
Author of *The Bible and Flying Saucers*

"Raymond Fowler, a veteran and highly respected UFO researcher, has written in *The Watchers II* a book that may well have deciphered the ultimate nature and meaning of the baffling but irresistibly intriguing UFO abduction phenomenon.... In my view, the achievement represented by *The Watchers II* is the unmistakable acme of Fowler's very distinguished career and marks a decisive turning point in the field of UFO studies itself."

Kenneth Ring, Ph.D.
Professor of Psychology, University of Connecticut
Author of *The Omega Project*

"While presenting additional detailed ET encounters from Betty Andreasson Luca, *Watchers II* goes beyond the relatively abundant encounter literature to examine important questions about the nature and meaning of ET visitation.... Well worth reading."

Richard J. Boylan, Ph.D.
Author of *Close Extraterrestrial Encounters*

"Fowler's meticulous exploration into the eerie labyrinth of alleged UFO abductions has led him into the paraphysical realm. He boldly considers the parallels with Near-Death Experiences and searches openly for answers in directions that few researchers have dared to discuss. Fowler's solid investigative background and scholarly review of information adds a credible dimension to this fascinating work. Pulling together details from the Bible, evolutionary theory, time travel, out-of-body experiences and religious events, Fowler presents a thought-provoking and challenging portrait of what may finally be the actual reasons for abductions...."

John S. Carpenter, MSW/LSCW

"*The Watchers II* offers interesting insights into comparative phenomenology. Clearly, our understanding of the true nature and complexity of the universe is in its infancy. This is a glimpse at some of the pieces of the puzzle."

John B. Alexander, Ph.D.
Past-president,
International Association of Near-Death Studies
Santa Fe, New Mexico

Other books by Raymond E. Fowler

UFOs: Interplanetary Visitors
The Andreasson Affair
Casebook of a UFO Investigator
The Melchizedek Connection [A Novel]
The Andreasson Affair, Phase Two
The Allagash Abductions
The Watchers

THE WATCHERS II

Exploring UFOs and the Near-Death Experience

Raymond E. Fowler

Wild Flower Press
P. O. Box 726
Newberg, OR 97132
800-366-0264

Library of Congress Cataloging-in-Publication Data
Fowler, Raymond E. 1933-
The Watchers II: Exploring UFOs and the Near-Death Experience/ Raymond E. Fowler.
p. cm.

Sequel to The Watchers
includes bibliographical refrences (p. 375) and index.
I. Title.
TL789.3.F682 1995
001.9'42---dc20 95-11066
CIP

ISBN 0-926524-30-5 : $18.95
1. Unidentified flying objects--Sightings and encounters.

DESIGN IMPLEMENTATION: Carlene Lynch
COVER DESIGN: Maynard Demmon

Printed in the United States of America

Address all inquiries:
Wild Flower Press
P. O. Box 726
Newberg, OR 97132
U.S.A.

Wild Flower Press has made the commitment to use 100% recycled paper whenever possible.

To Dr. Kenneth Ring for his tireless efforts on behalf of both researchers and lay people to document, scientifically analyze and present evidence for the common reality of the near-death experience.

Acknowledgments

Jerry and Peggy Black, Betty and Bob Luca, Fred Max and Armen Victorian for their direct participation in the preparation of certain segments of *The Watchers II.*

John B. Alexander, Ph.D.; Richard J. Boylan, Ph.D.; John S. Carpenter; Dr. Barry H. Downing and Kenneth Ring, Ph.D. for their review and comments.

Otto Binder; Ann Druffel; Dr. Thomas E. Bullard; Edith Fiore Ph.D.; Linda M. Howe; Raymond Moody, Jr., M.D.; Melvin Morse, M.D.; Paul Perry; Jenny Randels; Maurice Rawlings, M.D.; D. Scott Rogo; Michael B. Sabom, M.D.; Dr. Jacques Vallée and other researchers whose past efforts provided inspiration and material for this book.

Special acknowledgements to Whitley Strieber for his kindness in providing the foreword and to my dear wife Margaret, who continues to lovingly tolerate my addiction to UFO research *for better or for worse!*

Table of Contents

Foreword

The human mind is changing in fundamental ways, and the change is accelerating rapidly. We are beginning to reinvision reality, to see the world in a completely new way. And this change is much, much further along than anybody imagines. Because our established leadership on every level, from the political to the intellectual to the spiritual to communications, denies that it even exists, it has been buried beneath a cover of denial.

The remarkable experience of Ray Fowler and Betty Andreasson Luca is currently one of the most intense defining points of the change of mind. The new mind acknowledges its place in the unknown; it strips away all traces of assumption and expectation and regards the universe with open eyes.

No authorities lead it, no intellectuals interpret it, nobody owns its output or decides what it shall and shall not see. It sees, quite simply, what is there.

Thus this incredible explosion of new ideas, new thoughts, new meanings, new ways of thinking and new logic. If the material that Betty and Ray have created over their fourteen-year association was examined with anything like the loving care and attention that it deserves from the best minds in the world, the amazing depth of what is there would be discovered.

But it is not so examined, and in some ways, perhaps that is best. We can thus look at it and find its value for ourselves, each individually, without regard to "the critics," those awful voices that have been working to deaden mankind's sense of intellectual adventure almost since mind began to inquire.

I have observed over the years as Betty's narrative has developed and matured and become richer and richer. I have followed the trends in the narrative, which are always in the same direction: toward ever richer, ever deeper, ever more provocative questions. I have gloried in the love that spreads through these documents, and seen how it pours out of this woman's kind and faithful heart to dignify every detail of her experiences, and convert it into a human adventure of the highest order.

She has been to far places and we can go too, thanks to Ray's years-long struggle to keep up the chronicle. There is no demand made in these pages that the reader take them as a reflection of some concrete reality. Instead, the fundamentally indeterminate nature of our new view of reality is what sustains both the inner meanings of the chronicle and their exterior sense. This means that the information has literally thousands of different potentials. Potentially, every single reader can take his or her own meaning from it and in no way destroy its inner consistency.

They have, by being so faithful to Betty's vision, thus created one of the first truly metalogical texts, a structure so rich with inner resonance and yet available from so many different intellectual directions that it literally transcends linear meaning.

The collaboration between these two people is a genuine product of higher human consciousness, valid in literally every possible known way and in many ways that have not yet been discovered.

When the time comes that such chronicles can be created by intention and art rather than simply by faith to the inner narrative, perhaps even more potent metalogics will be evolved. But right now, if access to the production of higher mind is what the reader wants, this is among the very best places to go.

Enter the world of Ray and Betty as she has seen it and he has chronicled it. Be faithful to yourself. Blessings on your journey.

—Whitley Strieber
author of *Communion*

Introduction

This book is a sequel to *The Watchers,* which documented the reported UFO experiences of Betty (Andreasson) Luca, her husband Bob Luca and myself.[1]

What about *The Watchers?* Has it been successful since its publication in 1990? What effect has its publication had upon my research? Has anything of note occurred in the UFO research field since then? And, have Betty Andreasson Luca and Bob Luca had UFO experiences since its publication? The answers to these three questions provide the groundwork for and introduction to *The Watchers II: Exploring UFOs and the Near-Death Experience*. Let's address them now.

The Watchers has been successful in spreading the message given Betty by the aliens to many in the United States and abroad. Both the hardcover and paperback went into second editions. Thus far, it has been published in the U.S., Brazil, Germany, Hungary and Japan. Its publication resulted in a torrent of telephone calls and over a thousand letters from readers who shared their own UFO experiences with me.

Most correspondents were persons who exhibited typical benchmarks of the UFO abduction experience. Many, like Betty and Bob, were confronted by the paraphysical (beyond physical) nature of the UFO phenomenon. All were referred to local UFO researchers for possible investigation.

Such contacts provided me with an open window to incredible things happening to credible people all over the world. I was also faced with the paradox that some abductees received spiritual comfort from such unearthly visitations, others were utterly fascinated with them, and still others lived in utter terror of them.

Of the latter, I talked to people who were afraid to go to bed at night. They locked their doors and windows and left the bedroom lights

---

1. Fowler, 1990.

on throughout the night. Some feared for their children, who described the typical alien entity coming into their bedroom at night and floating them out to a craft in the sky. One even reported the untimely, unexplained, coincidental death of their child after such a visitation.

The printing of my name and address in *The Watchers* provided UFO experiencers with someone to whom they dared to relate their experiences. Telephone conversations, letters and one-on-one meetings proved to be a catharsis for the pent-up fears and emotions of many of these people. Some had attempted to relate their experiences to family and friends and were laughed to scorn. Others sought assistance from health professionals and were treated like psychotics. Some shared their encounters with their pastors, who explained the phenomenon as demonic.

In 1991, three major national surveys were taken by the Roper Organization in an attempt to determine how widespread the UFO abduction phenomenon might be. An analysis of the data from these surveys was published in a report by the Bigelow Holding Corporation.[2] It was made available to UFO researchers and sent to nearly 100,000 psychiatrists, psychologists and other mental health professionals. An analysis of the report's findings indicate that 2% of the adults in the American population have had a constellation of experiences consistent with an abduction history.

Included in the report is a commentary directed toward health professionals by John E. Mack, M.D., Professor of Psychiatry at Harvard Medical School. From the data, Dr. Mack concludes that:

> Hundreds of thousands, if not millions, of American men, women and children may have experienced UFO abductions or abduction-related phenomena.[3]

And, on June 13-17, 1992, an extraordinary meeting was held at the Massachusetts Institute of Technology (MIT) in Cambridge, Massachusetts, concerning the UFO abduction phenomenon. The abduction study conference attracted mental health practitioners, UFO investigators and abduction witnesses throughout North America and around the world. In the meantime, a number of significant things were taking place in the lives of Betty and Bob Luca and myself.

Upon the conclusion of the editing process for *The Watchers,* I immediately launched into an investigation of four highly credible persons who all shared the same conscious close encounter with a UFO

---

2. Hopkins, 1992.
3. Hopkins, 1992, p. 7.

during a camping and canoe trip along the Allagash Waterway in northern Maine.[4] All four witnesses experienced missing time and relived a detailed and complementary UFO abduction experience under hypnosis. Two of the abductees are identical twins and all four are artists who were able to draw many details of their abduction experience. My investigation revealed that each of the witnesses reported the typical benchmarks characteristic of other abductees, including physical examinations, sperm extraction, scars and earlier abductions as children.

I felt some sense of relief to get away from the seemingly aberrant aspects of the events that I had investigated and recorded for *The Watchers* during my investigation of Betty and Bob Luca. Instead, I found this latest case to be a straight-forward, highly significant textbook example of the *typical* UFO abduction scenario. I didn't have to deal with such atypical, mind-blowing experiences as confronting a Phoenix, a theophany, visits to other-worldly places, OBE-abductions and interrelationships with robed beings that looked more like reported angels than extraterrestrial entities!

It would have been easy for me to have ignored and not have reported on these things that did not fit the typical model that researchers have constructed of the UFO abduction experience. I am hearing that this is being done by UFO researchers who find these aspects reported by abductees too incredulous to believe.

Betty equates her abduction experiences with the Judeo-Christian tradition. She believes that her abductors love humankind and their intervention is for our own good. She also believes that there are entities who do not have all of humanity in their best interests. Why does she believe this? Because, as we have read in my books, the entities told her so. It was part of their message to people of Earth.

The religious, philosophical, spiritual and paraphysical facets of the abduction phenomenon are not being taken seriously by many UFO researchers. In their opinions, they do not fit the model and are arbitrarily rejected.

For example, let us listen in for a moment on a conversation that took place between major UFO researchers Budd Hopkins, Richard Hall and John Carpenter during a workshop at the UFO Abduction Study Conference held at MIT.[5] From time to time, I will interject my thoughts in brackets as if I were there at MIT commenting upon them.

---

4. Fowler, 1993.
5. Whiting, 1994.

Hopkins: One of the aspects of the conference which suggested a bit of [a] problem to me is there seems to be the tendency from time to time to slip into discussions of the nature of the aliens, quote, unquote, whatever they may be, as to whether they are helping us or pretty much—

Hall: The good guys versus bad guys?

Hopkins: The good guys versus the bad guys. And, of course, I think essentially that gets into almost a kind of *theological* argument. And I think we must concentrate our attention on what is happening to human beings and help them explore their own personal experiences, because I think if you start dealing with whether…these are enemies, these are friends, whatever, you're providing yourself with some kind of paranoia or rationalizations that you can see a certain kind of a denial. We've got to get people away from those judgments.

Fowler: [What you say, Budd, may be right in some or even all cases, but how do we know? Perhaps some data are not attributable to paranoia, rationalizations or denial on the abductees' part. Indeed, perhaps it is we ourselves who are doing the rationalization and denial of these aspects of their experiences because they do not fit our *rational* model of the UFO abduction experience.]

Hall: What happens when it's the experiencers who make that judgment? We see that happening.

Fowler: [Yes, Richard, we do see that happening. Have we the right to totally ignore their judgments? After all, it is they twho have had the experiences, not the investigator. What happens? It is incumbent upon us to devise models that incorporate all data no matter how strange or seemingly *atypical* that data might be.]

Hopkins: I think that one of the problems is that the investigator and/or a therapist, whoever's involved, can have an undue influence in that area. I think we've seen examples at the conference. I have—of a certain kind of theological line being played out by a therapist or investigator or whatnot which I think is not. In other words, it's almost as if we're trying to decide the nature and moral qualities of the germs without trying to figure out what the disease is.

Hall: That's the way the experiencers, certain ones, seem to be taking it. To them it's beginning to be a profound philosophical, religious issue. So they are introducing it.

Fowler: [Indeed they are so in my estimation, it is also imperative to concurrently attempt to decide the nature and moral qualities of the so-called germs so that we have a better grasp of who we are trying to deal with and how we should react to them. Perhaps there are reasons why abductees feel this way. Perhaps they are supposed to be introducing such issues. We do not know, but we certainly are not going to find out unless we pay attention to this side of the abduction experience.]

Carpenter: Perhaps that's their method of their coping with it. They choose that and it works for them and it doesn't hurt them or anybody else. It's OK.

Fowler: [This may be partly or entirely true. But, because we do not know this, we need to consider the possibility that it's more than psychological in nature.]

Based upon the above discussions, certain segments of the UFO and paranormal experiences reported by Betty and her husband would be ignored, patronized or rejected out of hand. When I was working on *The Watchers,* one of my close peers contemptuously remarked that "We didn't need any other *Andreasson Affairs."* Another researcher, Dr. David Jacobs, writes in his latest book that Betty's experiences are "so bizarre that UFO researchers were at a loss to separate reality from fantasy." [6]

Well, David, and others of like ilk, hold on to your mental hats, for here we go again. As I write these very words, a phase four enquiry into the seemingly never-ending story of *The Andreasson Affair* is nearing its end.

The material for this book began to be collected shortly after I finished my manuscript for *The Allagash Abductions.* The proverb that there is no rest for the wicked equally applies to UFO researchers, especially when one is involved with Betty and Bob Luca.

The experiences of the Lucas continue to manifest the ultra-high strangeness end of the abduction experience spectrum. Their accounts, coupled with those of others, provide paradigms for study and evaluation as we come to grips with the paraphysical reality of UFOs and their incredulous implications. Nothing retrieved during the many hypnosis sessions with Betty (regardless of their high strangeness) shall be left out of this book.

---

6. Jacobs, 1992, p. 42.

Also, I am in the midst of preparing yet another book. It will deal not only with Betty and Bob Luca, but with other members of their family. Again, I will open the doors of my own family closet to reveal some things that not even I knew of until *The Watchers* was published.

As in *The Watchers,* I will strictly follow a "what-if" line of reasoning in *The Watchers II.* If the following accounts are taken at full face value, the implications are mind-boggling. Such data, if reflecting reality, will demonstrate that the paraphysical nature of the UFO phenomenon is directly tied to humankind's real nature and destiny. What seems to be hiding behind the paraphysical nature of the UFO phenomenon and its consequences for us is beyond one's wildest imagination.

Prologue

Prior to launching into the high-strangeness accounts and speculations recorded in this book, I will dwell briefly upon the growing awareness of the UFO abduction phenomenon by both UFO researchers and the public at large and then comment upon its ramifications. Thus, this prologue, in effect, is my way of conditioning the reader for what one might dub the "Twilight Zone" component of ufology!

Today, abduction accounts are no longer relegated to the headlines of tabloids. In the past several years, serious treatment of them has been given in major newspapers and journals including the *Washington Post Magazine,*[1] the *Wall Street Journal,*[2] the *Harvard Magazine,*[3] the *Atlantic Monthly,*[4] and the *Boston Globe Magazine,*[5] to name just several examples. Steven Spielberg's *Close Encounters of the Third Kind* has been followed by a number of movies and TV documentaries on this aspect of the UFO phenomenon. The typical abduction scenario is now even creeping into the plots of TV sitcoms and major TV commercials.

The people that I have investigated and communicated with appear to be just a small fraction of those who have knowingly or unknowingly had an abduction experience. Studies relating to hundreds of reported abduction experiences indicate that this phenomenon probably has been going on under the noses of UFO researchers for decades, perhaps for centuries, prior to the advent of modern UFO research.

In fact, I was privileged to hear Barney and Betty Hill tell of their close encounter with a UFO and of Betty's dreams of an abduction. This took place long before they were investigated and their story made public. I listened politely and honestly and wondered how these two apparently sincere people could lie with such straight faces.

---

1. January 3, 1988, pp. 12-19.
2. May 14, 1992, p. A1.
3. March-April, 1992, p. 6.
4. August 1991, pp. 82-92.
5. October 11, 1992, pp. 20-27.

Looking back in retrospect, it should have been clear from the start that these objects seen maneuvering in the sky would have been piloted or controlled by intelligent entities. Thus, seeing entities in relation to objects seen close at hand should have been expected.

It also should have been obvious that in addition to an alien interest in earth's advancing technology, prime interest would be in the harvesting and examination of earth's life forms, including human beings.

Our past, and indeed present, blindness to such things can in part be attributed to our egocentricity and geocentricity. We consider ourselves as the dominant species on the only world we know. We routinely eat, control and study lower life forms. If we wanted to study a woodchuck, we simply would pump a little gas down its hole, lift it out, study it and place it back. When it woke up, it would remember little or nothing of what had occurred.

In the light of our deeply ingrained self-centeredness, how could we even begin to conceive of unearthly super-intelligent entities that are able to periodically and instantaneously at will pluck human beings out of a car, field or building with a beam of light, study them, experiment on them and place them back exactly as they had been found with little or no memory of what occurred?

It would be even harder to conceive of entities with the ability to do the same thing on an apparent *non-physical* level. Some abductees report being abducted via an out-of-body experience into another dimension that looks and feels just as physical as the reality we know on an every day basis! These things are reportedly happening not only to just a few, but also to perhaps thousands of usually unsuspecting people.

Such experiences, for the most part, have been and still are imperceptible to the general populace who, like the persons in Hans Christian Andersen's story about the emperor who wore no clothes, have been programmed by society not to perceive them. Let me illustrate.

Not far from my home, the Federal Aviation Administration (FAA) operates a huge radar control center. Radar operators peer at their screens around the clock guiding hundreds of aircraft from around the country and the world to safe landings at Logan International Airport in Boston, MA.

In addition to these aircraft, hundreds of other aircraft fly about the sky almost totally ignored by the radar operators. Why? Because only those equipped with transmitters called transponders are of interest, unless there is an imminent danger of collision with aircraft that they are controlling.

Society has equipped us with the transponders of social acceptance. Taboos do not only exist within primitive cultures. We who live in technological cultures are subject to them as well. Scientists create models of reality, the models soon are treated as reality, and we are told what can be and what can not be based upon a model.

Theologians, psychologists and philosophers also build models of reality. The models soon become dogma and we are told what can be and what cannot be.

Reports of UFOs (Unidentified Flying Objects), OBEs (out-of-body experiences), NDEs (near-death experiences), ghosts and a host of other "paranormal phenomena" do not fit these models. So, the reported experiences, like aircraft without transponders, are not being perceived as being part of reality.

People's preconceived models have seemingly tamed reality by exclusion of things beyond their ken. But if history has shown us anything, it is that such models have had to be rebuilt or expanded time and time again, as we discover more and more about ourselves and the universe we live in. Reality is far from tame!

Over the last several decades, a number of scientists, philosophers and even some theologians have begun to peek over and expand the artificial fences they have built to keep out nasty things that don't conform to the status quo.

Studies of the paranormal have moved from the grassroots of occultism to the study halls of universities. For a time parapsychology was recognized as a legitimate branch of science by the prestigious American Association for the Advancement of Science (AAAS) until conservative elements once again eliminated it.

Some medical doctors now conduct serious studies of the NDE and the related OBE. Their studies have been published in a number of books and journals. Hospitals now provide support groups for those who have had these experiences and find it hard to cope with them.

UFO sightings, of course, have been the matter of military and civilian studies for years. But the UFO abduction phenomenon is now in the process of finally being recognized and studied by both UFO researchers and health professionals.

A landmark comparative analytical study of UFO-abduction reports was conducted by Dr. Thomas E. Bullard and published in 1988.[6] It was commissioned by the Fund For UFO Research.[7] The 642-page, two-volume study catalogs, summarizes and then analyzes the se-

6. Bullard, 1987.
7. P.O. Box 277, Mount Rainier, MD 20712.

quence of events in over 300 abduction reports. In summary, Dr. Bullard writes that the reports show a great number of similarities, both major and minor—too many, in fact, for them all to be hoaxes or random fantasies.

Thus, the awareness factor of the UFO abduction and other paranormal phenomena is on the increase. Eventually, such phenomena may well become part and parcel of humankind's model of reality. However, history has shown us that such leaps of new knowledge and understanding of humanity and the universe did not take place overnight. The Copernican revolution and the Age of Enlightenment were painful processes. It took generations for humans to let go of scientific theories and theological dogma that had been held for centuries. New models of reality had to be constructed that would accommodate these radical new discoveries.

We who take their accomplishments for granted today may now be faced with a quantum leap of knowledge relating to the nature of humanity and the universe. Study of the UFO phenomenon may be the conditioning process that leads us to this end. The writing of this book and its contents are part of this process.

Like the proverbial donkey being led by a carrot, it would appear that those on the cutting edge of ufology, whether researcher, abductee or both, have been and will be the first to bear the brunt of the revolutionary changes that lie ahead. One can only wonder how these changes will impact not only our culture, but the cultures of the world.

For many of us who are deeply involved in UFO abduction research, the contemplation of losing our once sure grip on reality has resulted in a deeply emotional response akin to that of the grieving process over a lost loved one. What you are about to read may have the same effect on you.

If so, I am sorry. Remember that contemplation and firm belief in something are two distinct frames of mind. I cannot prove the reality of the experiences that you are about to read about or the inconceivable conclusion that results from their study. It is up to you to consider and perhaps correlate them in light of your own world view and belief system.

Again, I must repeat my disclaimer that this book, like its predecessor *The Watchers,* is based upon a "what if" proposition. *The Watchers II* may deal with experiences and a conclusion that many will believe incredulous. But, it is my conviction that the *paraphysical* component of the UFO abduction experience must be responsibly investigated, recorded and studied. It may not only prove to be a legitimate constituent of such experiences, it may be its very quintessence.

PART I

Paraphysical Paradigms

"The physical reality of UFOs remained a very problematical matter, which was not decided one way or the other with the necessary clarity, despite the mass of observational material that had accumulated. The longer the uncertainty lasted, the greater became the probability that this obviously complicated phenomenon had an important psychic component as well as a positive physical basis."

Dr. Carl G. Jung
Flying Saucers *(1959)*

chapter one

ET Primer

We go into this big theater.... Once we go there, we won't be the same. We will be changed. Our energies will be vibrating at a higher level.... Everybody's holding hands.... I feel tremendous joy.[1]

Linda (an abductee)

After the phase three investigation of Betty Andreasson Luca and the subsequent publication of *The Watchers,* I knew that there was much left undone. During my earlier investigations, we had explored Bob Luca's childhood UFO encounter at age five in 1944 and an adult UFO abduction experience at age 29 in 1967. However, during the phase three investigation, Bob had continually refused to be hypnotized. Reliving his 1967 adult abduction experience had been terrifying for him.

I was disappointed and felt that this forgotten memory might be of great importance to the overall database that was being collected on this fascinating case. There were other reasons that Bob's subconscious memories were of interest to me. During the phase four investigation, Betty had relived a shared OBE abduction with Bob in great detail. Bob could only remember what had happened just prior to when Betty said the shared OBE took place. Thus, he had no conscious recollection of what Betty had relived under hypnosis. I felt that it would be of great value to probe Bob's side of this fascinating abduction. In addition, there were still other areas in Betty's life to be explored.

Frustrated, I actually believed that the phase three inquiry marked the culmination of my then fourteen-year involvement with the Andreasson affair. As mentioned, my attention then turned to a new UFO abduction investigation which lasted several years. It resulted in a ten-

1. Fiore, 1989, p. 101.

volume, 702-page report which became the basis for my last book, *The Allagash Abductions*.[2]

During this period, I kept close contact with the Lucas and carefully made note of anything unusual that occurred in their lives. After my completion of the report and book manuscript on the Allagash UFO abduction, I again turned my attention to the Lucas in the hopes of persuading them to begin a new series of hypnotic regression sessions.

On the one hand, the weird paraphysical aspect of their experiences was a source of deep consternation to me. It had been a relief to put *The Watchers* behind me and work on the Allagash case, which fit the norm for abduction cases. But I also felt that the paraphysical elements of the UFO abduction experience were largely being ignored by my peers and that I ought to devote more attention to them myself.

In the last analysis, I decided that I could not terminate my long association with the Lucas. The data collected over the years and the possibility of new discoveries was too much for me to neglect. I had to make another attempt to initiate a phase four investigation.

In the fall of 1992, Bob finally agreed to undergo hypnosis. But each time that a session was scheduled, he always had a reason to cancel. Finally, late in the year, Bob came to behavioral psychologist Fred Max for the first of several phase four hypnotic regression sessions.

During these sessions, we again probed his 1967 encounter for possible new information. Bob's reliving of this abduction again revealed nothing new. After this, it was decided to probe Bob's mind chronologically. We started with his shared OBE abduction with Betty in October 1978 from their home at Meriden, Connecticut. Betty's relived account of this abduction was recorded in *The Watchers*. Now, finally, I hoped to obtain Bob's account of what had occurred from his personal vantage point for correlation with Betty's account.

The scene now opens in the office of Fred Max on November 21, 1992, as he places Bob under the final stages of hypnosis.[3]

OBE Abduction

October 1978

Fred: *[slowly, with pauses]* Very relaxed. As though you have been physically active for a period of time. And now it's time to

---

2. Fowler, 1993.
3. These hypnotic sessions have been edited for clear readability while still retaining essential content.—Ed.

allow yourself to take the wonderful trip inside where everything else is out—out in the distance, so far out that you're primarily aware that you are relaxed—deeply relaxed, deeply relaxed. You feel a rubbery feeling with your body as though you and the chair were one. You're very aware of feeling relaxed, so very relaxed. I want you to imagine 1978. Allow yourself to very gently settle in to 1978 in Meriden, Connecticut, and you hear a loud whirring over your bedroom. I want you to imagine that you have the ability to see this as close or as far as you like. You have the ability to be as involved as you like. Imagine having you there in 1978 in Meriden where you hear a loud whirring over your bedroom. What's happening Bob?

Bob: I'm on the edge of the bed, and Betty's over there in the bathroom brushing her teeth. *[sighs]* There's this noise over the house, and it's strange. I go on over to the door, to the bathroom where Betty is, and I put my hands up on the door sides—oh! *[pause]* Wow, I'm going up into something! A blur of...colors and fog and mist. *[breathing heavily]* And, ah, Betty is, Betty is taken off to my left. She's pulled away from me. She's kinda floating away up to my left and it's strange here. Wow, it's like there's no color.... She's faded. OK, OK, we stop. *[breathing heavily]* We're inside of something big here.... It's a white floor—this thing is big! You can look down from where I am—like on a rail—and you can look down there, and there's some of the gray beings. Oh, no! They got some people on tables there—girls. Oh, geez! They got the girls down there. *[almost crying]*

As related in *The Watchers,* Betty had been shocked to see some small gray aliens working with three members of the family. They were lying on tables far below the railed circular balcony that Bob was now was standing on. Fred suddenly interjected a question about these family members to see what Bob's reaction would be. Betty and Bob want their family members' names to remain confidential, so they have been changed.

Fred: What girls?

Bob: They got Brenda, Alice and Christy!

Fred: OK, relax.

Bob: And they're working—they're doing something to them. It looks like they're—

Fred: Are they awake?

Bob: I don't think so; they're lying very still. *[Bob is very upset about what he sees.]* ...They're down on the lower deck and they're just lying there. They don't seem to be too much affected.... One of...the greys right by Alice is.... He's holding up.... Looks like a little instrument.... I don't know, maybe like a forceps or something. And he's looking at something that looks like...a transparent, grayish-white, maybe...like a postage stamp size? It's...it's hard to tell here.... I don't know what the thing is; he's just looking at it. And...he puts it on her forehead.

Fred: OK. Remember, they're OK today. You're going back and seeing this, but they're OK today.

Bob: Oh shit, I can't help them!

Fred: I understand that, but remember, they end up OK. Keep that in your mind as you go through this. The girls are all right. How tall...are the ones near Alice?

Bob: They're...little guys. They're...gray guys.... From this angle, I don't know, because they're.... *[breathing heavily]* Awww, the people come out from my right and behind me and they take me over to the other side there—on the other side of the railing. And, ah, God! They...look something like us.

Bob, still in a state of shock, suddenly realized the presence of tall human-like beings that appeared from behind him.

Bob: They're tall people with.... *[sighs]* Gee! Really funny. Smooth complexion and maybe a foot taller than me. *[sniffs]*

Fred: How many of them are there?

Bob: There's two. There's one on each side of me.

Fred: What are they wearing?

Bob: ...It's just a white, long, *[sighs]* long thing. It's a white...gown, kinda, and it's pure, it's pure white and...it fits loose and it's.... I don't see any zippers or buttons or anything. And they.... Wow! They—on the other side in there—there's one on either side of me, and there's stuff on the other side.

Fred: What stuff?

Bob: It's, it's weird! *[sounds terrified]*

One can best appreciate what Bob was seeing by reading Betty's detailed and illustrated account of this very scene in *The Watchers*. Briefly, Betty witnessed herself being greeted by human-shaped beings of light who then touched hands and joined a circle. They seemed to be playing a fantastic game. They were alternately squatting and leaping. Each held different shapes of colored lights in their hands, which they playfully flung and bounced. Betty had also observed a cylindrical tower of whirling energy. It was encircled by bars of light. A single bar of light was held by one of the glowing entities.

As she watched the scene while under hypnosis, she recognized herself as one of the performing light beings. She also witnessed the light beings lean on a straplike device affixed to the edge of a counter-clockwise rotating wheel. When they did this, they instantly changed into a ball of light, rolled off the strap and changed into a light being once again.

The following description from Bob's vantage point complements Betty's equally vivid account of what she had seen during their shared OBE abduction.

Bob: Holy Jesus! This stuff is flying around. *[breathing heavily]* I, I don't know; it's like some white objects and some, like a dark pyramid—there's all kinds of activity on the other side there. And it's like people, but they're not people.... Wow! They're flying around and they're doing....

Fred: What's flying around—people?

Bob: Yeah, it's.... Oh, God! It reminds me of—oh, it was this old comic—the human torch? These guys, these people, look like that. They're doing...wow. They're having a heck of a time over there. It must be some kind of game or entertainment. *[Bob's voice is extremely excited.]* And there's a tower with...wow, look at the colors! Wow, they're vivid! Hey, this place is fun. This is unbelievable. Look at that stuff! Wow! It's, looks like...little stars floating around. I mean they're—some of them are going fast, some of them are doing loops...oh God, you can't keep up with them. *[breathing heavily]* Hey, this place isn't bad. Look at all the activity! Wow. There's...the people.... The light people are engaged in...I don't know, a game? ...Some of them can roll up.... Look at that, look at that! They're rolling right up into a *ball,* like a ball of light. Wow! God, this is—wow!

Bob was literally jumping with excitement. He could barely get his words out to describe the fantastic sight. Suddenly, he stopped. Something new had attracted his attention.

Bob: And, now.... *[garbled voice]* A door opens up in back. Over to the right. And it's...kind of an arched door and.... Gee, I didn't even see that before. *[The door was not visible until it opened.]* And we're going in here.

Fred: Where do they take you?

Bob: In, through this door. And, there's another room here. And...wow, it's clean and it's light. It's a lot of...light here. Geez, there's no lights again. There's never any lights. *[The room is bright, but Bob cannot see the source of the light.]* And it's light. *[sighs]* And...they're telling me to sit down. "OK, OK, OK." *[Bob is talking to the aliens.]* ...And to relax. Yeah, I'm relaxed.

As Bob sat down and waited, one of the tall human-like robed beings conversed with him telepathically. He explained to Bob what was going on and why he wasn't with Betty.

Bob: And, you know, those people out there...the light people.... I don't understand. They're being taught, being taught something. They're...growing; they're advancing their knowledge on another plane.... Yeah, OK, Betty was over there.... Betty was over there. And, they.... *[laughs]* OK. And...I wasn't over there because I still have to advance and grow some. Yeah, I just...I know. It's no secret. *[Bob is responding to what is being told him by the tall beings and was admitting his shortcomings to them.]*

Fred: What do you have to learn?

Bob: Well, you see Betty. *[laughs]* Betty. *[laughs and repeats what the tall beings told him about himself]* OK...I can get where Betty is, but...I've got a lot of studying to do. I need to advance spiritually because, well...I'm a little bit too caught up...in the world, and, I need to give myself over more spiritually to the.... Do you remember Betty a long time ago that they were measuring her for light? *[Bob is referring to Betty's abduction and examination by aliens from her former home at South Ashburnham, Massachusetts in 1967.]*

Fred: Yeah.

Bob: That's what they're talking about. It's not light-light, it's spirit. *[sighs]* Ohhh, I've got to relax a little bit.

Bob was overly excited now. He tried to gain his composure so that he could continue to tell Fred what the tall beings were telling him about himself and his relationship with Betty.

Bob: I'll advance, but I will do it at a slower rate. I need to be wise to the ways of the world. *[pause]* There are people in the

> world...that would do harm to Betty...not necessarily physical harm, but I'm there to block that because I...know people and I know worldly ways. And I see things. I see things in people—in people's personalities.... And, in their mannerisms. So...I'm a protector. I'm not only her husband, I'm her protector. *[pause]* That's why she's over there, and I'm over here. Oh...I'm relaxed. I have nothing to fear from them. I've nothing to fear from them at all. I am relaxed. *[deep sigh]*

Abruptly, Bob found himself back on Earth in their home in Meriden, Connecticut, at the bathroom door. It was at the very point that he had joined Betty in an OBE after hearing a whirring noise. Apparently, the tall beings had placed Bob into a state of deep relaxation and sent him back home with Betty at this juncture.

Bob: OK...I'm in the [bathroom doorway] and Betty's scrubbing her teeth. Whew, that was a kind of a strange [whirring sound] noise.

Fred: What was?

Bob: Over the bedroom there. Just kind of a whirring noise there for a minute. Kind of strange....

Just as soon as Bob reentered his physical body, all memory of the OBE and abduction dissipated from his conscious mind. All he could remember was the whirring sound. Typically, as with other abduction reports, Bob's return was a *mirror image* of his procurement by the aliens.

There were other things of interest that Betty had reported during this same experience which needed to be covered from Bob's vantage point. Also, the aliens had actually conversed with Bob. It was important to retrieve as much as we could of their conversation. So, Fred brought Bob back to the huge circular room once again.

Fred: Go back there a minute. Go back where you were with two tall beings beside you. OK? Back where you were. You have the two tall beings beside you.

Bob: *[sighs]* Yeah, all that stuff going on over there.

Fred: Right. How big is this ship? Trailer-truck size?

Bob: Oh, no-o-o. It's.... *[laughs]* It's like a football field. This is big. This is big. Betty's way over there...where those...things [beings] are.... This is a big, big place.

Fred: Right. Are you talking to anyone?

Bob: Myself now, I guess.

Fred: Are you free to ask them questions?

Bob: I guess I could.

Fred: OK.

Bob: But, but I don't.

Fred: OK.

Bob: It's just so—it's amazing what's going on here.... I can't believe this—that I'm seeing it. It's just amazing.

Fred: How did you get there?

Bob: I came up through...that mist and stuff with Betty and then when we got almost there...she went off to the left and just kinda floated away, and I came over this way and, all of a sudden, pow! I'm on...this white, white floor.... It looks like just white—pure, pure white marble.... It's spotless.

Fred: What's Betty doing there?

Bob: *[pause]* I don't know where Betty is right now.

Fred: OK, you did see her up there—right?

Bob: The...white, tall people in the room where I was sitting down told me that Betty was with the...*light people* on the other side.

Fred: What's happening?

Bob: She was gaining knowledge and growing. That was the purpose of what I thought was entertainment or a game. It is not; there are things being taught. The symbols, the symbols have meaning. The...way in which the game is played has meaning. It is knowledge. It is wisdom...a learning process. *[pause]* I think, I'm thinking to myself, Betty was taken to join in this and it's almost like I was here to observe, I guess. I am not as advanced to be over there with those people.

Fred: Are these beings astral in nature? ...Are they [physical] bodies or are they bodies that are projected there?

Bob: *[pause]* I don't know. They look like ghosts.

Fred: Do you mean that you could somewhat see through them?

Bob: A little bit, but interestingly, they are not white or gray like we picture ghosts. They're almost golden in color....

Fred: Is their body language friendly toward you?

Bob: One seems to be...but pretty much...*[laughs]* they ignore me.... This is a privilege, you know, for someone that hasn't advanced this much to be here. To be here and observe this is a privilege.... Not normally people that are at my stage of development would [be here].

Fred: How do you know that?

Bob: Because the two big guys told me.

Fred: Do they tell you together or separately?

Bob: *[pause]* It's hard to tell, they're almost like...what one thinks the other one thinks at the same time. I'm not sure of who says what. I don't think they're talking. I think...it's just thought. I'm...not sure.

Fred: What *form* is Betty in? Is she a light form or a solid form?

Bob: No. He said that...she was over there, that she was one of those people. One of those ghosts or...light people.

Fred: Light people. Did you ask this or was it offered?

Bob: No. They told me when they were explaining to me.... They told me that I'm not that advanced. I, I hope it's not a put-down. But...that's why I'm over here, and she's over there. *[pause]* You know...at first, I was real nervous there, and it's [now] so comfortable and relaxing. I, I didn't have anything to be afraid of. There's nothing at all to be afraid of. We're going to see them again. The tall white...people.

Fred: Does Betty know where you are?

Bob: She can't see me in here.... From where those light people are, they can't see behind the door. They could see me before...we came in here.

One wondered what Betty and Bob's physical bodies were doing back on earth in their home at Meriden, Connecticut. Were they just standing there at the bathroom door? Were they carrying on life and activities separate from what their other bodies were experiencing in the alien craft? Fred addressed this question to Bob. His answer was incredible.

Fred: If I were to [at this moment] now...that you're both up there, go into your...home—in Meriden—could I find you there?

Bob: You would find two shells frozen in time.

Fred: And if I were to shake them?

Bob: Oh, that's how.... Time? There is no meaning to time for them.... There is almost no time passing where the bodies are. This happens very quickly. While we're up here, it seems like a long time, but it's nothing...at the house. It's almost nothing. I didn't understand that.... Time is nothing.

There's no time up here. There is no time! And nothing changes....

Fred: Do they age?

Bob: No, they have been the same for years and years and years, they said—beyond my understanding.

Fred: Now, when you see Betty there—

Bob: Our years—what I call years—they have not changed.

Bob's answer tallied with what the entities had told Betty on previous occasions: "Time with us is not your time. The place with you is localized. It is not with us." Betty had explained to us in 1967 that "Time to them is not like our time, but they know about our time," and that they could reverse time. Interestingly enough, the theories being expounded by the "New Physics" indicate that "The flow of time...is an illusion."[4]

It would appear that Betty and Bob and probably other abductees have been undergoing a subliminal training process. This immediately raises some very interesting questions. When do these schooling sessions occur? Where do they take place? And, most importantly, *why* are they taking place? The answers to these intriguing questions will be addressed later. Suffice it to say that they are intimately connected with the paraphysical reality of UFOs and humankind, including humanity's origin and ultimate nature.

Little did we know that this initial philosophical discourse from an ET Primer was just a harbinger of the profound things taught to Bob by the alien entities. However, I have reserved that portion of Bob's experience for later on in the book, where it will be directly applicable to the subject matter under discussion at that time. Suffice it to say for now that Bob was willing to cooperate with us. There were a number of other curious things that had happened to him that cried for attention, and which will be the subject of the next chapter.

---

4. Davies, 1980, p. 185.

chapter two

The Rest of the Story

That completes Bob's account of the abduction at Trap Rock. Hopefully he will someday again consent to hypnosis. I feel that there is much more information waiting to be tapped from Bob's subconscious memory.[1]

Ray Fowler (1980)

During the rest of Bob's hypnosis sessions, a number of significant revelations were extracted. First, Bob had on a number of occasions encountered aliens in their various homes in Connecticut. Just after Bob and Betty married, they lived in Meriden between August 1978 and August 1979. They then moved to Cheshire and remained there between September 1979 and July 1985. From there they moved to Higganum. Other than a number of winter month stays in Florida, they still reside in Higganum.

I mention the above dates and places because, for the most part, Bob could not remember the exact dates when the following encounters took place. The above references will at least give the reader an approximate idea where and when they occurred.

Bob's encounters, for the most part, were linked to alien house calls that centered upon Betty rather than himself. Nevertheless, we did discover that Bob himself had experienced another abduction while he and Betty were visiting friends in Florida.

Let us now examine this two-fold breakdown of his overall experiences in the above order.

---

1. Fowler, *The Andreasson Affair—Phase Two*, 1994, pp. 63-64.

House Calls

The following are consolidated excerpts from Bob's sessions describing his brief encounters with aliens in their house, trailer and tent.

Fred: Relax. Deeply relax...where you're very in touch with your spirit and very in touch with who you are and how you feel. Very in touch. I want you to imagine, beyond 1944 and 1967 *[the dates of Bob's previous known abduction experiences]* and 1978. How many times did you actually have moments where you have been with beings?

Bob: *[lets out long sigh]*...They came one night to the house in Cheshire. They came to the house in Meriden and they came in '85 and '86, I think it was. They came to the trailer in New Hampshire. *[1981-1982 time frame]* They came [several times] to the trailer where we are—the big trailer. Sometimes...they talk to Betty. Sometimes they make me rest. *[They put him to sleep while they dealt with Betty.]* Sometimes they put pictures in my mind. The pictures...are thought-forms. The picture is a *thought.* It's not just a picture. It's...a thought being implanted.

After Bob quickly rattled off these brief incidents, Fred decided to home in on Bob's last experience before addressing the others.

Fred: What was the last time you were with the beings?

Bob: There's a grey. And he's at the trailer in Higganum.

Fred: What year?

Bob: 1992.

Fred: Month?

Bob: I think it's October. I wake up.... Something woke me up, and I looked straight downstairs. The fluorescent light's on, and there's one of the gray beings with a...blue uniform [on]. But, he's taller and thinner. He's a taller one than the rest. He's almost as tall as me. And he does have three fingers, three digits.... He's standing by the cabinet door, which is open, and I just had put the...motion detector sensor in the inside of the cabinet there, and he appears like he's looking at it, and he's got his right hand extended up toward it, and I kinda prop myself up in bed a little bit so I can look straight down at him, and he turns toward me. He doesn't turn his head. He kinda turns his whole body, his whole chest, and...pivots his body toward me, and he looks at me. He's different. His...eyes are just light...and he's telling me that I must go back to sleep.... I feel like I must go back to sleep like he's saying, and I go back to sleep. *[very long pause]*

Fred continued to probe Bob's memories for additional abduction experiences. But, again, Bob's subsequent encounters seemed to be connected with alien interest in Betty.

Fred: OK. Relax. We're going to take a look around in your mind's eye. How many times have the aliens visited you since the out-of-body experience with Betty?

Bob: They came to my house in Cheshire, but I was sleeping on one side of the bed and Betty on the other, and I woke up and saw one in the blue uniform, but he was on Betty's side.... And he didn't say anything to me, but I think...that I was just put to sleep. I fell back to sleep....

Fred: Can you somehow get back in your mind's eye? Can you see how many experiences you had?

Bob: That was at Cheshire. Betty and I were in Meriden *[1984]* watching a movie, *The Survivors,* on a video tape that we rented, and one of the beings suddenly appeared in the doorway between the kitchen and the living room.... Then Betty and I woke up and the tape was over. She fell asleep at the exact same time that I did. And we didn't remember any more of the movie.

I remembered that Betty had phoned to tell me about this curious incident on the following day. She told me that she had felt something stick into her head, but could not open her eyes. Apparently, Betty and Bob were instantly anesthetized upon sighting the entity in the doorway. It is interesting to note that on several occasions like this their telephone circuitry malfunctioned, perhaps as a by-product of UFO effects.

Bob: And, the next day, we had to call the phone company because the telephone quit working, evidently. And we couldn't call out. It just seemed strange that it happened when it did. And it took the phone company almost three days to get our phone fixed.

And another time we were up in New Hampshire in the trailer at the Oxbow campground *[1980-1981 time frame]* and something woke me up late at night or early in the morning. And this time it was one of the ones with the red uniform on with the lightning bolt like I'd seen back in 1967. *[pause]* But he didn't say what he was doing, why he was in the trailer, or [that] we're going anywhere. But...something just floating around. A big—I don't know what it is. It looks like...an artist's palette. It's just dark, like a shadow, and it went...in a circle around this little being.... He seemed to be moving this thing just with his mind or with his eyes.... Then there's just like a little sprinkling of light and he's gone. He's just not there anymore.

Lacoochee, Florida

Winter 1989

Since the phase three investigation, I asked Betty and Bob to keep me informed about anything strange that may have occurred in their lives. One such event had taken place in Lacoochee, Florida, where they were staying overnight at the house of their niece and nephew, Kitty and Terry.

Bob had awakened suddenly when a bright red light shone through the bedroom window momentarily. Simultaneously, the water bed that they were sleeping on began to vibrate. By the time Bob woke Betty up, it was all over. She neither saw anything nor felt the bed vibrate. Bob could not understand how she could have slept through the strong vibrations.

I felt that this event was a good candidate to examine under hypnosis. It turned out that it certainly was! At Bob's next session, Fred placed Bob under hypnosis and proceeded to interrogate him about this curious happening.

Bob: Betty's sleeping over there, and I wake up *[long sigh]* and there's one of those beings, the gray beings, with...the blue uniform. And...I think that they want Betty. *[breathing heavily]* He's on my side of the bed, and he's got something in his hands—looks like a...tiny spoon or something. *[pause]* And he's poured some liquid into it.... And he puts his hand on my forehead, and he pushes my forehead down. Aww...it makes my eyes hurt. He's pouring that liquid in my mouth.... He's squeezing my forehead! *[pause]* This will help me. *[exhales loudly]* Oh, there's...a ship right out behind the house. It's right out behind where the...bedroom window is. *[breathing heavily]* And he wants me to go into that ship!

This statement was enough for Bob's mind to temporarily break through the apparent sedative given him by the alien being. He broke into a raw panic both in his mind's eye and in the hypnotist's chair.

Bob: ...I'm not going to go, I'm not going to go! Oh, my will is strong. I won't go, I won't go, I won't go! They can't make me. *[breathing very heavily, panting]*

Suddenly Bob's body relaxed in the chair. He breathed out a temporary sigh of relief when the entity left, only again to be rapt in terror. The room was suddenly bathed in red light and the water bed began to vibrate violently. Fred immediately came to his rescue.

Fred: Remember, you're here now in March of 1993. You're remembering what happened then. You're OK now. You're OK. You're relaxed. You're in control. You're aware that your heart is beating calm and rhythmic. Your lungs are calm and rhythmic. Your mind and body are at peace. You are at peace.

Bob: Ohh, I shake Betty and...wake Betty up and I tell her, *[breathless]* "Did you feel that, did you see that?" I don't believe this. She didn't feel anything, she didn't feel the bed shaking, she didn't see the lights. How could she sleep through that? ...Oh boy! Ah, that's strange. *[tries to catch his breath]*

Fred: What happens next?

Bob: She didn't see anything; she didn't hear anything. And I cover up and *I don't want to know.* I want to go back to sleep. Ah, I didn't like that.

Based upon the typical abduction scenario, something just didn't seem right about Bob's insistence that he had not been abducted by the alien, that "he didn't want to know." So, Fred immediately interjected a tactical question hoping that it might break through a probable memory block induced by the alien.

Fred: Did Betty remain there while you were out?

Bob: *[in almost a whisper]* I didn't go. They couldn't make me. They couldn't make me. I wouldn't go.

Fred: Why not?

Bob: Because they wanted to put me on that table again. They wanted to put me on that table. And they wanted to do something to me.

It worked. Bob's mind shot ahead to a scary segment of his repressed abduction.

Fred: What table?

Bob: The one like I was on by the Trap Rock *[when he was abducted in 1967]*. That plastic or glass thing—like a table—in that room where it was all light. They wanted me to go in there again. They wanted to do something to me!

Fred: How do you know that?

Bob: *[sobbing as he speaks]* Because I saw the table.

Fred: Wait a minute. You were in your bed. You didn't go to the table, did you this time?

Bob: I don't know. I saw the table and I saw the inside for a minute, and I don't want to go.

Fred: So you were somewhere for a few minutes?

Bob: I don't know how I could see it. I saw the craft outside. It was on the ground right outside the window, behind the house. Oh-h-h-h, *[moans]* I saw the room, and the room is all white. And I saw the table. Oh-h-h, they want me on that table again.

Fred: Can we find out how you knew about that table...how you knew that they wanted to put you on that table?

The more Fred could get Bob to talk about his association with the table, the better chance there was that Bob would begin to remember even more about what had happened. Again, it worked. Bob began to describe the room where the table was located.

Bob: Because I saw the table for a minute. The room was a little bit different from the one at the Trap Rock, but it looked like the same kind of a table. And the beings have the blue uniforms. They were the ones that Betty saw, not the ones that I saw. *[The aliens that abducted him at the Trap Rock wore red* *uniforms.]* They were the ones that Betty saw. They have the blue uniform.

From time to time, Bob's mind would drift back to the safety of the bedroom. Fred kept him there temporarily by asking several questions pertinent to what happened in the bedroom.

Bob: They gave me some stuff—some liquid that was supposed to help me.

Fred: What are the immediate physiological effects you feel after having ingested it?

Bob: I just felt kinda more relaxed and that was before because...I wasn't about to go anywhere. I didn't want to go.

Fred: Why did you take the liquid?

Bob: Because I couldn't move.

Fred: OK.

Bob: He tells me again [that] he wants me to go with him, and I'm saying, "I don't want to go!" I'm not going to go. I'm not going to go, and my will power is very strong, and I won't go. And I go with him. And there's a...craft sitting in back, right in the "L" of the house behind the bedroom. And he takes me inside and it's funny because I don't...feel...much different as far as hot or cold or anything like that. And I go in...this room. It's real clean. It's all...white like and there's light. And it's almost like the one I saw [in 1967].... The light is coming from everywhere, but...there's no bulbs or light source. It's all like white, but you can't see where it's coming from.

Fred: Are you alone now?

Bob: No.... There's one in the blue uniform on the right hand side of me, and there's the other one across there by the table.

Fred: All right.

Bob: Oh-h-h. *[moaning]*

Fred: How long were you in some kind of contact with them?

Bob: I don't know. I thought I just stayed in bed. Because I don't want to go, I don't want to go. *[pause]* But, I see the table inside and there's...more of those guys in the blue uniforms, and I feel...real calm now...very calm.

Bob's statement indicated that he again was responding to the mental sedation induced by the aliens. But, not for long. His fear of being put on the table neutralized it.

Bob: And they want me to get up on this table again [like they did in 1967]. There's one on the other side over there, there's a table, and it looks...more streamlined, more modern than the one I had seen before [in 1967] because the base comes up from—it's almost like it's molded, right part of the floor. And the base comes up, and it seems like it's a little wider, like there's a rib in the center of the base about halfway between the floor and table part. And...it's angled...sharply—the base part that goes under the actual table itself...also [it] is white and clean.... I notice there's...nothing lying around.... I don't even think that there is dust in this place. This is really, really spotless. I didn't want to go in there.

Fred: All right.

Bob: *[long sigh]* They say they need to look at me.

Fred: Why?

Bob: To see how I'm progressing. I don't care. I don't want to be here. I don't want them to put me on that table! *[pause]* Aw...they do! They do!

Fred: They do what?

Bob: They put me on that table again!

Interestingly, just as soon as Bob's body lay upon the table, his whole attitude toward it changed. Apparently, alien control over his will and emotion was finally complete.

Bob: And I'm not...really feeling anxious, you know...it's almost like a pleasant friendly atmosphere...almost like if you went to your family doctor, you know. And, I'm on the table and...it's something like the other one [in 1967], because I can't really move. Only this time I'm not really frightened by it like...I was before. It doesn't seem that there's anything to be afraid of.

Fred: Uh-huh.

Bob: Oh, I can't move. One is leaning over. *[pause]* He's looking inside my right eye. And he's got a blue, blue light, and he's shining it in my right eye, and it hurts. It's giving me a headache. *[long pause]* I don't know what he can see there, but it's very bright.

And this one who is now on my right, one of the little gray guys, is looking into my right eye, and he's got a strange light. It looks...bigger than a pencil, maybe like a marking pencil.... And it looks like it's chrome or something polished. And it emits a strange, a very bright, blue [light].... Ah, it's a blue bright light, but it's not really blue. It's...like mixed colors of a blue and a white. They're not separate, but they're not...really one. It's two colors, but I don't know...how it [is] separated, but it's just blue-white. The other [grey] is standing on the other side on the left there. And he's just watching. *[long pause]* Oh, oh, they're putting something on my head. They're putting something on my head like a metal strap. It doesn't hurt, it doesn't hurt. It's making me see all kinds of sparkling things inside my eyes. It's...like a sparkler, like a fourth of July sparkler. I can see. My eyes are closed. And there's little symbols—there's circles and...little triangles. There's—butterflies?...There's white light. Oh, oh, I see the Earth. I see the whole planet. There's dark spots on some parts of the planet. And they ask me if I know, if I understand. I have no idea.... They say, I will, I will in time. *[pause]* They let me up off there.

Just as soon as he was taken down from the table, Bob seemed to come back to his real self again. He wanted to get out of there.

Bob: I want to go back to bed! I want to get back to the house! And now I'm standing up. I'm off the table and I'm standing up and part—Oh...look at that! I can see Kitty and Terry's house and we're up above it. We're up in the air. We're not on the ground anymore! *[pause]* I never even felt us move. I guess this is a little demonstration for my benefit. There's no feeling of movement or anything. And they explain that they did not want to stay on the ground because they might be seen. And the same one that takes me in, grabs my arm, my left arm, and we go right out and right through where the window is and we go back down. And there's...no feeling at all—no sensation. And it's like you can see...right through the wall. It's not like a window. It's like you can see

> right through the wall.... And we come back down. I go in, back into the bedroom with him, right through *[the window]*.... The windows are very, very narrow, and we're going right through that part where...the windows are to the bed, and I go back in bed, and he leaves with no explanation of what this was all about.

Bob then explained to us that for all intents and purposes, his remembered encounters just happened to coincide with alien visitations with Betty. He did not feel as if he had any further abduction experiences. At least, up to this point in time, we had retrieved the missing data from the other half of the on-going Andreasson affair. We had (as a well known newscaster often states) heard the rest of the story. Now we turn our attention back to the experiences of Betty Andreasson Luca.

chapter three

Return to Oz

> *The "Oz Factor" is a set of symptoms very commonly reported by a witness to an abduction…time standing still…all sound vanishing…the impression of temporarily having left our material world and entered another dream-like place with magical rules, just as it did to Dorothy in the famous fantasy story* The Wizard of Oz.[1]
>
> *Jenny Randles*

Over the years that have transpired since the publication of *The Watchers,* I have kept in close contact with the Lucas. There were a number of incidents Betty had told me about that I felt needed to be explored under hypnosis. My first curiosity centered upon an incident that Betty had written to me about in a letter dated June 26, 1989. Pertinent excerpts from this letter are as follows:

> The early [June 2, 1989] morning hours were still and quiet with a little fog. For some reason, I had tossed and turned and could not sleep. (This is unusual for me. I'm usually out like a light.) I kept sitting up on the bed next to the window and peering out. I kept feeling as if I were being drawn to go outside, and had to fight hard against it. My shifting around started to wake up Bob. I heard something like a tree fall deep in the wood and again was just glued to the window with a feeling I must go outside! About 10 or 15 minutes later, I heard another tree fall much closer in the woods. But, there was no wind or breeze. No thunder and lightning. Just dead calm. No bird or insects sounds. Just dead calm. Again, I felt I've got to

1. Randles, 1988, pp. 22, 57.

> quietly get up and go outside, and felt as if my resistance was getting weak to this feeling and that I must go. Evidently, Bob was wide awake [when] I started to move downstairs, he asked where I was going. I said, "I've got the feeling I have to go outside!" He said, "You're not going anywhere!" It seemed as if his command broke the pulling feeling to go outside. I lay back down, but it still was a while before I fell asleep. I don't know if the falling tree has anything to do with the feeling.[2]

Later on in the morning, Bob and Betty walked out into the woods to search for the two trees that she had heard falling. They could only find one. It lay in the woods about 200 feet from the trailer and presented a bizarre sight. A perfectly healthy oak tree looked as if someone had taken a giant meat cleaver and sliced it in half vertically from the top to near its bottom. The nearby surrounding trees were unscathed. Startled, they reported the incident to the manager of the trailer park. After inspecting it, he said it must have got top heavy with water from rainfall.

But, it had not rained in the area for days.

Bob examined the fallen tree very carefully and photographed it. [See Photographs 1 and 2.] The wood fibers where it had been split were strong and healthy. He did note that some of the upper leaves of the tree appeared to be blistered. I explained what had occurred to my friend, Dr. Tom Dent, who taught botany at a nearby college. He examined the photographs and wood fiber samples taken from the tree. He thought that the incident was very strange, and he could offer no clues as to what could have caused such sudden and violent damage to an otherwise healthy oak tree. Little did we know at that time what hidden mysteries lay behind this seemingly isolated, but anomalous, event. There were clues, nevertheless.

Betty's feelings and environment just prior to hearing the trees fall had struck a familiar chord with me. Her atypical restlessness, coupled with the compelling drawing feeling against one's will and the unnatural quietness of the usual nighttime sounds of insects, has been reported by many just prior to an abduction experience. I have examples in my own files, and one can find many references to both of these effects in the Bullard study mentioned earlier. Before proceeding further, let us now lay the groundwork for the subject matter in this chapter by examining some instances of these typical UFO effects.

---

2. Personal files.

Photo 1. The tree Betty heard splitting the night of an apparent ET visitation.

Photo 2. A close-up view of the tree.

The following samples were excerpted from several of the 300 reports analyzed in this landmark study of the UFO abduction phenomenon. The incidents are segregated by the Bullard study's numbering system. [italics mine]

Pinhal, Brazil	Bullard	034
A retired policeman felt an *irresistible urge* to walk on the beach at 9:30 P.M., and approached a large light.... He saw that it was a glowing disc.... Beings approached, and he lost consciousness.		

New York	Bullard	038
He took a drive on an *impulse* and 13-14 hours later he realized he had no idea where he was [or] where he had been. He...had memory flashes of approaching several tall beings in an open field.		

Australia	Bullard	043
Two young women...*compelled* to take a drive...to an indefinite place where they saw human shapes.... A large light followed them.		

Pennsylvania	Bullard	109
The witnesses awoke to a light-filled room and went outside in response to a sense of *allurement.* They floated into a...UFO.		

Pennsylvania	Bullard	180b
The witness awoke in the night, unable to speak or move, while a light shone into the room and a humanoid figure looked in at the third-floor window. When the paralysis passed, he dressed and went outside, guided by an *inner urge* onto the grounds of a deserted mansion where he met a group of humanoid beings.... He saw a landed craft like a flying saucer nearby.		

England	Bullard	E218
When driving between 8 and 9 P.M., the witness felt as if surrounded by a fog and drove to the coast without knowing why. He got out in a field to watch several luminous UFOs.... He arrived [home] at 3 A.M. [He had experienced missing time.]		

Indiana	Bullard	195
Kathy [then 17] felt an *urge* to drive to a church parking lot, oddly deserted...and sighted a silvery UFO...then, suddenly, she found herself driving along a street two hours later.[a]		

a. Bullard, 1987.

Betty herself had already experienced this same drawing feeling at age 24, in September of 1961. She was compelled by an overwhelming and unnatural urge to leave her two napping boys alone in her trailer home. Once she was outside the force drew her up a wooded hillside where she had an encounter with an alien entity.

The following is an excerpt from one of the phase two hypnotic regression sessions conducted by behavioral psychologist, Fred Max.

The Andreasson Affair Phase Two	Fowler	phase two
Fred:	Describe [the feeling].	
Betty:	I can't. I don't know what it is! I put the mop to the side and I'm going outdoors. I don't know what it is. My word, what is it?...I feel strange, like something is pulling me along. I'm walking up this hill. It's hard to get up here. There's all pine needles, and I'm slipping. I keep on walking and I'm climbing over this stonewall. I don't know why I'm doing this.	

Betty, under normal circumstances, would never have left her children alone, entered some woods and floundered up a slippery hillside.

Interestingly enough, I have another case on file where a single father unsuccessfully struggled against the same drawing force and left his sleeping adolescent daughter alone in the house. In this incident, he drove miles away to a deserted area where a hovering UFO awaited his arrival. The following are excerpts from my detailed investigation of this fascinating case. The witness prefers to remain anonymous.

Personal Files	Fowler	December 13, 1978
On December 13 [1978], I had a good day at work. And, on the side here at home, I give karate lessons. I had one of my students come over, and I guess he left about 9 P.M. I was sitting around paying bills, and...I don't know. I just felt uncomfortable to myself. My daughter was in bed and it was getting late. Around 11:30, I went to bed, lay there, and I just couldn't sleep. I got up two or three times to have a smoke and went back to bed. [Then, sometime between 1:00 and 1:30 in the morning, he finally succumbed to the overpowering compulsion to get out of bed and leave the house. He told me:] I just felt that I had to get out for some reason. I didn't know why. I got dressed, got in the car, and drove out of the yard. I've never left my daughter alone like that.[a]		

a. Personal file #78-01.

Another case in my files involves a truck driver who had no desire to deviate from his planned route to experience a UFO abduction at a remote place off the highway. He told me that:

Personal Files	Fowler	
I was driving on highway I-70...listening to the radio.... I was fully awake, and then I heard a tremendous...rhythmic hum from all sides. It scared me pretty bad.... I felt compelled to pull over. I didn't really want to.... I got off on a ranch exit. There's nothing out there.... I sat there for quite a while.... Then I saw this ship come down....[a]		

a. Personal file #75-UTAH.

Then, there's the eerie silence that is often reported just prior to a close encounter with a UFO. It has been reported so many times now that it has been dubbed the "Oz factor." One can find many references to it in the Bullard study mentioned earlier. The following are some examples from several of the 300 reports analyzed in this landmark study of the UFO abduction phenomenon. The incidents are segregated by the Bullard study's numbering system. [italics mine]

	Bullard	051
The car floated down about 2 meters above the ground. Miguel felt paralyzed and the men [were] *unable to hear* each other's voice.		

	Bullard	052
He attempted to report to his home office, but his radio malfunctioned and his car engine failed, so he approached the scene on foot. *Total silence* surrounded the area.		
	Bullard	110
A luminous object approached, and a *silence* fell over the house.		
	Bullard	165
While the witness hunted, he entered an area where he heard *no sounds of animals*...and he saw a humanoid being standing in the shade of a nearby tree.		
	Bullard	171
Sarah [became] aware again of an *unusual silence....* An arrowhead object moved in front of her.... Four floating figures came out.		
	Bullard	178
They saw a white spherical light.... A *silence* fell over the area.... The witnesses floated toward the object.		
	Bullard	187b
The area seemed *unusually quiet,* without squirrels or birds. They saw a craft...hovering about 75 yards away.		
	Bullard	193a
The witnesses...awakened at 2 A.M. to find that all sounds outside had ceased, and a blue-white light moving outside cast shadows on the walls.... Eight shadowy beings entered the house and [took] them to the ship.		
	Bullard	209
She saw a humming object...hovering above.... The engine died and she lost control of the car, which halted on the side of the road. Feeling as if *inside a vacuum,* she heard a voice inside speak.		
	Bullard	245
A UFO then appeared and paced the car.... *No insect sounds or engine sounds were audible.*[a]		

a. Bullard, 1987.

Betty had also experienced this typical phenomenon twice before, and relived it under hypnosis during our inquiries. One episode was her 1967 abduction at age 30 from her home at Ashburnham, Massachusetts:

The Andreasson Affair	Fowler	phase one
Betty: And it's a reddish-orange light [shining through windows overlooking a field], and it's pulsating like a throbbing heartbeat, and we knew something was the matter there. *[There was a power failure.]* And I said [to the children], "Be quiet and quick, get in the living room and whatever it is will go away." It seemed like the whole house was like a *vacuum* over it, like stillness all around.... There are beings standing there, and they are talking with me, but not with their mouths. They've got big heads!		

Another example of silence was just prior to the appearance of an alien entity in her bedroom while she was getting dressed to go to an anniversary party:

The Watchers	Fowler	phase three
Betty: I'm in my bedroom and it's the weirdest thing.... It's so quiet here and, and...a while ago, I heard...the kids out in the other room and the television going.... It's Aino and Alice's anniversary party tonight, today. That's why I'm getting ready. And...I just have to put on my shoes and I'm all set. But, it's just so quiet in here, and I just can't move.... There's...a *being* standing there. *[pause]* He's communicating with me.		

Still another example of silence concerns one of the Weiner twins who was abducted with his brother and two friends from a canoe on Maine's Allagash Waterway. Jim Weiner was ten years old as he hurried home from an afternoon of sledding. Not wanting to be late for supper, he took a short cut through an open field. It was snowing lightly. Suddenly a pheasant flew up. As he glanced up at it, he saw a huge spherical object hovering just above him. Note the described effects as Jim relived the event under hypnosis.

The Allagash Abductions	Fowler	
Jim: The air seemed...not heavy, but...pressure—like there's a pressure all around me. And it's's getting—it's increasing...and I feel like I'm going to explode! Everything—it's just real still. *I don't hear anything.*[a]		

a. Fowler, 1993, pp. 203-204.

Since Betty had mentioned both of these effects in conjunction with the mystery of the fallen oak tree, it was decided that Fred Max would concentrate on these factors during the first hypnosis session of the phase four investigation on November 6, 1992.

I will not interject my analysis of the regression transcripts that follow until later on in this book. This tack will help preserve the spontaneity of Betty's experiences. However, from time to time I will insert clarifications.

Fred took some time to place Betty at ease with general conversation. He then settled her into a comfortable chair and adjusted the recording equipment. Then, speaking ever so softly with long pauses between his sentences, he began to induce hypnosis. The following transcript picks up his voice just when Betty has reached a deep state of hypnosis.

Fred: Imagine yourself, in bed with your husband, in the summer of 1989. It's morning, and you feel this growing desire, something is drawing you, to go outside. What are you experiencing?

Betty: I'm in bed, and Bob is sleeping beside me, to the right of me, *[sigh]* and its very, very quiet. And I shift a little in bed there. And so I shift over to my left and...it seems...still, so quiet. And I'm getting a strange drawing feeling, like I have to get up. And I'm getting up and pulling the covers away and to the bottom of the bed and stepping out there. And I'm feeling like I'm being drawn, and I'm fighting a little against it. I don't want to have this feeling. But I'm moving, *[sighs]* moving downstairs past the bathroom and then into the kitchen, and I walk out into the living room area and then back again. Something is pulling me towards the door. And I don't want to go! It's dark outside, and I'm fighting against whatever it is that's drawing me. And I pull away, and I go past the bathroom again, and I get up on the other landing and get into bed. And I try to lie down there, and Bob is so very still now, and I'm still getting this feeling. I've got to go outdoors. And...as soon as I lay my head back, I'm up—like I sit quickly up, and I'm like being pulled, and I'm out of bed again. And I'm moving down the area where the bathroom is and...through the door, and I'm unlocking the door, and I don't want to go out, but I'm...being pulled to go out. The door, I'm opening it up, and I'm walking down the steps, and I'm standing on the landing. And it's so quiet all around, so quiet. It's so quiet. No insect sounds or peep frogs or anything. It's so quiet. And it's like haze down towards...the field. And it's so quiet. There's...a light over by the woods. It looks a light blue and.... Oh-h-h! *[panting]* There's a blue ball of light that's just...right around through the trees, and it's just there. And I can't move, I can't get back in the trailer! *[panicky voice]*

Fred: Do you see it clearly?

Betty: Yeah, just a ball of light just hovering there....

Fred: Does it have a shape?

Betty: It's a ball. It's a blue ball of light. Oh-h-h!

Fred: You're OK, you're OK.

Fred stepped right in to ease Betty's trauma. He instructed her to begin to observe rather than relive what happened next.

Betty: I'm inside...the blue light. That ball of light shot out a light toward me. I don't know whether...I'm standing in that light or in that ball—I'm in that ball of light now.

Fred: What do you see?

Betty: I can see the trees, and I can see the ground and...the road, the dirt road there. And it's just there, and we're moving now. The ball of light is moving with me in it. I can see the trees. I'm up, I'm up so high.... We're going into the woods. *[sighs]* The ball of light with me in it is going into the woods, and I can see the trees right past the blue. *[The blue ball is translucent.]* I see...some clusters of tiny, different colored, very light, pastel colored lights. Just hanging like in the trees, like clusters of lights, balls of light. And they're about the size of, I'd say an orange or...a small apple.... They're just hanging there. And some of them are rolling on the branch, and they're rolling down the trunk of the trees, down, and they're going right into the ground. [Figure 1] They're disappearing. *[panting and blowing out air]*

Fred: Take it easy.

Betty: Oh-h-h! I'm in another room.

Fred: Relax, relax. Go now into a nice deep inner space where you're feeling a basking and a feeling of love and peace that protects your inner being by your faith in your own inner being. What are you fearing—that someone or the light would injure you?

Betty: No, I'm just feeling that blue light is pouring off me, and I can see a little person, a little being there. And he's just standing there. Oh, that blue light is just gathering together, and it's just pulling together and condensing into a small ball of blue light. [The light] drifts around and settles into the area by my head. And that little being is communicating with me somehow through the mind.

Figure 1. Betty floating in the bubble.

Fred: What does he say?

Betty: He's telling [me] I'm going to go with them, and he says to kneel down, and I'm kneeling down there...and he's going off to the side, and another being comes in, and he's got two things in his hand, and he's passing one to him, the small one that was there. [Figure 2]

Fred: Passing what, please?

Betty: A hood of some kind.

Fred: Like a hood that you wear on your head?

Betty: Yeah, it's put on his head, and he's putting one on me. And there's a hole in it, a big hole. *[pause]* Another being's coming in with another thing in his hand. And he's putting [the thing] inside that clear...glass or what—hood—it looks like it clamps right in, and...it's weird, because it's got sections to it and looks like water bubbling in it now. [Figure 3] And I can breathe real good. *[long sigh]* Oh, wow, this feels better. Oh, it's taking away my headache. Oh-h-h, *[sighs]* they're telling me that I have to follow them—that one, right there,

Figure 2. Greys preparing Betty.

the small one, with the hood over his head. And there's a door over there, but it's a weird door. It looks...weird, and I've got to follow him and get in back of him. I'm getting up, and I'm following him, and I'm walking, and my knees feel funny. And we're going in, through that door, and I can see him but...it looks weird because it looks like he's in jelly.

And I got to follow him—being cold—right into it. And right there, and it looks like a long thing of gray jelly, and it feels weird but comfortable around me, like...plunging through jello or something, and he tells me to stop.... I'm just there, standing, in this gray mass of jello.... But it's weird. I can breathe really good. I see the thing that they put in there—that round thing. We're just standing there.

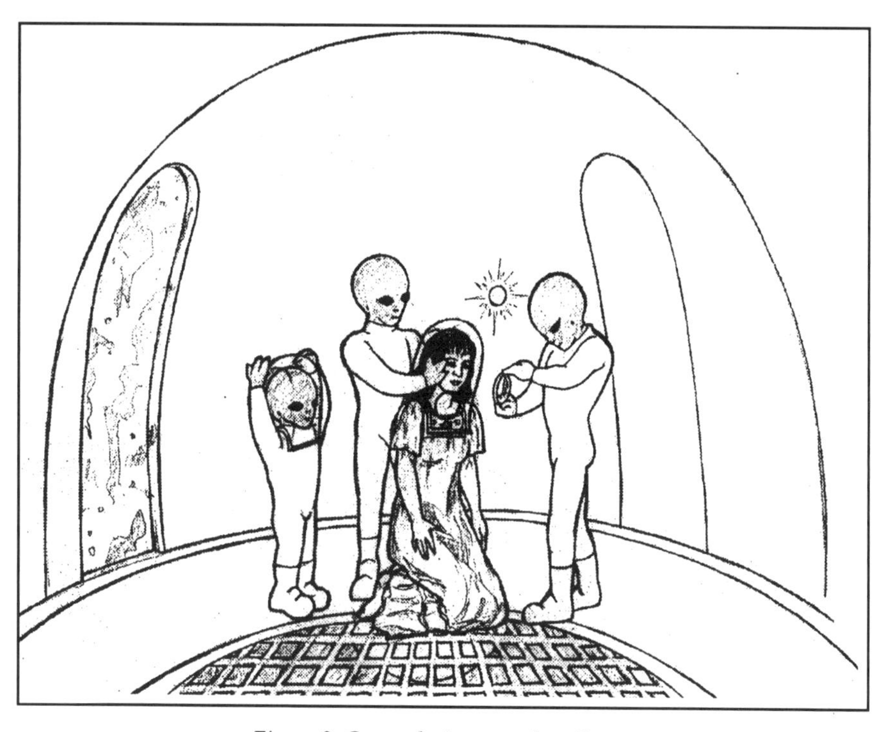

Figure 3. Greys placing a mask on Betty.

Fred: Are they friendly in the way they deal with you?

Betty: The small being just told me that they were going to take me some place.

Fred: Do they care how you feel?

Betty: I don't know. I don't know if they care or not.

Fred: Do they communicate with each other?

Betty: Yeah.

Fred: Do they appear to primarily agree with each other?

Betty: Yeah.

Fred: And do they appear to be as if they were giving each other new information or that they were acting on previous information?

Betty: It's as if...each one of them knows what's got to be done. And it's not as if they were deciding on the moment. It's like they know what has to be done.

Fred: What's the temperature?

Betty: It's very comfortable. I don't know. It just feels comfortable, but it feels weird because I feel like I'm in a mass of jello.

Fred: Could you draw this?

Betty: I think I could. I'm not sure.

Fred: ...When I count to three, you may open your eyes, while still in your trance. Give me an idea of what this looks like. One, two three—open your eyes without affecting your trance. Here's a pen.

Betty, under hypnosis, proceeded to draw what she was reliving in her mind's eye. [Figure 4] Fred then proceeded to ask questions about the scene that Betty had sketched.

Figure 4. Betty and grey with masks in place.

Fred: You're in this? Your whole body is covered with it? How are you breathing?

Betty: With that hood and that round thing. Right on the mask here, the hood, there's a round thing and...I think it's water on the bottom, and...there's some other stuff here, and the water's bubbling. It feels comfortable. I can breathe real good.... Ah-h-h.

Fred: Is it wet?

Betty: It's like jello, a little bit like jello, but...weird. I don't know, weird. Feels...like jello, like the water won't get on me, but...I don't know how to explain it. Jello—it feels like jello. But the water in the jello—I don't know how to explain it.

Fred: That's all right. Where are you?

Betty: I don't know. I'm in this room, and it's all like gray jello or jelly, and there's a little being right there by me, and he's got a thing. I can see him. I can see through this real light...very pale, clear jello, and I can see him, but he doesn't have one of these round things here. He doesn't have anything. He just has that hood over him. That's all. This thing has got something like...water, I think, at the very bottom there. It's bubbling, and...maybe that's...helping me to breathe. I don't know. It's other stuff in there, too. But, I don't know. It feels comfortable though. I feel comfortable.

Fred: What's on your feet?

Betty: I don't have anything on my feet. I got bare feet.

Fred: What else are you wearing?

Betty: Just...my white nightgown.

Fred: Are they...looking at you at this time?

Betty: That one's just looking. He's just there. He's just looking.

Fred: OK. Observing you for physiological changes?

Betty: I don't know. He's just...standing there, making sure I won't be afraid. I don't know. Because it's so weird. It's like being...surrounded by jello, like when you plunge your hand into a bowl of jello.... It's a weird feeling. It's just weird.

Fred: Did you ask them anything?

Betty: I don't know. I'm just standing there, because he's just standing there.... He probably could hear me, but I don't know...I'm just in there. And I feel comfortable in my breathing, so it's not bothering me, I guess. *[long pause]* Ah, he's starting to—oh, my head does feel heavy though. Oh, my head feels heavy, like lead. Phew! *[sighs]* He's moving a little bit, and I'm moving around with him, but I feel top heavy. Phew! Whoa, my head feels heavy. Whew!

Fred: How does it smell?

Betty: Can't smell anything but just fresh air, like clean fresh air.

Fred: Like very clean fresh air?

Betty: Yeah, it...makes me feel like spring—clean fresh air.

Fred: Are there any windows in this room?

Betty: I don't think so.

Fred: How is it lit?

Betty: I don't know—it's...a very pale watery gray, and it has light of its own, I guess, because I can see the little being there, and I can see my feet and my nightgown and my hands.

Fred: How many beings are there?

Betty: Just the one—the one in here with me.

Fred: The heaviness that you are experiencing—what do you attribute that to?

Betty: Oh, I don't know. It feels like a hangover. I don't...drink, but when...I was younger, I had beer one time, and I had a hangover, and this is what it felt like.

Fred: *[laughs]* Just relax. OK, its not because of the hood then?

Betty: I don't know. I don't think so. I don't know. It might be. It's not the hood on top of my head. There's space above me. It's on my shoulders; it...comes down over my shoulders and rests...beside my breast...and goes up and around my back. My head is loose in here, but it feels heavy.

Fred: Are there other beings around you? Are you doing anything, or are you just physically immobilized?

Betty: I'm just standing immobilized in this jelly, but my feet are on the floor. I can feel it. I feel it. It feels like they're on the floor, and the small one is just standing there by me. There's only that one being there right now.

Fred: Are you trying to walk?

Betty: Yeah, he's turning and slowly moving and stopped, and it feels weird, and I'm trying to move in it, too. My head feels so heavy, it's like it's bobbing in this glass or this clear thing that's on my head. Just feels like it's swaying, and I don't know why, but the heaviness is starting to go a little bit, and we're moving...and he's moving and I'm moving still in the same direction, trying to go a little faster because I don't want to be left there alone. And *[long sigh]* we're out of that stuff.

Fred: Where are you now?

Betty: We're in that room. I feel better, and that small being's taking that thing off his head. Then, another one's coming in—a taller one—and he's telling me to kneel down again. And he's taking out...the middle thing that was on the hood. That's better. Now he's moving that hood. *[sighs]* Ah, it feels better. My head doesn't feel heavy anymore.

Fred: Where are you?

Betty: I'm in...another room, and I see...something like lights all blinking over there and [that] looks -like-glass thing. The being's talking to me. He says that he's going to take me...someplace, but I don't understand what he's saying. *[pause]* The smaller one is going out now, and the taller one's just there with me. He set that...hood on the side there and that glass round thing over there, whatever it was, with the water in it. *[pause]* Another one's coming out. The other one's going over to talk with him.... They don't talk with their mouth, they just communicate through their eyes.... Mental telepathy or something.... It feels like something's stopping, like we might have been moving....

Fred: Is there anything with you physically in the room that you are in? What do you see?

Betty: The blinking lights over there. The blinking lights off to the side there. And I see those glass, I don't know, square things or oval things, I don't know what they are.

Fred: Could you draw me what the room looks like?

Betty: I'll try.

Fred: Open your eyes without affecting your trance. Here's a pen.

Fred looked over Betty's shoulder trying to fathom what the strange things were that she was drawing. [Figure 5] After the sketch was finished, Betty continued to describe what was happening to her, and Fred continued to ask her questions.

Betty: That tiny blue light is in here again, next to me.

Fred: What do you mean, the "tiny blue light"?

Betty: That blue ball of light that was there after. *[The large blue ball of light that carried Betty up to the craft that then shrank to a tiny blue light.]*

Fred: Is it alive?

Betty: I think it is. It seems to be by itself and moves around.

Fred: Do you think it has an intelligence?

Betty: Yeah, yeah. I think it does because it is, I don't know, it might run by a machine or something. I don't know.

Fred: Does it appear to follow anything?

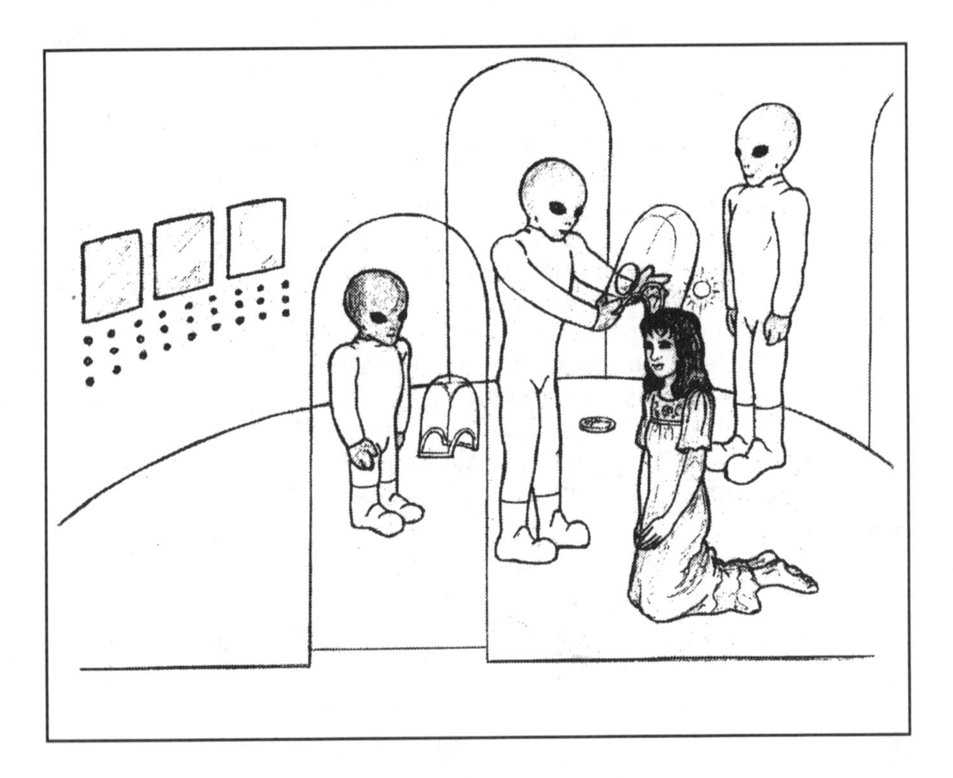

Figure 5. Grey removing Betty's mask.

Betty: No.... It's right up there. It's staying with me now.

Fred: What do you mean, it's staying with you?

Betty: I don't know, it's right up there. Right there.

Fred: Can you look at it easily?

Betty: Yeah, I can see it right there.

Fred: How physically large is it? Big as a basketball?

Betty: No, it's about the size of an orange.

Fred: Is it a source of illumination or is it something—

Betty: It's just a bright blue light, ball of light. It's just in the air there.

Fred: Do you feel a spiritual connection where you are and something you are interacting with in your environment?

Betty: I don't think so. It's all physical. I mean, there's beings. They seem...I don't know, just like the angel I saw before. They've taken me places before. I don't know if they're the same ones, but, they look similar. That light might be spiritual.

Fred: If you could focus on the light and focus in on the attitude that the light is emitting in your direction, what's it saying?

Betty: Nothing. It's just there. *[long pause]* We're moving now. We're being taken out of this room.

Fred: What makes you go?

Betty: Them.

Fred: How?

Betty: Through their mind, I guess—their eyes and their mind. They move me somehow.

Fred: Do they smile?

Betty: No. They don't. They don't have a smile like people do. They have like a thin slit for a mouth and they just...talk through their mind. There's no words...exchanged audibly.

Fred: Would their body language be classified as loose or tight or...?

Betty: No, they're sort of stiff, kind of stiff, rigid. And we're moving, moving out the room, and we're going outdoors, I think. Looks like outdoors or where it's awfully misty.

Betty was taken out of the craft by one of the small gray beings. The small ball of blue light moved along with her.

Fred: What do you smell?

Betty: Ah, a dampness.

Fred: Do they move like an animal or more like a robot?

Betty: More like a robot.

Fred: When they look at you, do their eyes appear more animal or robot?

Betty: *[pause]* There seems to be deep, deep intelligence, but seems like a robot.... I don't know how to explain it—seems very deep, like it goes right through you. But we're moving now, and we've left the area, and we're coming to something very

> bright up ahead, just moving along. And, we're stopping—
> I've been here before!

Betty gasped in amazement as she recognized the place where she had been brought as a teenager. It was the Crystal Forest!

chapter four

The Crystal Forest

Ray Fowler wrote three books on her experiences, but the events were so bizarre that UFO researchers were at a loss to separate reality from fantasy.[1]

Dr. David Jacobs

The Crystal Forest? Betty's past visit to this fairyland-like place is one of the bizarre events alluded to by Dr. Jacobs. Such a paraphysical experience would be dismissed as fantasy by most UFO researchers. Their reaction to Betty's description of her next visit will be equally incredulous. Let us now return to Betty as she relives her return to the Crystal Forest in the hypnotist's chair.

Betty's voice and facial expressions exhibited surprise as she recognized the place to which she had been brought in the fall of 1950 at age 13 from a field near her house in Westminster, Massachusetts.

Betty: I've been here before, and I know it. We're stopping, and…there's the things there—I've seen those before—and we're having to put on…shoes and stepping on them and [they are] sticking to my feet…. The little being's putting some on his feet, too, and we're going into that forest again where it's all glass. It's up ahead. I *know* this. After this mist clears, I know we must be going there, because this is so familiar to me. I've been here before. I know it.

Fred: Can you tell me what you're seeing?

Betty: There's…mist all around, but there's…these things that come out and there's the light in waves, like light rays. There's these glass—I don't know if they're glass. They're clear and they're just [like] clasp-on shoes.

1. Jacobs, 1992, p. 42.

Again, Fred left Betty under hypnosis and had her draw what she had just described. Betty had been made to wear these same type of glasslike shoes during the 1950 abduction. [Figure 6] A number of the shoes were laid out along a platform. Betty's feet stuck to the shoes as soon as she stepped on them. Concurrently, little lights and what appeared as waves of energy appeared within them.

Figure 6. Betty sees the glasslike shoes that they will soon wear to walk in the Crystal Forest.

After Betty had completed the drawing, Fred again continued the questioning process.

Fred: Now, where are you physically located? In other words, are you near where you live, or are you further out...?

Betty: I don't...know. I just know I've been here before. That looks so familiar down here. It's those glass shoes and those things sticking out. I don't know...exactly, but there's light, and there's a crystal forest around here somewhere. And we're putting on our [glasslike] shoes. They just stick to our feet, and we're moving along through the mist now, and there's light up ahead, and there's the crystal forest. I can see it from here, and it's beautiful! Oh, it's beautiful, and that blue light is following me, too. I can see the blue light following us.

Betty was led into a strange forest where she had been as a teen in 1950. Both trees and living creatures appeared to be made or encased in a glass or plastic-like substance. They seemed to be in a state of suspended animation.

During her last visit as a thirteen-year old, Betty found that everything she touched came to life momentarily and then returned to its former state. For example, when she touched a glasslike butterfly, it came to life and flew for a moment. Then its colors faded, its form disappeared, and a bright blue-white tiny spark appeared in its place. This in turn changed into what looked like a drop of water which expanded to reform into the glass butterfly. The glasslike shoes seemed to provide insulation against such effects.

Also during the 1950 abduction, one of Betty's eyes was temporarily removed and a probe placed within her head. This same place had been referred to as "home" by the alien entities. While there, she was taken to meet with someone or something called the One. The details of the 1950 abduction are covered in *The Andreasson Affair—Phase Two* and summarized in *The Watchers.*

Fred next turned briefly to the nature of the alien beings and then asked Betty to continue to describe what was happening to her.

Fred: Do you have a sense of gender in relation to the beings?

Betty: They seem like they're male.

Fred: All?

Betty: The ones that are here. That one seems like it's male.

Fred: OK. Go on.

Betty: We're going up to the forest, and that blue light's with us too. And, I can see off to the side...it rolls up into a mountain, like a glass or a crystal-like mountain that goes upward. And, it's like a big gully—I don't know what you would call it. *[Betty is describing a round tunnel in the mountain that egresses at its foot.]* We're moving now into the crystal forest, and we're on a path. And there's...a huge round ball that is moving up through the forest over in that deep thing that comes up all of a sudden and then just goes over [the tunnel] and just—I can see it over there, just hovering in mid-air. A big, big thing.

Fred: Do you have a sense of time?

Betty: No.

Fred: OK. If you could go back there, what questions would you ask the beings?

Betty: Not at this time, because everything is just unusual, and I'm just taking it all in.... That...ball of light—we're just walking along, and I see trees, and, oh, it's beautiful here! I asked him—I did ask him something! I'm asking him..."What is this?" And he's saying...something about light and refraction and, I don't know, I can't understand—something about dimension of light, the light, the refraction, I don't...understand what he's saying, and it's hard to repeat it.... We're just moving along now, and we're coming to something like a clearing off to the side here and trees 'round about it and we're—

Fred: Regular trees?

Betty: No, they're crystal trees, and now it's bright. It's bright in here and crystal all around. It's, it's fantastic! Oh-h-h, I hear...rumbling...off to the left there.

Fred: Is it day or night there?

Betty: It's very bright. It must be day. And I'm hearing rumbling off to the side. And, I don't know, but he's telling me to run! *[panicky voice]* I've gotta run! *[shouts in terror]* I've gotta run!

Fred: Just relax, just relax, relax, relax, relax. You have the ability to distance yourself from where you are. You have that power. *[long pause]* Imagine now that you are watching it with someone else. Now, where are you running to? Where are you going?

Betty: I don't know. I see...myself running...on a path and I think it was...because of that rumbling...that he was telling me to run. I don't know why, but I'm running on that path, and I keep on running and running. [Figure 7]

It was an amazing sight! Betty's facial expression and body language were those of someone fleeing in panic. Her legs went back and forth in the chair as if she were running for her life as she breathlessly tried to explain what was happening to her.

Betty: And...he's [the gray being] in back, but he's not catching up to me, and I keep running and, I'm running and running. *[almost crying]*

Fred: OK.

Betty: Oh, Oh!

Fred: All right. Relax, relax. relax, relax.

Figure 7. Betty running in a panic through the Crystal Forest.

Betty: I'm running from water—it seems like water. I've got to get out of this water!

Betty was now in a state of sheer panic. What we would find out later was that the glass shoes had come off when she had started to run. Apparently, she had been running over a glasslike body of water in suspended animation when the shoe came off her bare feet. This effected an immediate transformation. Betty suddenly found herself sinking into and wading in running water.

At this point, Fred had no idea what was happening. All he knew was that Betty was suffering intense trauma. It was decided that in Betty's best interest, we would bypass this upsetting segment of her experience and move her ahead in time. This segment of her experience would be addressed at a future session after he had discussed the matter with her out of hypnosis.

Fred: Hey, go back. Why don't you relax, and we'll get you back here. Take it easy. Relax. Sit back. Sit back. Allow your mind to suspend its feelings and thoughts for a few moments. Suspend your feelings and thoughts and allow yourself to feel a deep feeling of relaxation, as one who is committed to your feeling of faith, in that you are protected. Whatever happened, happened. You are OK. It's OK. As you imagine in your mind, fast forward this event. Go to the next significant thing and tell me about it.

For the sake of continuity, excerpts will now be used from that future session where Betty finally was able to describe what was happening to her. Then we shall move on to what happened next, using excerpts from both sessions.

Betty was very nervous about going through this ordeal again. The emotions felt during her first session still preyed upon her mind. Fred first asked her to relate from conscious memory what had happened up to that traumatic point of her experience. She did this with perfect accuracy. Then Fred took an extra long time relaxing Betty under hypnosis. When he felt that she was ready, he began.

Fred: You're here right now with Bob and me, and you are protected. You have been through whatever you have been through. You were running. What were you running to?

Betty: The little being told me to run because there's a rumbling as if there's an earthquake or something. The ground feels like something moving, and I have to run. I have to run. And it's so hard to run with these shoes. They're just too hard! I'm trying to run with them! *[very upset]*

Fred: You made it through, remember. You did make it through. You went through that OK.

Betty: The small, little being is back there. I'm way ahead of him, and all of a sudden, there's bright light all over the place. Streaks of bright light. Streaks of bright light every place. And I'm trying to run, and as I'm running, *[breathless]* I can see like a mirror or something from those streaks of bright light, and I hit the sheet of bright light and my shoes fall off....

Betty's voice again sounded terrified as she relived what must have been a horrifying experience. Again her legs moved in a running motion as she is relived her flight under hypnosis.

Betty: And [the glass shoes] went flying, and I'm falling backwards. I'm falling in some water! And...I've gotta get out of this water! I've gotta get out of this. *[screaming, breathless and can hardly get her words out]* And...I'm out of the water. [Figure 8]

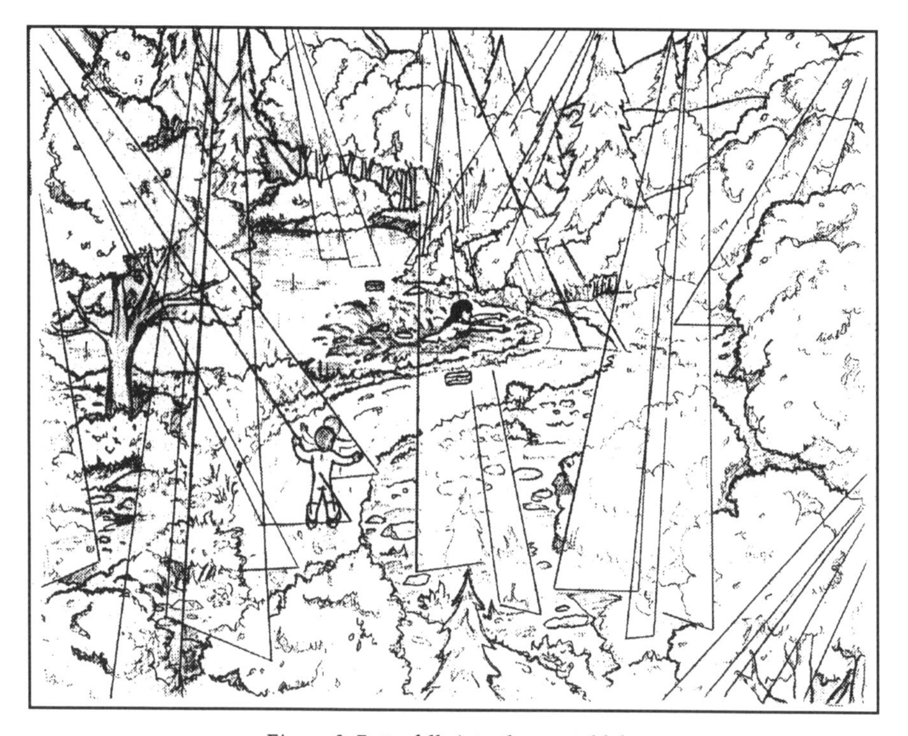

Figure 8. Betty falls into the crystal lake.

Fred: OK, you're all right. You're OK, you're OK.

Betty: And I'm...on the shore, and I'm just sitting there, and that small being is coming up to me now. *[out of breath]* And I'm asking him what happened. And he says—I feel so out of breath—Oh-h-h, phew! *[catches her breath]* That small being told me that.... Oh, there's bright light all over the place here. He says that the One has moved to open the Great Door. The Great Door is open. Oh-h-h, the Great Door has been opened. It's so bright! So bright in here. Oh, and I see...something coming. There's...such a bright light, and there's...beings coming and they're all light—they're *light* beings and they're...moving with something. Oh, I feel cold from that water. It's so strange. Oh, the ground around me and the water all is color. Everywhere I touch...turns to color. Oh, it's cold here. I'm cold. *[shivers]* Those...light beings are coming over, and they got this barrel that is moving, and it's revolving, and they're not even touching it. Two of them...have got some strange looking thing in their hands with...things on the end of it. They're moving over toward me. That small being is picking up that shoe that flew off my foot. *[pause]* That...light being is going on the water and picking up that other shoe that flew over there. Oh, I left a big hole in that water. *[The water had solidified back into the glasslike material that made up the forest.]* There's no water there. It's like glass, but there's like a hole of some kind. [Figure 9]

Figure 9. A grey helps Betty out of the crystal lake.

Fred: What is the temperature?

Betty: C-C-Cold. I feel very cold right now. I've got water on me. I'm drenched.

Fred: Remember, you are reliving this in part of your mind. The other part of your mind is here under a warm blanket, a warm chair and a warm room with warm friends. Could that be ice that you went through?

Betty: No, it was water, crystal water, and as I fell into it, it became...like water, blue water....

As mentioned, just as inanimate things of glass in the forest came alive when Betty touched them, the crystal or glasslike water became liquid water when Betty ran onto it with bare feet.

Betty: Everywhere I touched just came to life. The crystal is no longer there—it came to life like living water. It was splashing all over the place, and when I crawled up upon the ground, it turned colors. The grass turned green, and the pathway turned an orange color. Even now I can touch something, and it will turn color. All around me is...just in my area, is color, just color—all over there and all around me. I'm drenched. They're bringing that thing—that clear barrel—that's turning [revolving], and they want me to get inside it, and I'm getting inside that barrel.

Oh-h-h. *[sighs]* Oh, I feel very relaxed in here. It's warm. I feel as if...whatever that water [on me] is, [it] is just drying up into sparkly crystals—all falling [off me]...this barrel they got me in. And one of those light beings has those things, and they're leaving it to pick up all that ruffled water, I guess, or something. It's smoothing out that path, and there's two or three of them over there smoothing out the crystal lake part, or pond. [Figure 10]

The light beings carried instruments that were designed to restore the damage done to the crystal path and pond caused by Betty when she lost the insulating glass platform-like shoes.

Betty: Those tiny, tiny sparkles and it's smoothing out. And in here [the barrel] it is like all sparkles, crystals all around me like.... I'm inside that barrel thing that goes around. And it stopped, and they put me inside it, and I felt warm. It feels like it's drying me off. And there's...crystals forming from the water that has been on me, and they're all around inside here. *[The environment inside the barrel caused the natural water on Betty's body to change back into a crystal form.]*

I can pick them up and just hold them up in my hand, and they broke down in there into sparkly crystals. They're like sparkly crystals. And they're coming over. The small being is telling me to put my foot out.

Figure 10. Betty is helped into the barrel, as light beings repair the hole in the crystal lake.

And he's...putting that glass shoe on me again. And the other light being there is bringing over that other shoe, and he's putting that shoe on me, and it sticks right to my foot. *[The entities again insulated Betty's feet from the floor or ground of the Crystal Forest.]* It's so bright. They're telling me to get out of the barrel, and I'm getting out of the barrel now, and I'm standing up. The beings are taking those sparkly things out of the barrel and sprinkling them on the pond. They're just throwing them on the pond, and it's smoothed out.

The strange instruments carried by the light beings removed the crystal water that had materialized from the natural water on Betty's body and restored them to their proper place upon the glasslike pond in the Crystal Forest.

Betty: Oh, and there's that ball of blue light again right next to me. It's right there, and it's about the size of an orange. It's just there, and it's still like cleaning up or something. *[The light beings are using the instruments they carried to finish cleaning up* *the disruption in the Crystal Forest caused by Betty when she lost the insulating glass shoes.]* And they [are] finished. They turned around that barrel there, and they're going up the path. There's a path that leads up there. And still the ground feels kinda shaking, like something's moving, and I see that big ball over there—big glass ball. *[Apparently an on-coming glass ball was causing the ground to vibrate.]* And it's coming towards me. [Figure 11] It's coming over toward me. It's just sailing —coming nearer toward me. Oh, it just enveloped me. I'm just moving along. Oh, I feel so comfortable. I'm just moving, and the blue light is in here. And they left that little being back there, I can see him as we move. We're moving over the crystal trees, and I can see...mountains. They go up, curve upward, and we're going down into a circular thing [the tunnel in the glasslike mountain]. We're going down below, and it feels light in here with the blue ball of light, and we're going through a tunnel. [Figure 12]

Figure 11. Betty and a grey watching a giant glass ball roll towards them.

This appeared to be the same type of vehicle and tunnel that Betty had been transported in during her 1950 abduction as a teen.

Betty: And we're just moving along through a tunnel, and the tunnel is lit in some spots. We're moving along in this tunnel, and it seems like I'm very relaxed. That blue ball of light is in here with me. It seems like I'm suspended in the center of this huge ball, and it's moving, and I see light up ahead. And the ball is just floating, and I see the bright light and I can see...below there, there's all sorts of balls of clear glass, I think. I don't know. They're all sizes down there.

Figure 12. Betty floating in the giant blue sphere.

Fred: What are you in?

Betty: I'm in this big glass ball, I think, and it's all lit up, and there's that blue light right here, right beside me, and I'm just like hanging there inside and looking.

Fred: What are you standing on?

Betty: Nothing. I'm just—

Fred: Nothing?

Betty: I'm just in that inner thing, and I'm looking down, and I can see way down there those balls, all different sizes of balls, clear crystal balls, and we're moving toward it.

Fred: Is the blue light in the sphere with you?

Betty: Yes.

Fred: Is it the same size as before?

Betty: Yes, it's the size of an orange.

Fred: Has it the same intensity?

Betty: Yeah.

Fred: Does it appear to try to communicate with you?

Betty: No, there's no communication. It's just there. We're just moving along. It [the blue sphere] stays right with me, but I'm just...suspended there.

Fred: Something like in an apartment store?

Betty: I don't understand what you mean.

Fred: In an apartment store, they have video cameras that can move around.

Betty: [The blue sphere] is not attached to anything. It's just...free. *[It is floating in the air beside her.]* It's just a ball, a blue ball of light. We're moving downward. We're moving down by those other spheres, and we're stopping right by them. They're on top. I'm being lowered, and that blue light is still coming with me.

Fred: Is the blue light always in the same shape you first saw it?

Betty: Yeah.

Fred: Exactly?

Betty: I think so. I'm not sure. I haven't been watching it all along.

Fred: Do you feel protected by the blue light?

Betty: Yeah, I think I do. I feel better that something else is in here with me than being all alone. We're stopping. I'm being moved out, and there's another ball there, and... there's beings coming out of it, only that one's metal. *[This ball is made of metal.]* They're standing there, and we're just looking over at all...the...crystal-like balls that are there and light all around. And I'm asking what they're all about, and he's telling me. He says they are intelligence. Those are intelligence. Those...orbs—he called them orbs—they are record keepers of intelligence, they can become small as what we know as atoms, or they can become large, but they each are intelligent, just as the earth and the moon and the sun are intelligences and all the planets are intelligent. They have an intelligence of their own. They're living.

Fred: Are they a good intelligence?

Betty: I don't know. There's one popping up right now, with bright light. It's just popping right out of there. [Figure 13]

Fred: Did the ball of light seem like a secretary recording your experiences?

Figure 13. The greys explain that the tiny orb of light is a record keeper of intelligence.

Betty: *[Betty thinks that he is talking about the glass spheres.]* They're saying that they are record-keepers of all intelligence, and that they're all around us, everywhere around us...but our eyes cannot see them. And they collect all knowledge and intelligence. They're record-keepers...recorders of it somehow. They're around about everything and everybody. That one popped up with bright light. It seemed as if it got out amongst all the others there. It popped right up and with bright white light. It just popped right out of there. There's like a light around, too, and, and stuff like steam comes up. *[pause]* They're telling me that I've got to go with them now.

Fred: Have to go where?

Betty: Go with...the beings there and having to get in back of one, and the other one is following. We're going into that round metal-like craft.

Fred: Will you tell me what the craft looks like?

Betty: Round and it's real big and round, and it's silvery.

Fred: Does it have windows?

Betty: No. No windows at all. There's a door, but you can't see that door until it opens up. It's very shiny, almost like a mirror. The silver is so shiny, it looks like a mirror, and in a matter of fact, it reflects a lot of...those [spheres] down there and that tiny ball of light there is showing up as it follows me. They're telling me that they're going to take me some place to see somebody. And I get in back of one and the other [in back of me], and we're moving along and taking me into that ship.... *[pause]* We're going inside that craft, we're just swooping in, and I'm standing there, and he said that I'm going to a very high place.

As Betty repeated his words, we could never have guessed what he meant by them. First, we wondered where she was physically located right now in her mind's eye. Secondly, where was this very high place where they were taking her? Let's take these one at a time.

First, where was this crystal forest located? During her 1950 abduction, we found that it existed somewhere within an underground site with an icy underwater entrance. Earth is the only planet in our solar system that has oceans. Its icy regions are located at its poles. Could it be that Betty was still on Earth somewhere under the Arctic or Antarctic circles?

A hint of this possibility came out during a hypnosis session when we were investigating Betty's UFO abduction experience in 1967. This was, if you recall, our initial enquiry into the Andreasson case. At this particular hypnosis session, questions were raised about the origin of the aliens. We were interested in what Betty may have been told of this by the aliens. The following is a pertinent excerpt from that session.

The Andreasson Affair	Fowler	phase one
Betty: Some...come from realms where you cannot see their hiding place. Some from this very earth.... Yes, there is a place on this very Earth that you do not know of.		

And, where was this very high place that Betty was going to visit? Again, it seems as if Betty may already have been taken there during the 1967 abduction.

In 1967, Betty was apparently taken by a small craft to a larger craft where she was cleansed by a machine prior to a physical examination. From there she seems to have been prepared for a further trip to a strange realm. After arrival, the craft seemed have butted up against a tunnel carved out of stone. Betty, accompanied by two beings, floated down the tunnel above a black track. She egressed briefly into an area with a red atmosphere where strange red creatures were kept. From there she moved into a huge expanse with a green atmosphere. As she floated above one of many tracks that resembled a roller coaster, she could see what appeared to be domed structures in the distance. She also saw water, plant life and a strange pyramid far below.

When we asked her if she had been brought to another planet, Betty replied:

The Andreasson Affair	Fowler	phase one
Betty: I was taken to the high place, higher than their home planet.... It is not a planet, it is a place.		

These curious answers given by Betty at a hypnosis session held in 1977 coursed through my mind as I pondered about the whereabouts of the Crystal Forest and the very high place. Were the high place of 1967 and the very high place of 1989 one and the same place? Were they different terms for different places? What was meant by the word "high" or the remark "higher than their planet"? The complete answers to these questions are yet to be resolved. But, in terms of a common definition of the word "high," the place to which Betty was being taken was very high indeed. The craft carrying her was on the way to dock with a huge mother ship drifting somewhere in the recesses of outer space.

chapter five

Mother Ship

Some of the most startling formation cases on record are those in which a large central object is observed in the process of launching or taking on board smaller objects, very much like an aircraft carrier or mother ship.[1]

Richard H. Hall

The above statement refers to witnesses who observed a distant interaction between a mother ship and its brood of smaller craft. Betty Luca is about to describe an incredible experience. She was privileged to experience this dual interaction not as a mere observer, but as an on-board passenger! Now, we have the wonderful opportunity to share this marvelous experience as Betty relives it under hypnosis.

Betty stood submissively within the bright silver spherical craft for a short time before she felt it begin to move.

Betty: We're just standing there. And the [craft] is moving along. And we're moving away from that bright light, and it's very dark now outside. They've got...a window, but...it seems to blend right in with the wall. But you can't see the window from the outside.

Betty was surprised. The window through which she was gazing, like the door, had not been seen on the outside of the craft. The window behaved like a one-way mirror.

Betty: It's...open [transparent], and we're moving. We're standing there. Oh, and my fingers hurt from whatever is moving or—ow! The tips of my fingers hurt. We're moving along. It seems like we left the very bright area where the orbs were,

1. Hall, 1964, p. 15.

and we're moving out into darkness, real dark. It looks like space, like there's stars there or lights—scattered lights all around. There's one being on both sides of me. And we're moving along...and it's very dark outside. It's light inside, but it's dark out there, and I can see lights go by...a lot of lights now out there, a lot of lights. We're just moving. *[pause]* They're taking me...some place. Somebody else wants to talk with me or see me, I think. They...don't say who it is.

Fred: When you say "they," are you saying that more than one being is talking to you at a time?

Betty: The two of them think [alike], you know? Like when...one is talking to me, it's like they're both talking to me because they have the same thoughts.

Suddenly Betty stopped and paused. Even with her eyes closed, the expression on her face showed utter amazement. We wondered what in the world she was looking at. We soon found out that what she saw was definitely not in the world. Far from it!

Betty: Oh, wow! Whoa!

Fred: What's happening?

Betty: Ah-h-h, it's a thing up in there in the darkness, and it's huge! Oh, we're coming up to something that is big—really, really big. Hanging in space. It's long, and it has like wheels, on this long thing, that moves. There's wheels, two wheels right in the front and the back that move one way and the middle wheel travels this way...and there's an end that is lit up. There's lights all over the place. We're just moving closer and closer toward this long thing.

Betty drew a picture of what was astonishing her. [Figure 14] The sketch again depicted a gigantic tube-shaped vessel floating against a jet-black backdrop punctuated by hundreds of stars. It dwarfed the tiny craft carrying her. The huge ship had a metal-capped transparent enclosure in front that contained many red and white lights. Within the enclosure, Betty could see three protruding tongue-shaped tiers. The cylinder itself was girdled by three rotating rings, which Betty referred to as "wheels."

One ring was located near the front end of the craft, another one in the center and the other near the end. The three rings had evenly-spaced orifices along their left sides. The orifices on the rotating rings

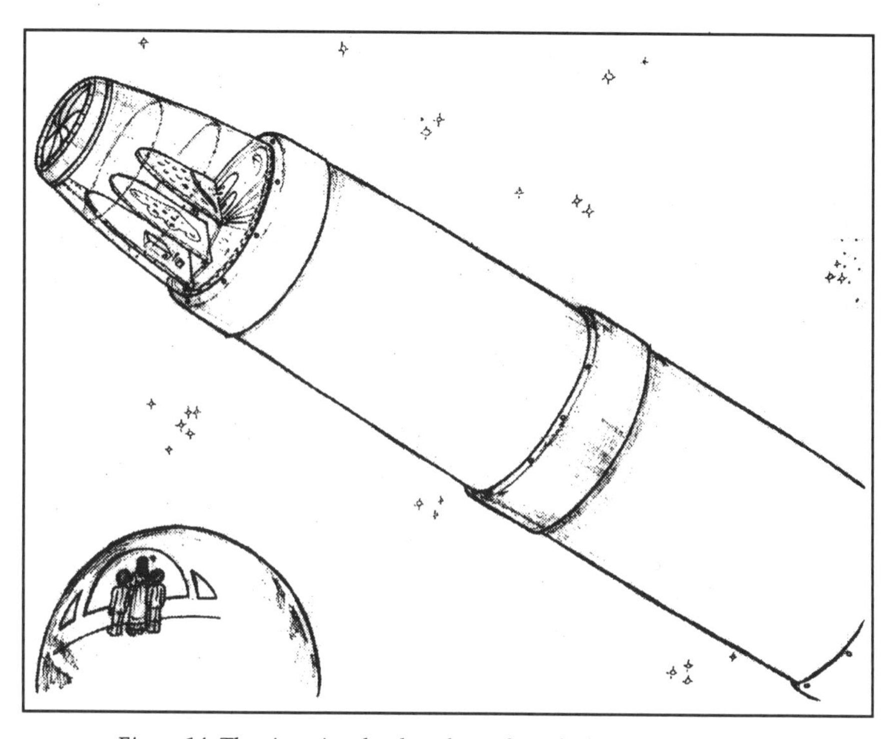

Figure 14. The gigantic tube-shaped vessel to which Betty was brought.

provided reference points for Betty to note that the outer two rotated clockwise and the inner ring rotated counter-clockwise.

Fred, as usual, gave Betty a strong post-hypnotic suggestion to remember and make detailed drawings later. The figures in this book are those drawings.

What is extremely interesting, if taken at face value, are these subsequent detailed drawings of the craft. Betty has a near-photographic memory, and her graphic drawings depict several descriptions not extracted during the hypnosis sessions.

When queried about these apparent extra details, Betty told me that somehow she knew that they existed, but she could not explain to me how she knew. Perhaps we should have been more thorough in asking her to describe the craft, because subconscious memories of these details apparently existed and surfaced in her drawings.

These new surfacing memories may be a result of Fred's post-hypnotic suggestion to remember more details, or they may be products of Betty's imagination. Betty indicated in one drawing that the orifices on the rotating wheels could release a steamy vapor that would envelop the whole craft in a cloudy mist from stem to stern. [Figure 15]

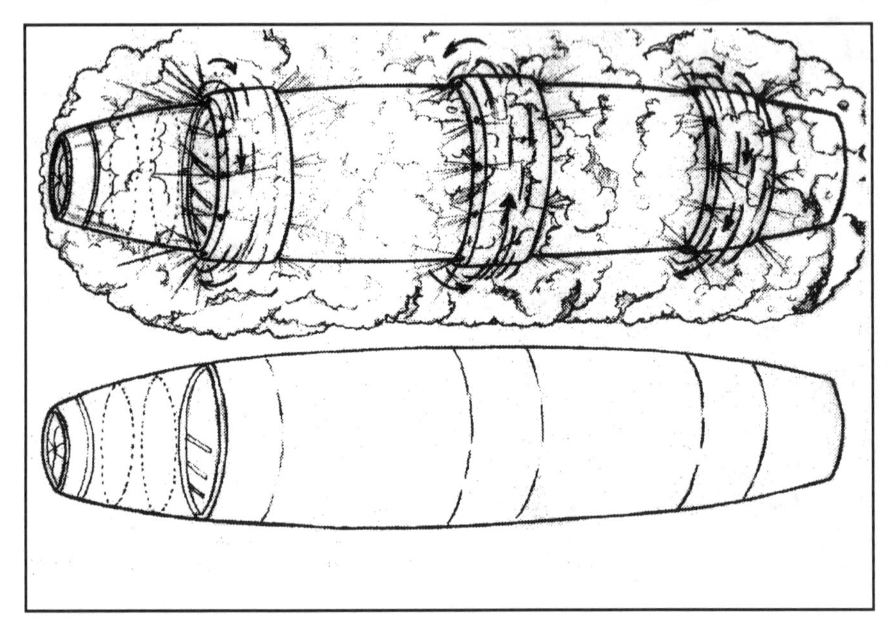

Figure 15. Rotating wheels of the space craft released steamy vapor.

This description certainly matches one of the major characteristics of what are called Type II Cloud Cigar UFO sightings. Such cloudy vapor is often noticed during daylight UFO sightings involving huge cylindrical-shaped objects. We will discuss this similarity in detail in chapter fifteen as one of a number of pertinent parallels to the Lucas' UFO experiences.

Betty also related to me a number of other descriptions of the huge vessel. She noted that:

1. The metal-capped glass enclosure and the rest of the elongated craft remained stationary when the three rings were rotating.
2. The two inner sections of the ship flanking the center wheel rotated when the rings were locked in place and not rotating.
3. The whole craft could rotate as one unit.
4. One or more rings could move independently of each other depending upon what direction the craft traveled.
5. The rings could be deployed outward or withdrawn into the craft where they could barely be seen on the outside.

6. The inner part of the craft was not affected by the outer rims and exterior skin.

As the craft containing Betty approached closer to the massive cylinder, she continued to describe it in detail.

Betty: We're...coming closer and closer to this long...cylinder thing. And it's lit up red at one end—low light. And there's lights around those wheels. And we're moving closer. It's got a...long...glass-thing there...that we're headed toward.... I can see that it's like...a glass enclosure all over...through that window. I can see it through that window. It's a glass enclosure. Wow! Oh-h-h, we're going inside. We're going to go inside. I can see it. It's like clear glass—but it's not clear glass. It's red because of the light.... There are red and white lights there.... Something is opening up for us to go inside.... It looks like there's three levels that stick out, and we're going into something that opens like...a steamer. I don't know how to explain it.

A *steamer?* I asked Betty what she meant when she used this term to describe where the smaller craft was about to enter the large cylindrical craft. She explained that it was similar to the sectioned diaphragm that lets out steam in an appliance used to steam vegetables.

Later, when she sketched this device, it laid my confusion to rest. The entrance to the huge craft reminded me of a camera diaphragm that opens to let in light to expose a film and then closes. Similarly, the huge diaphragm at the front of the hovering vessel swung slowly open.

Betty: It opens, and we're getting ready to go in.... I can see it even closer now. There's three levels there, and there's big indents. The craft is moving with us, and we just keep on going. We're moving up closer. Oh, there's some other crafts there too, in those indented bowl-like things. And it looks like there's some pipes or something close by. In each one of those indents is some pipes. We're moving along slowly, slowly and I can see big doors and stairs that curve around and lights all around the edges. There's a lot of stuff here.... The craft is setting down in one of those indented [berths], and it's slowly settling down there, and we've landed. We're just slowly going in, going, going in...slowly setting down.... And it looks like there's steps there, too. We're just standing there and waiting...until it's settling down in that [berth]. It looks like steps, and it looks like there's some silver there, too. Some silver and some gold.

Fred: What are you seeing?

It was hard to visualize what Betty was seeing, so Fred stopped Betty again and had her draw what she was viewing while she was still under hypnosis. [Figure 16]

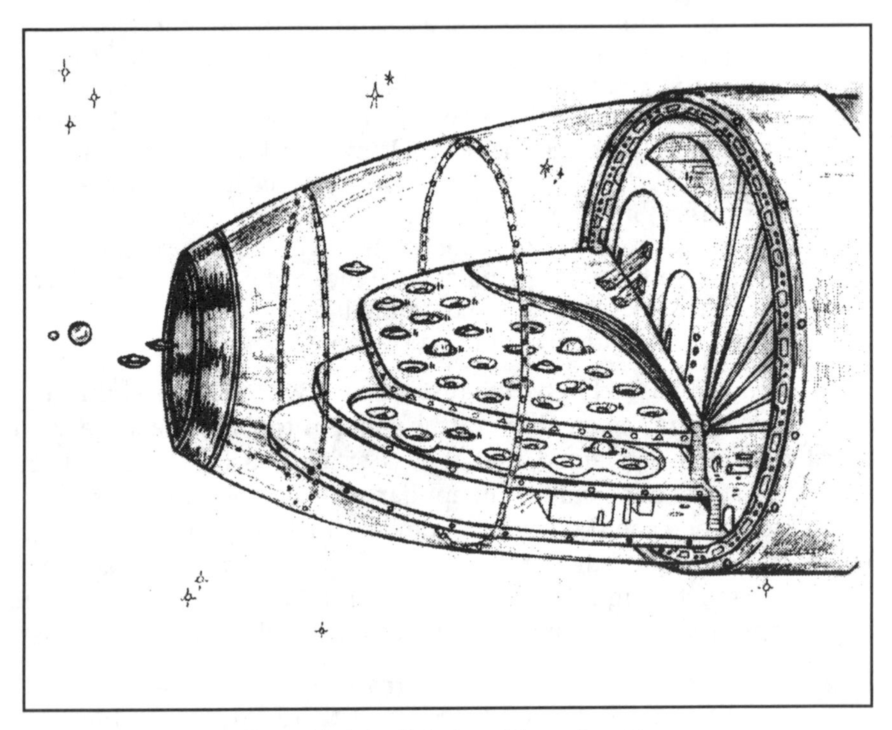

Figure 16. A detailed view of the mother ship.

The end of the gigantic mother ship that the small craft approached appeared to be constructed of glass reinforced by metallic rings. She observed that the surface of the three protruding tiers within the glass enclosure contained indented bowl-like docks of disk and globe-shaped craft. Each dock had one long and one short upright pipe located beside them.

In her drawing, Betty sketched several alien craft to show how the craft she was on had entered the mother ship. Betty explained to me that the three tiers containing the multiple landing berths for smaller craft could be withdrawn into the craft's body. Later, Betty was able to provide other detailed drawings of the craft's exterior and interior.

A tinge of envy swept through me later as I gazed at her final artwork. I imagined how I would feel if treated to the magnificent sight that greeted Betty's eyes.

Once the smaller craft docked, Betty and the two entities disembarked. One could never have guessed what she would experience next while aboard what seemed to be an alien mother ship floating in outer space.

Fred: Where are you now?

Betty: I'm inside that silvery craft looking out the window at everything there. Beautiful. It's huge. We're just there standing—waiting, I guess. *[pause]* Looks like those are stars out there. Think it's black with stars out there. And I'm looking through this window and through another. *[pause]* We're just waiting there. I...see someone coming now. There's someone—there's a tall person coming, dressed in white.

Fred: Human person?

Betty: Yeah, real tall and coming down those stairs.

Fred: A man or a woman?

Betty: It's a man.

Fred: Do you know him?

Betty: N-n-no, it looks like someone I've seen before though, some people that were real tall. They're real tall.

Betty had met tall persons like this during her abduction experience as a thirteen year old in 1950 and again during a shared OBE abduction with Bob in 1978.

Fred: What color hair?

Betty: Whitish.

Fred: Age?

Betty: I don't know. Probably...I don't know.

Fred: Caucasian?

Betty: Pale. White, pale skin.

Fred: Friendly?

Betty: I don't know. He's coming up to the craft and we're coming out. *[pause]* Yeah, he seems friendly.

Fred: What's he wearing?

Betty: Just a long white robe.

Fred: Something you'd buy in a department store?

Betty: No. No. But...I've seen people like him before.

Fred: Does he look like someone you'd meet on the streets of a city?

Betty: No.

Fred: Why not?

Betty: He's unusual looking.

Fred: Well, aren't there a lot of unusual people?

Betty: Not like this. This man's real tall with white hair down to his shoulders and pale skin.

Fred: What's on his feet?

Betty: Nothing. No…shoes. Just bare feet.

Fred: Is he near you?

Betty: No.

Fred: How far away is he?

Betty: He's just outside that…silver craft-like thing. He's motioning for us to follow him.

Fred: Is he wearing any jewelry?

Betty: No.

Fred: Are you still dressed the same as you were?

Betty: Yes.

Fred: You're still in your nightgown?

Betty: Yes. We're just going up those stairs.

Fred: What's the temperature like—comfortable, hot, cold or what?

Betty: Comfortable, very comfortable. Very comfortable, and we're following him.

Fred: How well lit is your view?

Betty: Oh, it's bright here. Very, very bright. But you can see outdoors, and it's like space or stars or lights.

Fred: What's the source of light [inside the craft]?

Betty: I can't see its source. It's everywhere.

Fred: Does this man smile at you?

Betty: No.

Fred: Or say hello?

Betty: No.

Fred: Does he in any human way acknowledge your existence?

Betty: Yeah. He looks at me. I'm just following them and we're going up the stairs. We're on top of the stairs now and walking over. We're going over to the door that leads inside this...long thing. The two...are staying in there to the side, and he's telling me to come along. I'm walking on my own! *[sounds very surprised]* I can't believe it. Most of the time when I'm with [them] they float me along, but I'm walking all on my own.

Fred: What does the ground feel like underneath your feet?

Betty: Smooth, very smooth.

Fred: And is it warm or cold or...?

Betty: Very...comfortable. We're just walking, and I'm following him, and we're just walking along, and I can see.

Fred: Is it hard or soft?

Betty: No, it's hard. The floor is hard, but it's smooth, and it feels comfortable. I can see some things that we just passed there, and there seems to be other rooms. There seems to be some doors open there, but they're not like our doors. We're just moving along. It's very bright in here. We're walking up some more steps. And I'm just following him.

Fred: Are your surroundings more earthlike or crystal-like?

Betty: It's more crystal-like. More like I'm in...rounded rooms.... There are rooms off to the sides, and there's some doors, and I can see some different things as we pass by. *[pause]* We're...stopping after we get up that flight of steps, and he tells me to wait there, that he'll be back. So, I'm just waiting there, and it's on another...level—the steps we went up. And there's a room over there, and I see a light coming from it. I'm walking over toward it. I was going to look there, but I go back after I look what's in there. Ah-h-h! Oh, there's...some people...that are sitting on the seat, [on] chairs. It's not a chair. It's like a long thing that goes out, and they got their heads bowed, and they're dressed in black.

Fred: Men?

Betty: Yeah, they look like men. And they've got sort of scraggly hair, white scraggly hair and they got their heads bowed, and there's, ah, one of those little beings standing right next to them, and he's got his head bowed, too. They're dressed in black. Oh, oh! Oh, oh! The one...is looking up and looking over at me. [Figure 17] And he...pointed, and the other ones turned their heads up and looked at me. They...look old—old and gnarled. I better get back there [where she was told to wait by the tall entity].

Fred: Were you able to move around by yourself?

Figure 17. Entities seen by Betty within the mother ship.

Betty: Yes.

Fred: What's moving you around?

Betty: My feet.

Fred: How do you move from one place to another?

Betty: Me. I...looked into that room where it was light. Oh, another being stuck his head out around the corner to look at me. Like I wasn't supposed to be over there. I'm waiting right here now, but I can see other rooms, and I can see way, way up there. It's...beautiful, but like a big hall, and there are adjoining rooms to it. I can see that other...tall one coming now. He's leading me...up the hall, telling me to come along with him. *[pause]* He's taking me to another room off to the side here, and it's lit, and I see three beings [the small gray type] just standing there. [Figure 18]

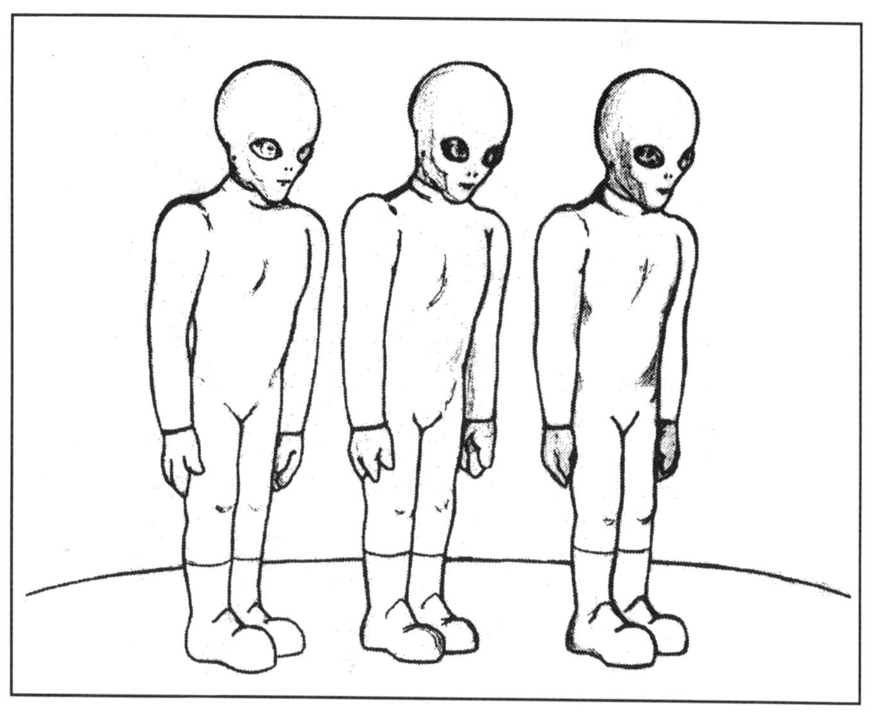

Figure 18. Three greys with strange eyes seen by Betty on the mother ship.

What's strange is their eyes. Their eyes are all gray, like they have cataracts or something. They're just standing there, and I asked him, "What's the matter with them?" He says that they're here for *biobics.*

chapter six

Biobics

Not just the sperm and the egg carry all the developmental information needed to create a finite organism. The wealth has been spread around to whole embryos, parts of embryos and nuclei.... Some animals retain portions of the development program all throughout their lives, which permits them to regenerate sections of themselves when the need arises.[1]

John Medina, Ph.D.
Molecular Biologist

This statement about the regeneration of body parts is directly applicable to what Betty was about to witness. Such a capability would answer a baffling question related to weird animal-like creatures she witnessed during a 1967 abduction. We will review this pertinent episode shortly, but first, we return to where we left off in the last chapter. At this point during the hypnosis session, we hadn't a clue to what Betty meant by biobics. Betty had been just as perplexed by this strange term.

Betty: And I said, "What do you mean? What is biobics?" and he says that their natural sight or eyes are no longer useful. They have to receive biobics.

Fred: *[checks pronunciation]* Bi-o-bics?

Betty: That's what it sounds like he said.

Fred: *[spells phonetically]* B-i-o-b-i-c-s?

Betty: I don't know how to spell it. It's biobics, biobics. He said biobics. *[pause]* They're just standing there, stiff, and their eyes

1. Medina, 1991, p. 129.

aren't black, they's like gray matter over them. They said that they've...been burned out because of the natural use, and they have to have them removed, to have biobics [and] would I like to see how it's done? "I don't know." *[Betty answers the entity.]* He says, "Come on, come in here, and I will show you." And, we're walking again up the long hall, the lit hall, and we're continuing to walk, and there's...a room over there and...I see that...some of the beings are in it.

The gray beings are there standing and there's...one being on...the table there. I can see it. [Figure 19] And we're continuing walking, and as we continue to walk, there's another room up there ahead that we're going to go into, and the door's closing, and we're heading towards something, and it looks like a wall, but the door opens, and bright red light comes out. Whew! Wow! Red, red light there. And we're walking inside. I'm just following him, and it's red in here.... Oh! And there's all sorts of...tubes with—I've seen these creatures before, too!

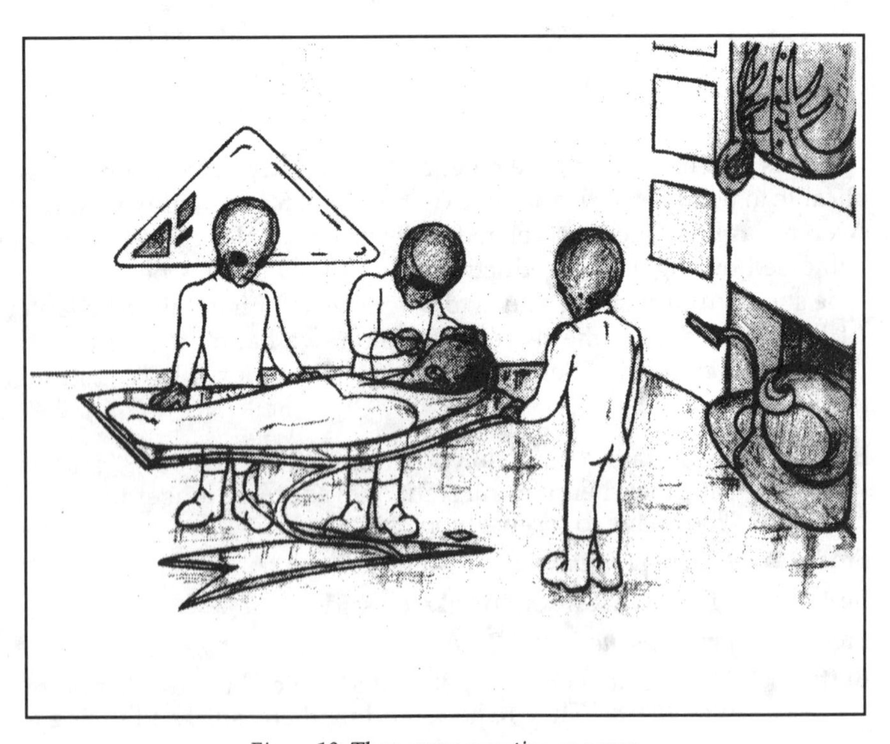

Figure 19. Three greys operating on a peer.

Betty had indeed seen these creatures before. A summary of the preceeding events is in order. During her abduction in 1967, she had been taken from her home in a small craft that had landed at the edge of the field behind her house in South Ashburnham, MA. This craft rendezvoused with a larger craft, and Betty was brought to a round examination room where she was first placed on a platform which rose into a bright light. She was told that this would "cleanse" her. The aliens then had Betty enter a small wedge-shaped cubicle to disrobe. She was given a white, loose-fitting garment to wear, and then, she was floated onto a table and subjected to a number of strange instruments.

After the examination, Betty was led to a cylindrical room and placed within one of several glass-enclosed chairs that lined the sides of the room. She again was subjected to light rays. Then she was removed and placed in a tank where she was given a liquid to relax her. Tubes were placed in her nose and mouth, and the tank was filled. It is assumed that this procedure was to protect her from G-forces caused by the craft's high acceleration to an other-worldly place.

Following this procedure, Betty was removed from the tank and dried off in an unknown manner. She then was floated out of the cylindrical room between two entities in the opposite direction from where they entered. The trio floated above a wide single black track which led through a dark tunnel. Prior to moving down the tunnel, the two small gray beings put black hoods over their heads.

To properly set the stage for what is about to follow, let us now go back to Betty's reliving of this experience under hypnosis. It is excerpted from one of the sessions conducted during our phase one investigation in 1967. Those questioning Betty were MUFON investigator and telecommunications specialist Jules Vaillancourt, electrical engineer Joseph Santangelo, hypnotist Dr. Harold Edelstein, and myself.

The Andreasson Affair	Fowler	phase one
Betty:	And we are—going through a tunnel. Looks like a dark tunnel. They have hoods over their heads, and it's a dark tunnel. Their suits look shiny, but because of that dark thing they have on, they look like they don't have any heads. Look *[whispers]* headless. I wanna go back!	

None of us could figure out why the aliens placed hoods over their heads at this particular juncture. It was just a foretaste of bizarreness that began with the abduction and steadily built up with a crescendo of higher and higher strangeness. We asked Betty to describe these so-called hoods.

The Andreasson Affair	Fowler	phase one
Betty:	Just black. No shine to it. Just black cloth, because it blended right in with the tunnel, so that all I saw was just the silver shining suits.	
Jules:	What was the source of illumination in the tunnel? You said it was really dark.	
Betty:	Their suits...were the only illumination.	

The aliens' silver suits glowed in the dark, barely illuminating their way. But the soft glow lighted the tunnel enough for Betty to see that it had been chipped out of stone.

The Andreasson Affair	Fowler	phase one
Betty:	I can see things that are chopped out. Oh, my head feels heavy. I'm still going in that tunnel. I'm just going with them.	
Jules:	Did it seem like a tube, like the inside of a garden hose, or did it seem chipped like a coal tunnel?	
Betty:	Chipped, like a coal tunnel.	

As they floated above the black track in the tunnel, Betty noticed that they were passing entrances to other intersecting tunnels. It was obvious that wherever they were, it was carved out of rock. We wondered how Betty could see these other entrances.

The Andreasson Affair	Fowler	phase one
Jules:	How could you tell? It was so dark.	
Betty:	Because of their suits. The illumination came from those suits, and we would pass other tunnels, openings. I could tell that there were other tunnels there. As we would pass, I would see...a darker hole.	
Ray:	You never touched the track? You were always above the track?	
Betty:	No, I couldn't touch anything with my hands or my legs and feet because they were too heavy.... Oh, my head feels heavy. *[sighs]* And we're going—now we're going upward a little bit.	

Abruptly, the black track slanted upward. Ahead loomed a shiny, mirror-like obstruction.

The Andreasson Affair	Fowler	phase one
Betty:	And we are coming to some kind of a glass—mirror, or glass.	

Betty braced herself for a collision, which never occurred. The three passed through the silvery membrane-like material without encountering any resistance.

The Andreasson Affair	Fowler	phase one
Betty:	And they are going through it! We are going through it—through that mirror!	

Betty squinted her eyes as they passed out of the tunnel into a place where the atmosphere was a vibrating red color. "The red looked like infrared light," she later explained. "It vibrated. It was like vibration through the air." The entities' silver suits reflected the shimmering color of this new environment.

The Andreasson Affair	Fowler	phase one
Betty:	I'm in a place where it's all red. The atmosphere is all red, vibrating red.... And their suits look red. Only their head-thing looks blackish red.	

The black track stretched on ahead, between two square buildings with openings.

The Andreasson Affair	Fowler	phase one
Betty:	We are going in this place, and there are buildings—square buildings with openings.... All you can do is make out the forms of things. And now we are passing.... Oh boy, we are coming where there's some beings!	

Betty gasped in horror at groups of weird red creatures crawling on the buildings.

The Andreasson Affair	Fowler	phase one
Betty:	And these beings...got two eyeballs...and they're loads of them. Oh, they're scary! And they have skinny arms and legs and kind of a full body. And their eyes can move every which way, and they can climb just like monkeys. They can climb up quickly and swiftly and down and around and in and out of windows. They are all over the place!	

We all sat transfixed at what Betty was describing. I wondered if the effects of hypnosis were somehow causing Betty to have some kind of psychedelic hallucination. We did not have time to dwell on this because Betty and her captors moved along the track through another membrane-like door into a huge earthlike area with a green atmosphere. There the track jointed a network of similar tracks stretching like interconnected roller coasters above land and water. From this point Betty sighted distant domed buildings, vegetation and a strange fish-like aerial craft. She passed over a strange pyramid, and a bright crystalline structure loomed ahead directly in their path. This is where the apex of her experiences's high strangeness lay. This is where she experienced the holographic-like life and death cycle of a huge phoenix-like bird. This is where she was told by a booming multi-voiced unseen personage that she had been chosen "to show the world."

Since the publication of *The Andreasson Affair,* I have received many letters and phone calls offering interpretations of the phoenix experience. Few, however, including my peers, could offer any convincing explanation for Betty's brief glimpse of the strange creatures seemingly caged in an area with a shimmering red atmosphere. We suspected that the red creatures were a kept food source for the aliens, or that the hoods were worn by the entities to disguise themselves from the creatures. After all, it was surmised, if the entities periodically grabbed and took away these stalk-eyed creatures for food, they were probably frightened by the appearance of their captors. Thus, the entities donned the hoods to avoid panic among the creatures as they transported Betty through their caging area.

Over the years, I left Betty's experience with the red creatures for others to ponder. It was certainly beyond my ken and completely atypical of the usual UFO abduction scenario. However, during this current phase four investigation, the totally unexpected took place. We found out the purpose for which the mysterious red creatures were raised. It was revealed to Betty by one of the Elders while aboard the huge mother ship floating in outer space.

Betty: They're red and they...look like small bodies with...thin limbs and four fingers with...nodules.... They're just hanging there, and they got two stalks by the neck, and they got big eyes! They're in tubes. They're in glass things.... Ah, there's one...that's got its head bowed, and it has *no eyes*.... It's all shrunken-like and just a little tiny, tiny thing that, a little ball is there. Another...tall man is coming in with white hair, but it isn't like white hair. It looks pink in this [red] light. And there's something in his hand, and the other one tells me to come closer and to go on over by one of those red creatures inside those glass things, and they're opening up the top of that glass thing. *[pause]* And...that red creature has its eyes upward. And that tall being that's going over and and he's taking out the eye, the black ball—eyeball—I guess, from that red thing, red creature, and there's all little things on the bottom of it.

Fred: Bottom of what?

Betty: That black ball, the eyeball of that red thing. It doesn't seem to hurt that red thing. He's setting it aside...on a table and a sort of a round type plate. *[pause]* Now he's taking the other one out. Uh-h! And he's setting it on the [the round type plate]. Oh...it comes out so easy. *[pause]* Oh boy!

Fred: Does that mean these red things can't see now?

Betty: I don't know, but they don't have any eyes—that one doesn't have any eyeballs, but that other one over there with it's head bowed...it's got a little tiny...black ball and it's just a little tiny...thing that comes out and has a little ball on the end of it. Then there's more of them over there...that's just inside the tube and—

Fred: Are they going to get *new eyes?*

Betty: I don't know..... They're just removing them, and I'm just watching. They said they're going to show me. And now...they're putting the top back on [the glasslike tube that contains one of the red creatures]. And there seems to be some kind of steam or...gas or something filling up inside the one, inside...that glass thing there where they took...the two eyeballs out of that red thing. And it's just getting...very filled with...a smoke or reddish-colored steam.... Oh, they're telling me that...I'm not to fear because it will grow back another eyeball.... Evidently, that's what that one over there is doing. [Figure 20]

Fred: Growing eyes?

Betty: Growing eyeballs. Yeah. And, they're saying that they use these for when the natural eyeballs go. They implant these because they control through them.

They're telling me they have to do this because sometimes the natural eyes of the Watchers become burned from being in too much light and open all the time, so they have to replace them.

Fred: They become what, please? Too much light?

Betty: They become burned out.

Fred: Oh, I see.

Betty: They're open all the time and view everything and so the light is too bright at times, so they have these biobics done to them.

Figure 20. Elders showing Betty one of their laboratories.

Fred: Did they tell you how long that process takes?

Betty: I don't know.

Fred: So [the Elders] are more like people?

Betty: They are, yeah, they're people.

Fred: Do they look like *people* people—like us?

Betty: Yeah, but different. They look...pale with white hair and pale blue eyes and very little color.

Fred: Those with the pale blue eyes—do they move around like a person would or an animal would? Do they appear to move around?

Betty: Oh, they move around just like we do. They're very, very tall and they move quicker....

At this juncture, Fred interrupted Betty and had her draw what she had just described while still under hypnosis.

Later, Betty made an attempt at a cut-away drawing of the mother ship. She based it upon her movement from the time she entered the ship up to the time she observed biobics. [Figure 21]

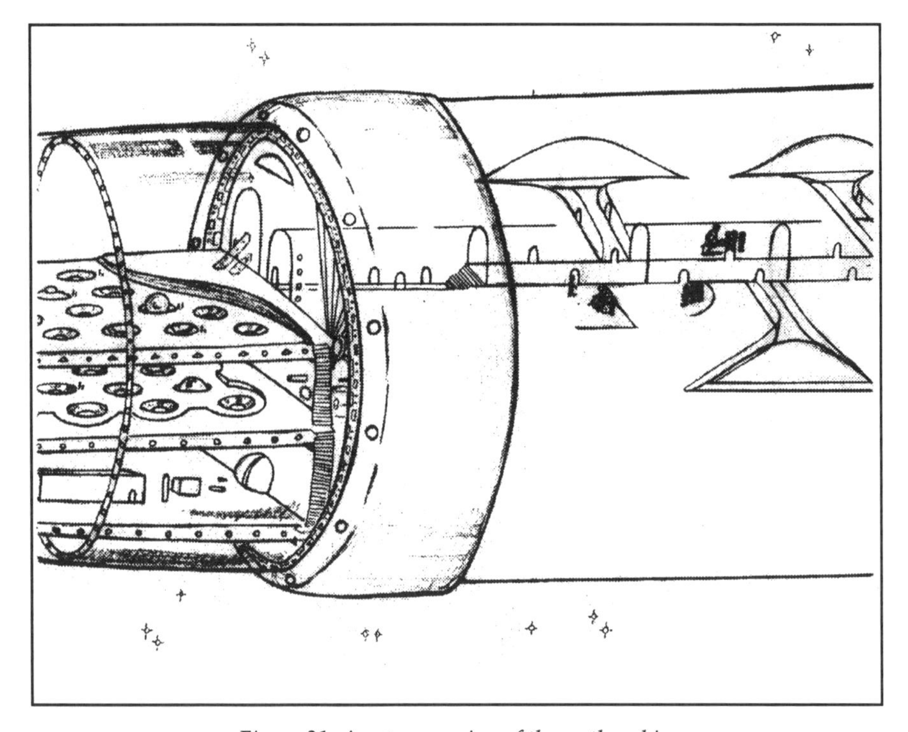

Figure 21. A cut-away view of the mother ship.

After Betty had finished her drawings, Fred continued the questioning process. Interest first centered upon the interaction exhibited between Betty and the aliens and between the aliens themselves.

Fred: Relax. Do you feel a warmth around these people?

Betty: Uh-huh.

Fred: Of love?

Betty: I, I don't know. It feels like a *peace.*

Fred: Do they interact with each other?

Betty: They...talk with each other. Yeah.

Fred: Do you feel them or hear them when they talk with each other?

Betty: Yeah, I can hear them. They're talking audibly. They're not talking through their minds and—

Fred: What are they saying?

Betty: Well, they're there and taking those eyes. They're going to do biobics, whatever. And they were showing me how they do it, and they said that they will grow back.

Then Fred asked the proverbial $64,000 question.

Fred: *Why* do they take the eyes?

Betty: They're going to use them [so] that...they will have control over them. Through them, they will see and perform, make happen, with...the greys. But they don't last as long, the natural eyes, because they are open for so long and become blind, but they can communicate right through the eyes.

Let's stop for a moment and take stock of these astonishing revelations given Betty.

1. The red creatures were raised as living eye banks.
2. Eyes removed from the red creatures regenerated.
3. The ever-open eyes of the gray Watchers degenerated over time due to prolonged exposure to natural light.
4. The worn-out eyes of the gray Watchers were replaced with newly-grown eyes removed from the red creatures.

Equally astonishing was the disclosure that the Elders could somehow see through the eyes of the Watchers. The Watchers in effect were living monitors for the Elders!

Although mind boggling, it all made sense. Betty was told during her 1973 abduction that these small fetus-like creatures were in actuality *mature fetuses* apparently in various stages of alien/human hybridization. She had witnessed the removal of two fetuses taken from a human mother abductee. The aliens used Betty to help them comfort the mother during the process. Betty had watched in horror as the aliens quickly performed a number of operations on the removed fetus.

The Watchers	Fowler	phase three
Betty:	Oh no! They're putting something on that baby's mouth! It's so tiny. *[Betty began to breath heavily and her voice was anxious.]* Oh! One of the beings is saying [telepathically] they have to do it . They can't allow the baby to take a breath of air. Oh! Oh-h-h! Don't do that.... They're putting needles in the top of its head and its ears!...And they're cutting the eye lids away!...And they're really pleased with...this little thing because its eyes are big and black when they cut the lids—*like theirs....* The fetuses *become them*—like them.	

Thus, it becomes quite apparent why the red creatures were kept in a red light environment. Their eyes, like human eyes, are less sensitive to the red end of the spectrum. This environment kept their eyes in a healthy condition for biobics. Why the two entities that led Betty through this red environment in 1967 were hooded still remains a mystery. It appears that neither they nor the red creatures were supposed to see each other's eyes.

Questions continued that related to the interaction between the two types of alien entities. Of prime interest was ascertaining the alien chain of command. Betty was asked if she knew the answer to this question. The answer was forthcoming as she continued to describe the final stages of biobics to us.

Betty: They're servants. The greys are servants to them. They said...that they are ambassadors of "Oh," masters of rings, cycles and orbs. *[long sigh and pause]* They are Elders.

Fred: Where do they live?

Betty: I don't know—I guess in this place where they have me. In this space thing with long main halls to it, long halls and many rooms. *[sighs]* They're taking...that round thing with the black eyeballs [removed from the red creatures].... They're picking them up, and they said come along, they're going to show me what they do. *[pause]* We're going out of the room and we're going down that hall again, going back, and that door just closed up so you can't even see that red area any more. It was all red in there—that atmosphere. And we're just walking down. Oh, we're going—now we're turning into that room to the right there. We're going in. Now the greys are moving away from that one being that was on the table. And they've removed...those eyes. *[gasps]*

Fred: Do the greys interact in a warm friendly manner with each other?

Betty: They just seem as if they're doing what they had to do. I, I don't know. They are…friendly, I guess, but they don't make any motion as if they're friendly. They're just there all working together as if—

Fred: You're the only human being there, right?

Betty: I don't know, those two in white seem human.

Fred: These beings, like people—do they seem to be workers for the greys?

Betty: No, the greys are working for them [the tall human-like beings]. And how they can see everything, is through the greys' eyes, and they can command them to do whatever they want.

Fred: What is this?

Betty: I don't know, but they're standing now, the two are standing over that grey on the table, and all the other smaller beings are over by that wall there…. And they have their heads and their backs turned. And…the tall ones are leaning over and—it looks like they're working on that grey [on the table] with the two black eyeballs. Oh-h-h, that one lying on the table…. Oh, it's gross. His eyes are gone. The tall one is putting those eyeballs that he took from the red creatures, and he is somehow putting those in that being [the grey] that's lying there. He's got some kind of instrument and connection, and light, makes light. And all the other ones taking the hood that was around that one that they put those eyeballs in. He looks better with those eyeballs in.

After the Elder transferred and implanted the black eyes from the red creatures into the Watcher's empty eye sockets, he pressed his fingersto its head and tiny lights appeared in the black eyes. [Figure 22]

Betty: And they're…touching his head in different spots. Is that weird! *[pause]* They touch his head in different spots and tiny pinpoints of light—different colored light—light up in those black eyes.

Ah-h-h, is this strange! Whew, whoa! And they're just touching the top of his head with their fingers.

They're touching and…. Oh, is that something! Those…eyes are lighting up…two points of light all over. Different colors of light in…that black [entity's new eyes] as they touch certain spots on his head. Ah, it's amazing. It's beautiful. They keep touching him with their fingertips in different spots, and the eyes light up in different spots like it had hundreds of sections to it—like pinpoints of different color light is happening. The other one is stopping and going over and pulling some kind of a machine over to the edge by the Watcher's head.

Figure 22. An Elder implanting new eyes into a grey.

Betty then described a machine-like chair that was pulled from the wall. It backed up to the operating table where biobics was being performed on the reclining gray Watcher. A glass hood was put over its head, which was to the back of the chair. An Elder then on the chair, tilting his head backward. It was hard to visualize what Betty was describing verbally. Betty produced a detailed drawing of this operation. It depicted a close-up view of the operating table and its connection to the chair where the Elder sat. In the upper right corner of the drawing, Betty inserted the overall view that confronted her. [Figure 23]

Betty: The other one's bringing over something and pulling it over and placing it right over the whole head of...the grey that just had big...black eyes of the red [creature] put in it. I, I don't know. It's just coming over them. And they're just standing back. One of them is going over and sitting in—what he pulled over has like a chair attached to it and a thing comes down on top of his head. *[pause]* The being's just sitting there. And I'm just standing back with that other one—the other tall being, and they pull it upward and out and down over his head, and this glass thing has got...things that reach around it. They're pulling it down and around him and adjusting it, I guess. Then one of the beings is going, and there's a seat on the other end. And there's something down there, too, that that one touched, but I don't know what it was (a bar or something that comes out).

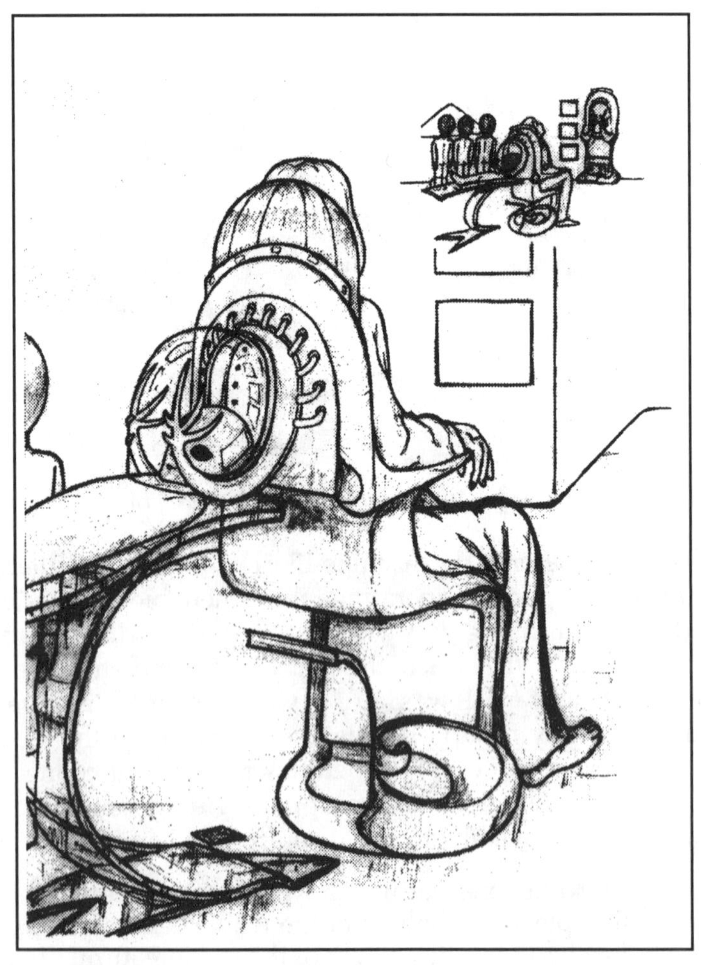

Figure 23. The Elder's chair connecting to the operating table.

The other one's steadying the chair, tilting his head back. He's just sitting there with his head tilted back. He somehow controls through the eyes—the new Watcher's' eyes—the workers. *[pause]* He's still sitting there. Now he's getting up, and the other three Watchers, the beings, are turning around and coming over to where that other one [the being on the table] is. They're doing something to him. They're lifting up that glass thing, that hood or whatever it is, off his head. They're putting it back by the chair. The other tall being is pushing it back into...the wall over there. *[pause]*

Fred still was confused about the chain of command during this operation. He wondered what part the red creatures played in it.

Fred: The [red creatures]...do they control the human-like beings?

Betty: *[emphatically]* No. The tall beings in white, with white hair, control the gray ones to a point through the eyes and the brain evidently. Those eyes are evidently like cameras for those tall ones to see through [the greys' eyes remotely]. But, much more sophisticated than saying they're cameras.... The greys are like walking or living cameras...and do the bidding of those tall ones.

Fred: Do the tall ones move more like people?

Betty: Uh-huh. Just like people.

Fred: Are [the] eye-beings [the red beings] the controllers? *[Fred still was confused about the chain of command.]*

Betty: In some respects, but they're only given orders.

Fred: Who controls? In other words, who's on top? Who's on first?

Betty: The tall beings.

Fred: The tall beings, the eye-beings, the greys. Is that the order?

Betty: No. The eye-beings? You mean the red beings with the eyes they took from?

Fred: Yes.

Betty: No. Those red beings are grown for their eyes. The greys can't look upon them, because they are what the tall beings use, and the greys. Oh, I don't know.

Scheduled time was running out. Slowly but surely, he brought Betty out of the trance back to his office on November 6, 1992.

Betty: *[slowly comes out of the hypnotic trance]* I feel like I'm so relaxed.... I'm *[sigh]* just about to fall asleep.

Fred: *[laughs]* You'll sleep well tonight, I assure you.

Betty: So something did happen that night.

Fred: *[laughs]*

Betty: Well, I didn't know. I know that the two fallen trees—but we still didn't find out why those trees fell.

Fred: I got the feeling—you said that there was a couple of points of light coming out when they put their hand on the head? That was connecting nerves and endings and stuff inside, I think. That's the feeling I got.

Betty: It was weird! To see that. Those little red beings? They're farming those little red beings!

Fred: Right.

Betty: It was weird.

This was an understatement. Weirder things were to follow as Betty continued her odyssey aboard the giant craft far above our planet Earth.

chapter seven

The Blessing

> *The things that flashed back came in the order of my life.... The scenes were three-dimensional.... It was like the little girl I saw was somebody else.... Yet it was me.... They were the exact things I had done, because I remember them.*[1]
>
> *(a near-death experiencer)*

Betty's description of biobics was fascinating. It indicated that the alien entities were able to genetically engineer and produce a creature specifically programmed to create replacement eyes for the small gray beings called Watchers. The creature in turn was able to replace eyes taken from it by a process similar to a frog's regeneration of a missing limb. This was perhaps just a glimpse of the aliens' capabilities in their overall genetics engineering program.

In any event, after the biobics demonstration was completed, one of the self-named Elders with Betty asked her to follow him. As Betty walked down a hallway, she could look out big windows and see stars against the blackness of space.

Betty: We're going out the door. One of the tall ones is staying in there, and I'm walking with the other one. He tells me to come along. We're walking up the hall, and I can see other halls down that way, and it looks like windows—big, big windows, and you can see it. It's like the night sky with stars out there, and there's doors in different places. We're walking up the hall and I can hear something like tinkling, like music or strange sound of music up ahead, and we keep walking. He says, "Come along, come along." And we're

1. Moody, 1976, pp. 66-67.

> walking up...and we're coming toward a room, and I hear that music. It's so peculiar, but beautiful. It's a strange sound, like tinkling.... A combination of xylophone...and a harp or—I don't know what it is. Like tinkle all over, and I can hear it. We're going in that room, and there's another tall being over there. Ha! And that's...what's making that music.

What Betty is now about to describe is so strange that it needs some clarification. Figure 24 is her detailed drawing prior to reading her relived description under hypnosis.

Figure 24. An Elder working near the inclined cylinder.

As Betty entered the room that was emanating musical sounds, she noticed a number of things. First, the room had an inclined cylinder running out of one of its walls. It was made of a transparent material and looked to be several feet in diameter. Large and small balls of white light raced up and down within it.

She also saw an Elder standing to the side of the cylinder with his back to it. He was waving his hand over what appeared to be an inverted hemisphere-shaped holder that contained different sized upright two-pronged (tuning?) forks. The tops of each of these forks held crystal, pyramid-shaped objects. As the Elder waved his hands over the forks, small balls of light zipped upward from the pyramid objects as the strange music continued to play.

Concurrent with this scenario, a table rose up from an opening in the floor. Its surface was indented like a shallow basin and contained liquid of some kind. The balls of light emanating from the forks floated over and immersed themselves in the liquid.

A triangular glasslike shelf lay midway between the forks and the cylinder. It held a ball of pointed crystal that hung in the air. Under the shelf was a row of what looked like hieroglyphics. Betty penned these in on her drawing, but she felt that her representations were probably not exact.

The Elder watched with Betty for a while and then went over to the basin-like table. He removed the tiny balls of light from the liquid and placed them somewhere within the upper part of his white robe.

Betty: He's got something that is from the wall and...there's the things that come out and over and there's like...these diamond things that he's touching and just waving his hands over—and music. Oh, it's just beautiful. As that music is playing, there's these tiny balls of light coming out of it. We're standing here watching, and there's...something coming up out of the.... Oh! there's five indented things there! And there's something coming out of...the floor. It's like a table, and it's.... Oh! and look it! There's something that came in, too. There's...this long hatch. *[A slanted, square hollow shaft that is coming down from the ceiling to the floor.]* It's...got these balls of white—still, white, bright light that's bouncing back and forth, tiny ones and large ones, and they're going back and forth. This is fascinating! And there's something there, too. There's...a diamond thing with...a beautiful, beautiful ball with these crystal things coming out of it. It's beautiful! Oh! And...that music is causing all those tiny [marble-sized] balls of light that are just floating all around. They're coming over, and there's...liquid or water or something in that...table that came up. *[The table top is like a basin and has liquid in it.]* It just came up in a circular form, and the balls of light are falling into it. Oh, this is fabulous! *[whispers]* This is fantastic!

Those diamond-shaped things, those triangular-shaped things...he's just moving his hands over them. Music is coming out, and there's these balls of light—some out of those triangular things. A ball of light appears around it, and it just goes up and goes around and comes over that table there and goes into the water. Those...little tiny balls of light [are] about the size of a big marble. And he's sitting in there, and the music is so strange, so unusual, and that [the cylindrical hatch] over there—the balls of white light [are] just coming in and going out and coming in all different sizes, going out and coming. We're over there, and the tall being goes over, and he puts his hands in the liquid [in the basin-like table top]. He's washing his hands, and he's holding up the balls of light that are in there, and he's lifting them, and he must have pockets, as he's putting them in his side, on the side of him....

After the Elder had somehow secreted the tiny balls of light within the folds of his robe, he again approached Betty.

Betty: He's coming over to me, and he's saying somebody wants to see me. *[pause]* We're going out of that room now and in the hall.... The hall is so long. You can see...way down there, way down there and way back. And we're just standing there. I don't know why. Oh! I see why. He's watching down the hall. Way down the hall. They're taking...those old men that were in black, that were all bent over. They're moving along.... There's a being in front of the three, and then there's another being that...looks like it's not very pleased at something, and then there's one following it. They're going out of the room, and they're marching down. They're going down by the stairs. There's a red light following each one of those men in those black robes. That's what [the tall being] stopped for. He's watching them as they go down the stairs. They're way down the hall there. We're just watching them walk down the stairs. I guess they're going to be taken outdoors or out...front.

Farther down the hall, two Watchers were ushering three aged Elders in black robes and a smaller Watcher. A small plum-sized red ball of light hovered in front of the heads of those being escorted. It appeared that they were being taken out to where the three-tiered landing decks were located. The Elder stopped awhile with Betty and watched the procession until it descended the steps. Then he motioned again for Betty to follow, and they continued on their way. [Figure 25]

Betty: But he's turning now and saying, "Come along." We're moving again and we're going into another room. And...is this strange! We're going right through the door! It's like the

Figure 25. Greys leading aged Elders away.

door...is a *picture* of a door, and there's nothing there. We walk right through it! And we're walking through and going into...this room, and there's another tall being, another Elder, and he's bringing me over to him. We're standing there.... I asked him, "I don't see any ladies in this place at all. Is there any women in here? All I see is men." And he says, "No, we are neither male or female here. Humans are male and female, and the male is the dominant one." And I asked, "Well, what am I doing here then?" And he says, "Don't you remember your blessing?" And I said, "No...what blessing? What are you talking about?" He says to come here and move over by him, and he looks over at the other one.... In this room, there's some light with letters on it over there, and there's another one of those...things that come down *[what she had described as a cylindrical hatch in an-*

> *other room],* with balls of white light of all different sizes going up and down and up and down. And there's chairs there, like glass, and there's a thing right out in front there. Oh, yes, over there, there's like...a light that comes down by the door. And there's a thing up ahead there, like it's a round thing that goes in like a tunnel almost, and there are...rings of light in it...that go way, way back. And that other one is touching some...lights...on the thing that's back there. I don't know what it is.

Again, without some clarification and Betty's drawings, it was hard to visualize what she was describing. This room was large. It had a round, conelike indented circular area in one of the walls that looked like a tunnel emanating rings of light.

A clear, glasslike platform extended out in front of the tunnel-like opening. Round designs with lights on them lay on the floor on each side of the tunnel-like opening. In a corner to the right of the opening was a stand with four upright clawlike prongs. To its right was what appeared to be a wide doorway filled with what looked like vibrating water. A row of four clear-glass or plexiglass chairs faced the tunnel. Each had a square or rectangular cover on the floor in front of them. An inclined tubular hatch angled out of the wall behind the chair. It, like the one she had seen before, was filled with balls of light shooting up and down. A large window lay between the doorlike opening and the hatch. Betty could see the stars through it. [Figure 26]

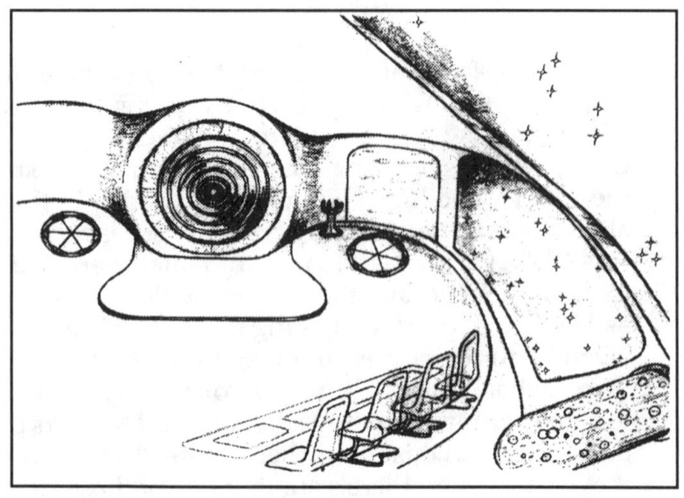

Figure 26. Stars were visible through the windows of the mother ship.

As Betty gazed about the unearthly room, the Elder told her that she would now know what he meant by her blessing.

Betty: He says, "You will remember your blessing now." And all of a sudden, there's a ball that comes rolling through that tunnel, and it's collecting all those rings of light. And that ball has got lines all through it and rings that are moving—colored rings of light moving every which way around it, and it's stopping. This is so strange! *[whispers]* This is so strange—everything! It's stopping there, and all the rings of light are coming together, and one toward the center.

Betty watched in amazement as a large ball of light moved out of the cone-shaped tunnel in the wall and stopped at its entrance. Astonished, she watched the big ball take up the shimmering rings of light around its mid-section. [Figure 27]

Figure 27. The big ball of light with shimmering rings.

What reportedly happened next is precisely the kind of thing that was discussed by a panel at the UFO Abduction Conference held at MIT.[2] I mentioned this panel discussion briefly in the introduction to this book. Abduction researcher Budd Hopkins and others were discussing the "theological" overtones of some of the abduction experiences. The question revolved around what to do about them.

Budd, if you recall, felt that these overtones represented the "biggest cloud on the horizon...a kind of theological argument which is...essentially a waste of time. It misses the point all the way around." Moderator Richard Hall responded that "To them it's...a profound philosophical, religious issue, so they are introducing it." MUFON's Director of Abduction Research, John Carpenter, retorted that "Perhaps that's their method of...coping with it. They choose that, and it works for them, and it doesn't hurt them or anybody else. It's OK."

Betty's experiences, although not specifically mentioned by the panelists, are among those that contain such theological overtones. They have appeared consistently since my investigation of Betty started in 1977. Recording these aspects may prove to be either a "waste of time" or an abductee's "way of coping" with an unearthly experience. We do not know for sure.

Thus, in my opinion, this unpopular component of some abductees' experiences should be accurately recorded. They should not be prejudged or arbitrarily dismissed. After all, it's part of the reported experience. If we decide what to record and dismiss in abduction experiences, we are left with abduction reports created in our own image.

At the same time, the investigator must be very careful to remain neutral concerning these seemingly atypical components of the abduction experience. One must remain an objective recorder of what an abductee reports and not be influenced in either a positive or negative fashion by personal world view prejudices.

Now that the ground work has been laid for what is to come, let us return to Betty as she stared at the big ball of light that has just appeared at the mouth of the cone-shaped tunnel.

Betty: And, we're standing there.... All of a sudden that ball of light is opening. It's opening up and I—this is so.... *[whispers]* I can't believe this!

What Betty saw next was hard to believe. An opening appeared in the big ball of light to display what appeared to be a three-dimensional

---

2. Whiting, 1992.

movie complete with audio. She then described the scene that played upon the screenlike opening in the ball of light.

Betty: There's a scene there with people.... I see two of the tall beings. *[The tall beings are not visible to the humans in this place.]* There's a stage there, and there's a man...and a podium, and there's in the background...a woman, and she's looking down into [what] looks like a Bible. And the man's standing up there, and there's all people [humans] in the audience. It's strange, because some of the people [have] a light around them. They're just sitting there, and I can hear the man...saying...how much...we love God. It must be a church meeting.

The people in the congregation were oblivious both to the presence of the invisible Elders as well as to the radiation Betty saw around the heads of some people. Betty was able to see both. Suddenly, she recoiled with shock in the hypnotist's chair. She recognized the place. It was a lower room in an old stone church in Ashburnham, MA. She recognized the pastor, brother Lee, and his wife, sister Lee. Then she saw herself with her mother and father!

Betty: Ah-h-h! *[gasps in amazement]* There's my mother and father! There's my mother and father, and that's me when I was younger! We're sitting there, too! There's a person standing up now, and they're giving a testimony of what God has done for them.... But there's one tall being standing there, and then there's another tall being...up on the stage. I can see myself now. I'm standing up and I'm giving testimony. I can hear what I'm saying.... I'm saying that God has been with me through everything, through all the hardships that I've had to endure. And that although I don't have any money to give—I'm crying there—I can see myself crying.... The gift that God has given me to draw I will give back to Him and glorify Him somehow. [Figure 28] And I see that...tall being [invisible Elder] is bending down and whispering in that woman's ear. And all of a sudden she jumps up, and she's running off the stage and down the steps.

The minister's wife rushed down into the congregation and went directly to Betty. She placed her hands on Betty's head and began speaking in tongues. Then, one of the unseen Elders placed his hand on the minister's shoulder. Instantaneously, seemingly in response, the minister began to interpret the strange ecstatic language being uttered by his wife.

Betty: And now that tall being is after the minister...and...he's putting his hand on his shoulder or something, and...the minister's talking in tongues...and the woman is coming running down and she's putting her hands on my head, and she begins to talk in tongues as she has her hands on my head.... She stopped, and now that other tall being is standing by and...that man at the podium is saying, "You have given...all that you have.... Thou shalt be blessed above women...." Oh, the scene is fading. It's so strange, because there's a man that's sitting there too, and...there's black surrounding him. Oh, this is so peculiar! The whole scene is starting to fade.... Oh, and that ball is starting to close.

Figure 28. A church scene from Betty's past is viewed by Betty while on board an alien craft.

Fred decided to end the session after this unexpected turn of events. I wondered what Budd Hopkins would think of this? I also wondered what my peers would think of my including such incongruous material in my report. This, however, was just a tiny taste of what was to come. Later I shall devote a complete chapter to discuss what one might generally call the religious overtones of Betty Luca's UFO abduction experiences.

Betty slowly but surely came back out of hypnosis.

Betty: Ah-h-h. Whoa, I feel so relaxed.... I remember [the incident in the church] now. I remember going to that church meeting with my mother and father in Ashburnham, and standing up, and giving testimony and that prophecy. Weird, huh? This thing gets more and more weird! I'm beginning to think I'm nuts with all this weird stuff. I really am. Maybe I need to get a psychiatrist. *[laughs]*

I laughed when I heard Betty make this statement. It brought me back to 1977 in the office of Dr. Harold Edelstein. Betty had said the same thing to us after coming out of her initial hypnosis sessions after reliving her 1967 abduction. She found it impossible to believe some of the memories that were surfacing. In a sense, the investigating team was glad that she felt this way. We accommodated her wish and arranged sessions with a doctor.

The doctor was a board-certified, clinical, medical specialist in occupational medicine. This man had a rather unique educational background that seemed to especially suit him for the task. He had undergraduate and graduate degrees in both aeronautical and astronautical engineering and a doctorate in environmental health science and engineering in addition to his M.D. degree. Following are some pertinent excerpts from his analytical report based on his initial 1977 and 1979 psychiatric interviews with Betty:

The Andreasson Affair Phase Two	Fowler	phase two
I spoke with Betty...at times informally, but with the conscious attempt to observe her behavior, language, thought content, cognitive functioning and affect. The conversation was directed toward matters unrelated to her alleged abduction experience specifically, although the topic of the similar experiences of others and the subject of UFOs in general did come up briefly.... I found that the overall elements of Betty's personality...were consistent with the 1977 interview. As before, I found no clear evidence of a thought disorder or impairment in cognitive functioning.... I certainly have no new information to endorse the authenticity of Betty's alleged experience, but I can medically continue to support the stability of her general life perceptions and her interpretive functions. This may not qualify her as an unbiased scientific witness to the experiences which she has described, but then, who among those with such credentials would necessarily perform better?[a]		

a. Fowler, 1994, p. 217 (and personal files).

It was mutually comforting then, as it is now, to at least have confidence that these experiences, aberrant as they might seem, nonetheless come from a mentally healthy personality, especially in the light of the astounding things that are yet to be reported within pages of this book!

chapter eight

Odyssey to the One

The most incredible common element in the accounts I have studied...is the encounter with a very bright light.... Not one person has expressed any doubt that it was...a being of light.... The love and warmth which emanate from this being...is utterly beyond words.[1]

Raymond A. Moody, Jr., M.D.

Betty arrived at the office of Fred Max for a hypnosis session. Prior to hypnosis, she was asked to describe the immediate events that led up to the "blessing." We wondered how much of the data extracted by hypnosis was now part of her conscious memory. It soon was apparent that she remembered what had happened. However, she was still concerned about the falling trees she had heard. As mentioned, one of these trees had been found and photographed. It had been mysteriously split right down the middle. Betty had hoped that what caused the trees to fall would have been revealed while under hypnosis.

Betty: I'm still trying to find out about those trees—why...they broke, why they snapped like that. 3:00 in the morning when there was dead calm—no rain, no wind no nothing. It was dead calm, dead quiet—no wind sounds.... We haven't got to that part yet. That must have been when I went back *[when the entities returned Betty to her home]....*

Bob: Do you remember in the beginning when you saw the blue lights go over the trees...?

Betty: Uh-huh.

Bob: Was it the same tree?

1. Moody, 1976, p. 58.

Betty: I don't know. It may have been.

Betty also wondered if she had any encounters prior to the mother ship incident. She felt that the possibility should be explored that something might have occurred. However, she agreed that for continuity it would be best to continue on from where the last session left off.

Betty: We haven't found out if there was...any other encounters before this. We were just trying to find out about these trees [in the last hypnosis sessions]. You know, there may have been something before too.... Maybe we should just try and finish up and see what happened....

Fred sat Betty in a comfortable easy chair and proceeded to induce hypnosis. It was decided to have Betty go back to the church in her mind's eye and proceed onward from that scenario. This process would accomplish two things. It would lead her naturally into the next events of her experience, and it would serve as a benchmark against which to compare what she had relived during the prior session. We have found in the past that Betty's mind was like a human tape recorder. Time and time again she was able to spontaneously relive the same events when called upon to do so, thus demonstrating that the events are firmly embedded in her mind, and providing compelling evidence that the events actually occurred as described. Fred placed Betty under hypnosis and brought her back to the events that transpired in the church.

Fred: Tell me, what's happening?

Betty: It's a...time when I was in a church and...it looks like it is happening just now. It's so real-life, and there's people sitting in the chairs, and there's two tall men in white robes, [with] white hair. One is over by the door, and the other one is standing up on the stage part there. And the minister's wife is looking in the Bible and sitting down, and the minister is standing at the podium, and he's asking about testimonies of what Christ has done for each person. And there are people that stand up and tell how good God has been in their life. And what is so unusual is, I see light around different people and around the tall beings there. There's white light around some, and I see some with red light, and...there's a person there that has black around him. And there's a person standing up telling what the Lord has done for him. And I see myself now, standing up and telling how much the Lord has been with me in all the troubles I've been through. And I'm crying as I'm standing up there and I'm saying that...I don't have any money to give right now, but

I can draw, and I can give that to God—to glorify God. And it's strange because I see that tall being—looks like the Elders—bending down.... It looks like he's whispering in the minister's wife's ear. And she's suddenly jumping up, and she's coming off the stage and coming down the stairs. And she's going over to where I am, and she's putting her hands on me, and she's talking in tongues. And...that tall being has his hands on the minister's shoulder, and she's talking in tongues over me as I'm crying.... The minister...talks in tongues a little, and then he interpreted what she was talking in tongues, and he said I would be blessed above women.

I must interject here that Betty did not want the above remark made about her by the minister to be recorded in this book. Betty recognized it as a near quote of how an angel had described the virgin Mary in the Bible. It was deeply embarrassing to her. She felt it would be misunderstood and make her out to be more than she was as a person. But I wanted to record an accurate record of everything, and I finally convinced her to allow the remark. The Bible-oriented minister may have embellished the remark with his religious fervor. We now reach the point where we had left off at the last hypnosis session.

Betty: And that's the blessing that the tall...Elder was telling me here. It seems like...the picture is starting to fade or pull back...into that ball.... It's just disappeared. And those rings...were straight, vertical around that ball, and now they're starting to twist and turn around that ball. They're twisting and turning, and as they do, they pull inward a little bit, and they keep on twisting and turning, just staying there. And the Elder beside me is...saying to me, "Now you remember your blessing given you."

At this point, Betty's attention was drawn to the sudden appearance of three other tall human-like beings coming through the door. She was about to witness a strange, mystical ceremony, the likes of which were beyond her wildest imagination.

The three walked over to a round design on the floor and stood within it, forming a triangle. Then they each stretched out their arms to each other, touching their hands palm to palm.

Betty: There's other Elders, tall beings with white hair and white robes, coming through the door. And...there's three of them standing over on that design over there, that round, circular design that has like points on it. And they're just standing...in a diamond-like fashion. Three in a diamond fashion. And as they're standing there, they stretch out their hands, arms, and touch each other's hand so their hands...and their fingers are pointed upward and their arms are stretched outward...forming a triangle, and they're bowing their head.

Betty and the Elder standing beside her stood watching the three beings, when suddenly the seemingly impossible occurred.

Betty: A ring of light forms...right in the middle of them! They're just standing there. Oh, there's light coming out of their foreheads, and touching each other's foreheads...making a triangle. Oh, this is beautiful!

The expressions on Betty's face revealed the wonder of what she was seeing. As usual, we needed Betty's drawings to provide us with the visual content of her experiences. Some have been so other-worldly and complex that it would have been impossible to understand what she was describing without them. [Figure 29]

Figure 29. Betty sees a group of Elders meditating, which causes beams of light to appear.

The complexity and weirdness of the ceremony continued to evolve. Betty watched, dumbfounded and incredulous.

Betty: There's some other Elders coming in. Four of them. Three of them are going over to where those men are, those Elders, and they're going right in between them. Is this unusual! They're crossing their right arm over and their left arm under the other arm, and they're touching their hands with their fingers pointed upward. *[excited voice]* All of a sudden, there's a ring of light that forms around all of them.... And they're bowing their head, and as they do, I hear them saying, "Oh, Oh, Oh, Oh," but low, like a low "Oh" for a man's sound. Light is coming out of...their foreheads, and it's touching those other two that were with them. And they keep on saying, "Oh-h-h."

Betty excitedly described how three other Elders joined the three in the circle. Each placed his right arm over the one next to him on the right and his left arm under the one next to him on the left. All, like some medieval choir, chanted the sound of a long "Oh." Instantly, a ring of light materialized around them. Two V-shaped beams of light burst from their foreheads and formed a six-pointed star with a smaller ring of light in its center.

This was almost too much for me. My mind was rebelling in disbelief at what Betty was describing. I wondered if I were in my right mind myself, recording and writing about such outlandish things as this. I could empathize with those who felt such aberrant components of the abduction experience must be a product of the abductees' minds. But, nonetheless, a question continually addresses my UFO-weary mind: "What if these components are a valid part of such experiences?" So, even now as I write, I grit my cerebral teeth and remember what was promised in the introduction to this book: Nothing retrieved during the many hypnosis sessions with Betty and Bob (regardless of their high-strangeness) shall be left out of this book.

I imagine that similar thoughts may have played across Fred Max's mind as he tried to remain professionally aloof to what was being described. Seemingly nonplussed, he continued his questioning.

Fred: Real sounds? Out-loud [not telepathic] sounds?

Betty: Yes, it just is low. It's "Oh-h-h."

Fred: Can you draw me a picture of what you're seeing now, so I can try to relate to it?

Betty: I'll try.

Fred brought Betty back, and her eyes blinked open. He gave her a pen and some paper. One could see that even she herself was presented with some difficulty in trying to draw the complex scene that she had just described. She took some time preparing her rough sketch. Later, she provided a finished drawing of the mysterious scenario. [Figure 30]

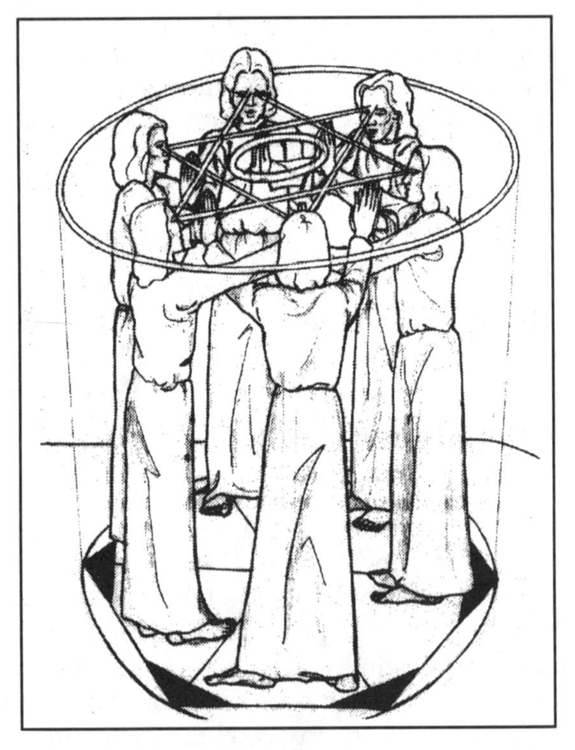

Figure 30. The Elders performing a mysterious ritual.

Betty: It's hard to draw it.... It's...a ring of light around them and in the middle and it's like a star.

Fred, although keeping his composure, was still confused about what and where this was happening. His first thought was that this ceremony was taking place in the little church in Ashburnham. He confused the lights around the Elders with the aura-like light that Betty had seen around some people sitting in the church. Betty corrected him and continued.

Fred: Are you sitting in church? Could those colors be auras?

Betty: No.

Fred: No? Why not?

Betty: Those colors coming out of their forehead? I...don't know, it's just like long light, and they touch each other, and one touches the other, then the other touches the other, and then the other, and they keep on going "Oh-h-h." They have their heads bowed down....

Fred: Are they praying with their sound? Is that like a monk?

Betty: It could be. I don't know. Yeah, I guess it is. I don't know. Their hands are together, but their hands are not together themselves—they're touching the next one...*[not individually clasped together as a human would pray].* They just keep on saying that "Oh-h-h." And we're just standing over, watching....

Again, Betty's face expressed astonishment, and her voice took on a high pitch of excitement.

Betty: Oh! The ring of light is moving upwards.... I can see it move above their heads, and now...it's getting smaller and coming and going into that ring of light in the center. *[pause]* And...the center light is blending together with it. The light [has] stopped coming out their heads now, their foreheads, and they're raising up, they're letting go [of] their hands. They're raising their hands high in the air and again, each one of the is going "Oh-h-h."

Fred: What's their mood?

Betty: Their what?

Fred: Mood. Are they happy?

Betty: I don't know. They're just there, and...they seem like they're concentrating or something. I don't know.

Fred: What's your mood?

Betty: I'm just surprised that that's possible.

Fred: Are you being noticed?

Betty: No, I'm just standing there with the other one, and he's watching, too.

Fred: Can they see you?

Betty: No, they're not looking at me. They're concentrating on whatever...is going on.

Fred: So, what's the ceremony about?

Betty: I don't know. They're raising up their hands. They got their hands way high in the air, and they keep on saying "Oh-h-h," and that light keeps swirling around in the center.

The beams of light emanating from the Elders' foreheads suddenly vanished as they lifted up their arms. The outer ring surrounding them moved upward and shrank to a size similar to that of the inner ring. It then moved down to join and encircle it. Together they orbited around each other in every direction before forming a beach ball sized orb of lavender-purple light. [Figure 31] Then it stopped and floated in the center of the Elders, who remained standing and chanting with up-stretched arms. [Figure 32]

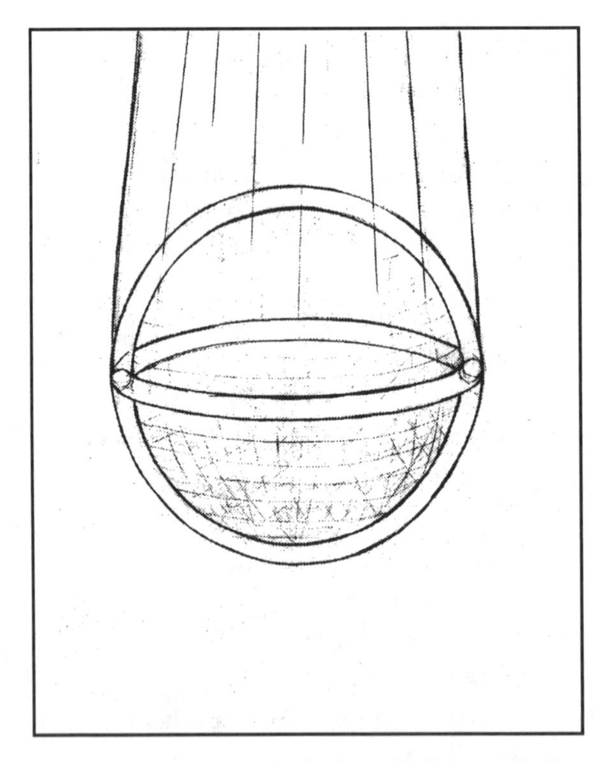

Figure 31. A beach ball sized orb of lavender light seen by Betty.

We wondered whether there was any communication between the Elders and Betty during this strange alien rite. But Betty, totally awe-struck at the sight, had remained tongue-tied.

Fred: Can you talk to the one that you are with?

Betty: I suppose I can, but I don't.

Fred: Why not?

Betty: I'm just watching it.... It's so fantastic to see that. Oh, it's turning into a ball. It's turning.... It's like going in all different directions and turning into a ball of light.... It's in between them. They're putting down their hands, and it's a ball of light now.

Figure 32. Elders chanting around globe of light.

Fred then asked questions about the appearance of the Elders and how they compared with human beings and the Watchers. However, Betty, despite answering such questions, was still very much reliving the experience and observing things. As soon as the questions ceased, she continued to describe what was happening in her mind's eye at that very moment.

Fred: Those people that you drew in your drawing—were they more human-looking or grey-looking?

Betty: Human-looking, but pale skin with white hair and white robes—just like this one. *[She points to her drawing of one.]*

Fred: Like hybrids?

Betty: I don't know.

Fred: Are they mostly human?

Betty: They look human. I don't know if they're human, but they look like…tall men. But…he told me that they're not men…not like earth men…not male or female. That ball of light is just getting bigger. It's in the center, and it was light blue, and all of a sudden now it's turning into a lavender color. It's beautiful, and there's just something circling in it all the time….

The circle of Elders broke up and began to disperse. One of them brought the large purple ball of light over to the Elder with Betty and handed it to him. [Figure 33]

Figure 33. An Elder bringing Betty a large ball of light.

He in turn brought it over to the prong-shaped holder that was located to the right of the cone-shaped tunnel (that was protruding out of the floor). Betty was then asked to sit in one of the glasslike chairs. As she sat, she underwent an out-of-body experience! [Figure 34]

Figure 34. Betty undergoing an out-of-body experience in front of an Elder.

Betty: Now…one is reaching out and taking [the lavender ball of light] with his hands, and the others are just stopping and dispersing. They're just moving away from it, and some of them are going out the door…. This one is telling me to sit down on one of the seats here to the side.

Fred: This one what?

Betty: This Elder that is standing, this tall Elder. He told me to sit down for now.

Fred: Does he speaks speak in words out loud?

Betty: Yeah, I'm hearing him speak.

Fred: Does he have an accent?

Betty: No, it just sounds like English to me.

Fred: Soft?

Betty: Kind and soft and loving, yes. Pleasant.

Fred: Is this a *person* person?

Betty: No, he said he's not male or female. He's a person, but he's not male or female. *[pause]* That other one's now coming over with…that lavender ball of light, and he's talking with him about something…and now he's going over to the side there…placing that ball of light inside that…prong thing there, that thing [holder] that goes up and has four things…. He goes over again to the tall one that's over here and talks with him.

Fred: Balls of light—what do they contain? Do they contain information?

Betty: That purple one?

Fred: Yeah, do they contain information?

Betty: I don't know what that purple one does, but they told me that those [orbs Betty had seen earlier] way over [on] the other side…were record keepers of all intelligence recorders.

Fred: What were? The lights? *[Fred is getting the crystal balls or orbs that Betty had seen at another place mixed up with the purple ball of light she was seeing where she was now.]*

Betty: The balls…that I saw before I came here with the gray ones.

Fred: Are they like brains from something? Elders or something?

Betty: I don't know what they are…just recorders of knowledge and intelligence, those balls that I saw before with the gray ones.

Fred: Where did the balls go?

Betty: I just saw them there, and I saw one pop out before. One popped out in bright light and took off. They were crystal clear like.

Fred: Now you could be talking while you're there, right?

Betty: I am talking to them at times.

Fred: Can you ask questions?

Betty: Yes…. I asked him who "Oh" was.

Fred: And what did he say?

Betty: He said they were the ambassadors of "Oh," and that "Oh" was the internal, external, eternal presence. *[pause]* Now…he's coming over to me, and he says that we are going to journey to Earth. And he says that I will have [to] disrobe. Oh! Oh! And I'm coming out of myself . *[Betty is in an out-of-body state.]* My body is like a robe!

Amazed, Betty found herself slipping out of her body as if she had just taken off a coat. The Elder then passed the purple ball of light to her, and they walked toward the wide doorlike opening that shimmered with patterns like heat waves.

Betty: We're walking over to...that purple ball of light, and he's taking it and passing it to me and telling me to hold on to it, and what we're going to do is go through...that wide door that looks like waves.... He has his hands on my shoulder, and we're walking through. Oh, just bright light. *[pause]* We're...someplace where it is dark, and there's people lying down.

The very instant that Betty passed through the shimmering door, she found herself in a wooded area with the Elder. They appeared before some human men sleeping on the ground. They looked like hoboes. One of the men awakened. He was glowing and stood up to meet them. [Figure 35]

The Elder then took out the balls of light that he had earlier secreted in his robe and put them on his left fingers like rings. He put out his hand toward the glowing hobo, who reached over and took some of the balls off the Elder's fingers. As he did, they coalesced into one tiny ball of light. Simultaneously, the color within the large ball of light in Betty's arms changed from purple to blue for a moment.

Betty: It's like in the woods.... There's people...and there's a man that's getting up. He's coming over. Oh, he's got light around him. It's just a [human] man, and he's coming over to the Elder, and I'm holding this purple.... Oh...it's...just so beautiful! Something in it keeps on moving.... *[pause]*

That Elder's talking to that man, and...the Elder is drawing something out from his white robe in front and holding out his hand. Oh, it's balls, tiny balls of light, that he has like rings on his fingers. Is that weird! And that man is selecting some. He's pulling some off and they turn into a tiny ball.

Betty's experience again was interrupted to ask questions about the large ball of light that she carried in her arms.

Fred: What is the physical sensation of touching the ball?

Betty: I don't know. It just seems smooth....

Figure 35. An Elder and Betty greeting a human man.

Fred: Is it cool? Warm?

Betty: No, I can't really tell. It's just like purple light, but it's like moving in motion in the ball, like smoke or something, but it's purple [like a clear ball with purple, moving smoke inside]. And it just keeps on revolving, moving.... The ball doesn't...but the stuff inside is revolving or moving all around.

Fred: Do you feel the sensation of motion when you hold the ball?

Betty: No. I'm just standing there, and now that man is going back, and he's smiling.... He's going over and sitting down. No one else is moving over there.... There's some people sitting over there. They look like they're hoboes. That man [the one that came to the Elder] does, too. He's dressed shabbily...but, there's light around him, and he's got a beard, and there's others lying down there. *[sighs]* Now, the Elder says we must go to another place.

At this point, the Elder touched Betty's shoulder. Betty experienced a brilliant flash of light and found herself in what appeared to be a hospital room.

Betty: He touches my shoulder again and whew! Just bright, white light. *[pause]* Oh, we're in another place. It's like in a room.... I don't know what it is. There's a light on. It's like a hospital room.... There's a bed there. We're going over to it. Oh, there's an elderly man lying in the bed, and there's a black woman, kind of heavyset, and she's sitting next to the bed. She has her head bowed. I don't know if she's watching out for this man or what, but.... Oh! Is that weird!

Fred: What's weird?

Betty: There's some...*black things* that are trying to pull that [man in bed] out.

Fred: What do you mean, "black thing"?

Betty: Oh! *[Betty is so excited she can hardly get her words out.]* Wait a minute, there's...a light being that's pulling the opposite direction. Oh, I'm getting chills from this. *[whispers]* This is weird. Oh, it's so weird. It's like there's a tug of war going on for that old man. Oh!

The scene that Betty was now describing was terrifying if real. From my perspective it appeared that two types of entities were struggling over a dying man's essence or soul.

Fred: Is the old man being hurt?

Betty: No, he...looks sickly though. He's just lying there. The tall [Elder with Betty] is taking out some of those tiny balls...of light that he has in his shirt, his breast part, and he threw them—there were two of those black things—he threw those tiny balls of light at them, and they just took off, disappeared.

Fred: Who was being pulled? Was he being physically hurt?

Betty: No, it doesn't seem it.

Fred: That seems inconsistent, right?

Betty: Yeah...it seems like they're pulling something out [of] him or trying to pull [his essence, his spiritual body] out of him.

	Like...I came out of my body—it was like something was trying to be pulled out of his body, and there were two.... There was a tug of war going on.
Fred:	Are [the black things] symbolic of being evil?
Betty:	Is what?
Fred:	Is it...two forces, like good and evil?
Betty:	Yes, it seems like that. It seems like there was a black [thing]...at the head, two black thin things with no features or anything, just like long arms and skinny bodies and a head and some legs, and they were like hovering in the air, pulling at...something. And there was a light being that was at the bottom, by the chest, and it's pulling at something, pulling back.... And the tall...Elder with me threw two...tiny marble-like balls of light at those two black things, and they took off. *[Fred had Betty draw what she had seen while maintaining her hypnotic trance.]* [Figure 36]

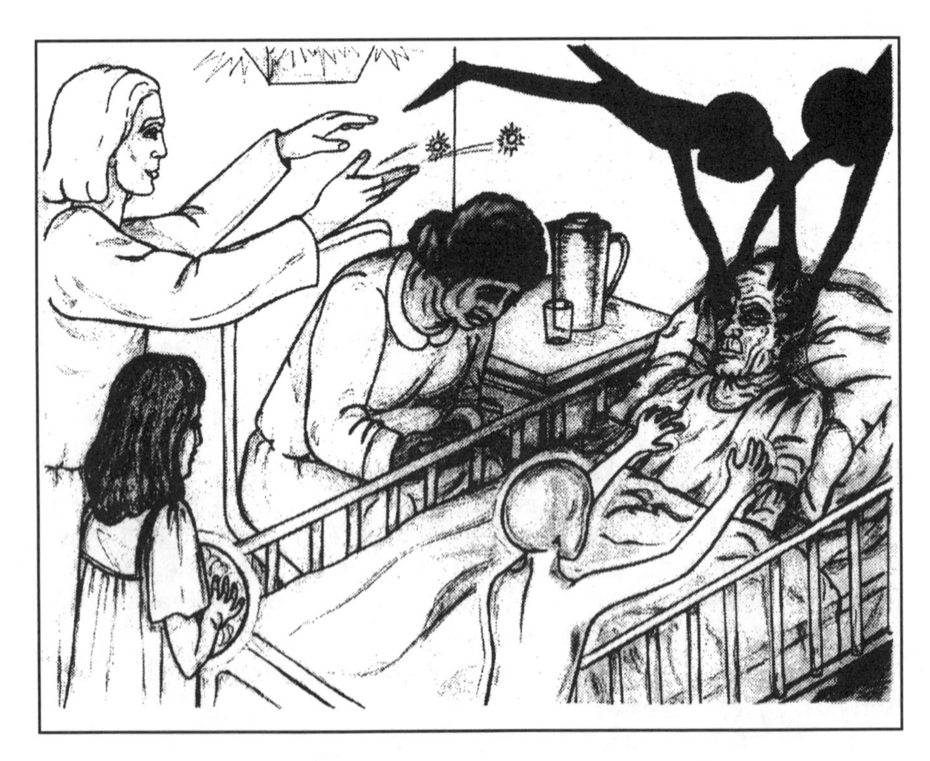

Figure 36. Betty and an Elder look on as good and evil forces fight for a dying man's soul.

Fred soon continued:

Fred: What kind of an expression does the person being pulled, so to speak, have?

Betty: Nothing...he looks like he's asleep. It's an older person, older man.

Fred: Do you really have a reason to believe that one side was good and one side not, other than the symbolism?

Betty: Those...black things—the Elder threw a tiny marble light at it, and it went...in the bed—the older man—they didn't take something from him. I don't know what they were after.

Fred: Why did they not get it?

Betty: Because of the Elder throwing...those lights. The lights hit them, I guess, or went toward them, and...they didn't like it. *[long sigh]*

Rather than break up the continuity of Betty's odyssey, this ominous scene along with OBEs and NDEs will be discussed in some detail later.

Fred: OK, what happens next?

Betty: We're standing there. He puts his hand on my shoulder and that ball of light, that purple light, turns green, and it still has those things in it. He says, "We go again." All of a sudden there's a bright white light again. *[pause]* And we're in the woods....

Fred: A regular garden-variety tree-woods?

Betty: Yeah, and we're walking along, and now that ball of light has changed to blue in my hands. Oh, this is so beautiful! Oh, I'd love to keep this.

Fred: Does it have a shape?

Betty: It's round like a ball, but...it's like something is moving in it, and it's beautiful, and I can't tell what it is. It is so beautiful in it. It seems powerful or something....

It seemed that Betty had somehow materialized back on Earth once again, but still in the OBE state. Both she and the Elder walked a short distance before sighting two blue-suited Watchers standing beside a silver oval craft sitting on the ground. I wondered at this point whether the entities and the craft were, like Betty, in an invisible existence that coexisted with what we call physical reality. If one were walking through these woods, what would one observe? Would anything be seen, or would the entities and craft be observed but not Betty? These scenes described by Betty were literally blowing my mind. It was no wonder that my wife accused me of looking like I was in another world when I arrived at the dinner table from the task of writing this book!

Betty: We're in this woods, and...I see a craft over there. It's...silver, and there's a couple...gray beings...in blue suits. They're coming over, and...we're going over to meet them.... We're going to go into that craft for some reason. We're following the greys in those blue suits over to the *[sighs]* circular-type craft.

Fred: What's moving you?

Betty: My feet are, right now.

Fred: Regular walking?

Betty: Regular walking. And so is he regular walking, it seems, only I don't feel anything under my feet.

Fred: Do you feel like you weigh less?

Betty: Yep, there's no weight and no restriction.... *[Betty is still in an OBE state and thus, feels weightless.]* Oh, this is beautiful. This ball of light now is turning like a light blue into a white [light], and we're going up into that craft now and into a lit room. We're just standing there. The gray beings have gone to another room, and it's just me and that tall Elder there and that ball that's turned white. *[pause]* We're just standing. He's not saying anything to me, and I'm not saying anything to him. I think that the [craft] has lifted off, but I'm not sure. This room is very empty and bright light.... Oh, that's beautiful. Now [the ball] is turning back to purple light. It's just so fascinating that...there's something [inside the ball]. I don't know what it is. We're just waiting there. *[pause]* And I asked him, "Where do we go now?"...He's saying that we're going to see the *One.*

This statement, needless to say, elicited tremendous interest on our parts. Betty had introduced me to the "One" once before. When she relived her visit as a teen, Betty's face manifested a beautiful expression of sheer joy. It had been emotionally overwhelming and even uncomfortable to watch this. At the time, even though mere observers, we felt caught up in the grip of something immeasurably and wonderfully beyond our comprehension. Try as we may, we could not persuade Betty to tell us what she had experienced. It seemed to be a combination of a promise not to tell combined with an inability to describe the indescribable. And now, as we listened, she again was going to meet the One. We waited with bated breath to see her reaction this time around.

Betty: We're just standing there. Oh, now...there's that one grey that is coming out with the blue suit on. *[pause]* Why do I have to give it? Why? Why do I have to give this up?

Fred: Give what up?

Betty: I have to give that beautiful purple ball to the gray being. I'm handing it to him.

Fred: Reluctantly?

Betty: Yes. It is so beautiful. And he's taking it into the other room. And the Elder just puts his hands on my shoulders to the side. I'm just still standing there. It...looks like light all around us, and I think...we're coming to a stop or something. *[The craft is coming to a stop.]* A door is opening. And that grey is coming out with the blue suit on, and he's coming over to us, and we're...going out of this craft. Oh, is there bright light around here! Whoa! It is really, really bright! [Figure 37] We're going to enter [the Great Door], and the grey stands back. He...doesn't seem as if he's going to be able to go. But, the Elder goes over to him. *[pause]*

He's talking to him, and he's touching him on the shoulder, but he's not talking verbally, it's like he's talking somehow to him through the mind or eyes. I don't know. And two of them are coming over, and The Elder says, "Are you ready?" And I say, "Yes." Oh-h-h, whoa! Is this beautiful! Oh! *[exhales loudly]* Oh, we're running toward the light now. Oh-h-h! *[breathless]* I can see...the Elder is changing to a white light being and...the grey is changing into a light blue one *[blows out air]* as we're running closer to the light. Oh, I'm starting to change into a golden-colored light! Oh, this is beautiful! Oh-h-h, this is beautiful. Oh-h-h! *[Betty can hardly catch her breath.]* Oh-h-h. *[long sigh, exhales, sighs again]* Oh, this is wonderful, wonderful, wonderful. Oh, there is such love. *[Betty is in pure unadulterated ecstasy.]* Oh, there is such peace. *[long sigh]* I'm just engulfed in light and blending into that light. Oh!

Fred now recognized another possible window of opportunity to afford all of us a glimpse of what Betty was describing. He stopped Betty midway through the experience and asked her to draw what she was observing.

Figure 37. Betty and her alien friends are humbled before the Great Door.

Betty took the pen and paper from Fred and sketched herself and her two companions running toward a brilliant source of light. As they did, their forms also changed to light. [Figure 38] But that was it. She would not draw what was observed in what she called the "world of light" that existed behind the Great Door. She also refused to describe the One. Again, it was a losing fight. The secret of the One still remained tightly locked within the recesses of Betty's mind. After her sketch, Fred allowed her to continue in what appeared to be an intense and spellbinding experience.

Betty: That's wonderful, beautiful here. Oh-h-h, it's beautiful! Oh, and I hear like a sound like music. Sounds like singing...of beautiful, beautiful music. I can't even explain it. It is so wonderful, beautiful. *[sighs]*

Fred: Do you need protection? Is it so bright?

Betty: Oh, no, it's just permeates me. It just is...wonderful. It's just—I can't explain it. *[breathlessly]* It is just fantastically beautiful. It's just so much love, so much peace and so wonderful. It's so wonderful. Oh, it's just wonderful. Oh. It is. It is. It is.

Figure 38. Beings of light seen by Betty beyond the Great Door.

Suddenly Betty's countenance abruptly changed from joy to disillusionment as she felt herself being pulled back against her will.

Betty: Oh. Oh. Oh, I don't want to go. I don't want to go back. I want to stay! I want to stay!

Fred: Are you alone?

Betty: Oh, this is everything, everything, everything.

Fred: Are you alone...?

Betty: No.

Fred: Who else is in the light with you?

Betty: Oh, the light is all over. It is wonderful.... I cannot explain the wonder and beauty and love and peace. It is so joyous! Oh, glory, glory, glory! Glory, glory! Oh, I'm going to have to go back. *[almost crying]* I have to go back for others so that they too will see, will understand and know. *[pause]* Oh, I'm having to turn. Oh, it is so warm and peaceful and wonderful. Now...I see that tall, white, light one [the glowing Elder].... That light blue one [the glowing gray entity] is coming out of the light, too, coming over, and...the tall white one is in the middle and...I'm a golden color light. We're walking away, but it's so bright still. It's still wonderful. We're...walking away. We're walking out.

As Betty walked out with the Elder and the Watcher, their transfigured bodies of light changed back into their visible forms. [Figure 39]

Figure 39. Their bodies of light took on physical forms.

Betty: Oh, we're coming out.... I can see myself. I'm not golden light anymore. It's bright here, but I can see myself.... Whoa! Oh, is that something! Oh, right over there I hear like singing, and I can see...the balls...of light are just like dancing...and making song or music. Oh, it is beautiful. Oh, it's beautiful. Oh, it's beautiful. [Figure 40] Now [the orbs] are moving away. They are moving away, and we're moving on. I'm me again. And the Elder is in his white robe again.

Figure 40. Orbs of radiant light dance for Betty, an Elder and two greys.

Betty had changed from a body of light back into her other self or essence. Note that even in the OBE state, Betty recognized her features as if she were actually in her physical body that was left behind in the mother ship. As we shall see in a moment, her physical body had been transported back to her home awaiting her essence's return to it.

Betty: And...the grey is over there, but his skin looks very pale. And he's in that blue uniform. We're walking now...over to where that craft was.... We're getting inside the craft. The Elder isn't. Just me and the grey. The Elder is touching my head. He's...passing me three balls of light about the size of a marble. And I'm taking them before I go inside that craft.... The Elder is just standing there. *[sighs]* I'm in that room with the grey. We're going into another room. And...I see some kind of instruments on the wall there. I guess we're taking off. *[The craft is taking off.]* Because I see...out of a window like all the brightness. *[A bright aura of light surrounded the craft as it began to move.]* We're starting to go. We're lifting up.... It looks like the night sky is out there.

We're just moving along. He says that I will have to get in an orb. I'm being brought into another room and there's an orb there, and he says to move into it, and when I do, I don't even feel...any separation. I'm just in the center of that orb.

Betty again found herself automatically moved inside a transparent ball of light similar to the one that initially carried her away from her trailer.

Betty: All of a sudden that orb shoots out...of that craft with me in it, and it's like I'm in mid air! [Figure 41] Oh, I feel something or see something like...trees underneath. And it seems like I'm coming down, down towards those trees.... Oh...I see the trailer there. I'm coming down, and I'm...on a platform, and that...clear ball just...goes away from me and takes off...over towards the woods.

Betty watched the ball disappear and then, like an automaton, trudged toward the familiar sight of her trailer.

Betty: And I'm just...going in the door. I'm going up by the bed. I'm in the trailer. There, I see Bob there. He's sleeping.

Betty saw someone else sitting on the bed and was shocked to the core when she realized that it was herself, her physical body. The last time she had been in her body was in the mother ship. She had left it in one of glass chairs in the room where she had witnessed the blessing. She had no idea how her body had got back to the trailer while she was still in an OBE state of being.

Figure 41. The orb carrying Betty shoots out of the craft and takes Betty home.

Betty: Oh, and I see myself just sitting there on the side of the bed, and yet I'm here! I'm going inside myself! [Figure 42] Oh, I'm sitting right by the window, and I'm looking out, and I'm getting this feeling like I've gotta go outdoors. Something wants me to go outdoors, and I...get up from the bed, and I go down toward the foot of the bed, and I'm walking down to the living room area, and...I'm coming back up again, and...I'm not going to go out there. I'm coming back up, and I'm sitting on the bed again, and I'm looking out the window, and it is so dead calm. There's no insect [sounds]. What is going on? And, all of a sudden, I'm hearing something in the woods, like a tree is falling. A tree fell. And I'm looking out there.... What is going on? And I'm still looking, and I'm getting this feeling that I gotta go outdoors. I don't wanta go outdoors. Oh, I hear another tree, another tree fell closer by. Down there...down in the woods. I hear it *snap.* Oh, I gotta go outdoors now. I got to. I'm getting up, and...I'm getting down at the bottom of the bed, and Bob's stirring, and he's saying, "Where are you going?" I say, "Honey, I feel as if I gotta go outdoors. Something's making me feel like I gotta go out." And Bob is saying to me, "You're not going anywhere!" And so I...got back up into bed, and I'm lying down and I told him, "Oh, I had this awful feeling I had to go outdoors. I kept on getting up and fighting against it, and I heard two trees fall. I heard two trees fall down...in the woods." And, all of a sudden I'm just, *[sighs]* lying down there, and I'm getting tired, and I said, "Hon, we gotta go look for those trees tomorrow."

Fred: Were you concerned about going outside?

Betty: No, I don't feel as if I gotta go out anymore.... Because [Bob] said, "You're not going anywhere." And it seems as it makes me feel better, so I could go to bed.

Figure 42. Betty steps back into her body.

When Betty entered her body, all memory of the abduction immediately vanished from her conscious mind. All she could remember was the strange drawing force and the sound of the two falling trees. She was still left with the feeling that she had to go outdoors, but Bob prevented her from doing so. This type of mental illusion has been employed time and time again by the alien entities. The abductee is placed back in the same situation that existed just prior to the abduction. This, coupled with induced memory loss, effectively conceals the existence of alien intervention into the lives of human beings. Sometimes, in cases like Betty's, memories are allowed to surface purposively. In other cases, recollection of the abduction may occur in the form of mental flashbacks and nightmares.

In any event, Betty's reliving of her 1989 odyssey had come to an end. Fred slowly but surely eased her back from the past to awake in the familiar surroundings of his office.

chapter nine

A Never Ending Story

Many witnesses have not seen the last of UFOs when the abduction craft flies off.... A few abductions recur within days or weeks, but more than often the gap is months or years, the heaviest concentration lying at 1.5 to 3 months and especially at 4-5 years.[1]

Thomas E. Bullard, Ph.D.

A few other curious things remained to be investigated in the lives of the Lucas. One involved a 1988 incident in their car while on their way home from a drive-in movie. For some reason they had taken a rather lonely route home. As they passed an apple orchard, a bright light enveloped the car. Then inexplicably, Betty and Bob found themselves driving along, miles from the orchard. Upon arriving home, they noticed it had taken much longer than it should have to reach home from the drive-in. When they called to tell me about this incident, it became one of my primary candidates to be explored under hypnosis.

Another incident in 1989 involved Betty's awakening to see a strange multi-appendaged object float right through her bedroom window. As she recoiled in fear at the sight, a bright flash of light filled the room, and she fell fast asleep. On the following morning, she phoned to tell me about it.

I instructed Fred to simply ask Betty if there had been any other UFO-related incidents in her life other than the ones already covered. Nothing was said about these two incidents. If they represented alien encounters, it would be best if they were recalled without any prompting. Fred relaxed Betty and directed her attention to the period between

---

1. Bullard, 1987, pp. 158-159.

1986 and 1989. Instantly, Betty found herself sitting in the car with Bob at the drive-movie!

Betty: In 1988. It's at night, and Bob and I are starting to enjoy it.... It's warm and there's a lot of cars. The first movie just got over, and we're sitting in the car—just looking around and talking. Windows are open, and there's the car off to the side of Bob and there's another car off to the side of me here, and we're parked in the front of the refreshment and bathrooms building where the movie comes out of the projector. And the car on the side of me...[has] their window open, and there's a man at the driver's seat and a woman. And over beside them is a bunch of people. Looks like a van. Must be about four or five people there and a couple of them sitting out. It's so warm and so nice out. And it's intermission right now, and we're just waiting for the second movie...*Short Circuit*.... We're sitting there, and this woman—sort of lean woman and about my height, with blonde hair and glasses...wearing shorts—and she comes over to the side of the car and she's got a camera in her hand and she flashes a bright flash of light. Evidently took our picture.

This brought to mind another time that something similar had taken place. Bob and Betty were washing clothes in a laundromat when suddenly, a sports car pulled up outside. A man jumped out with a camera, opened the door, took their photograph and rushed back to the car and drove off.

Betty: It's weird. It's strange she did that. And now she's just walking as if nothing happened and walking by the car and by Bob. She's going over by the refreshment stand, and I can't see her anymore. "What do you think that was all about?" I asked Bob, and he didn't know. "Do you think she was taking a picture of those people at the van?" And he says, "No, she was right in front of our car and took our picture." We're still trying to figure it out.

As if that were not mystery enough, suddenly something hit the back of their car with a loud noise. Bob reacted to the matter completely out of character. It was if he could care less what had happened to his car. This seemed extremely odd to Betty.

Betty: Oh, all of a sudden there was a loud thud on the back of our car. Whoa, was that loud! What in the world was it? That was weird. The man [in the car opposite them] is...looking, too, and I...said, "Hon, why don't you go out and check and see what that was?" and he...didn't want to. He just sat there. He didn't want to go out, but I see the man opening his door and he's...going out to check, because they heard it, too. There was a loud thud. He's going in back and checking...the back of his car. He's coming back to his...car and getting in, and he says, "It seems all right. Those tires seem OK." Evidently he thought a tire blew out or something. I don't know. But it sounded like a real loud thud like if you took a ball of soft clay and just threw it at something. And so, we're still wondering what happened, and we're waiting for the movie.... We're watching the movie.

Fred: What's the main features?

Betty: *Short Circuit* and the other that we saw, I think the name of it was *For Keeps.*

Fred: This was the Southington [CT] drive-in?

Betty: Yeah, it was at the Southington. After the movie is all finished, we got...right out there, instead of waiting for such a long time with the cars all going out. Bob...gets out on the highway, and we're going down the highway, heading back home, and we keep on going along...quite a distance on the highway, and we decided to go the Durham way. And so, we went over towards Lyman orchards and passed...Lyman's store and...we're moving past...the house that's off to the right, that big house. We're going on into Durham, going toward that way. Shhh-Whew! What a bright light! Whoa! Whew, oh wow! It hurts my eyes! Oh-h-h! *[long pause]* I'm looking at Bob, and it seems as if his arms are out straight on the steering wheel and he's staring straight ahead, not moving. And I'm not moving either.

As I observed Betty, I wondered what was about to happen next. Surely it wouldn't be as strange as the other encounters had been. I was wrong. It was really bizarre. On the surface, it didn't make sense. It just served to show me that UFO researchers perhaps have only the smallest inkling of what is really going on in the lives of abductees.

Betty: There's a bright, bright light here, and it's...half in me and half out of me. [Figure 43] This is weird! I can see my body just staying still, and I'm looking around. Oh, I hear something on the roof! I hear something on the roof. Oh-h-h! It's one of those beings. It's...on top of our roof, and it's...leaning down. It's taking something from the back of the car. [Figure 44] The light is getting dim now. Whatever...they had on the back of the car lit everything up, and we're...in some place. *[confused]* Oh, there's a couple more of the beings coming over, and I can see over there now...a green van with the back doors open. It's sort of rusted. It's just sitting there. We're in a huge, huge...huge room, and there's another car over there...that's just parked there. Nobody's there. It's a small car. It's just like a maroon colored car, and it's just sitting there...abandoned, both of them.

Figure 43. While driving with Bob, Betty undergoes an OBE and notices a menacing grey.

Incredibly, they had been abducted with their car, and from what Betty was describing, another car had been taken too. Even more astounding was the fact that Betty was observing these things during an OBE while their physical bodies were in a state of suspended animation!

Betty: Oh, here comes another one of those...beings. It's walking over to the car. I think it's going to come and open the door. Oh-h-hh! I see bright light again. Oh, wow! I hear some clashing or crashing.... Oh, and I see a strike of lightning in here. Wow! It's lit right up. And out of the light, I see now a tall being wearing a white robe and white hair and...he's got...about four or five of those...beings with him, and he's looking...at those...who were trying to get in our car.

Figure 44. Greys, possibly evil ones, surround the Lucas' car in order to kidnap them.

He's looking at them trying to get in our car, and...he's pointing and sending those five that are with him over after them. [Figure 45] Those others are running, it seems. They're trying to get away into a room over there. *[long sigh]*

Fred: Where's Bob?

Betty: *[pause]* Bob is right here beside me. He has that steering wheel.

Fred: Is Bob aware of anything unusual occurring?

Betty: He looks stiff. His hands are like on the wheel, gripped to the wheel. His eyes are wide.

Fred: Is the car moving?

Betty: No, we're still. We're just still. We're very still...both of us. And that was the weirdest thing. It was like I was half out of me and half [in] me. I don't know how to explain it. And I could see what was going on. Those beings must have taken us [with the car] into a craft. They were not good. The man in the white robe with the other five were...holding them off or something. I don't know, but it seemed like he...waved his hand over and pointed, and all five of them went running after those other beings. And it's bright light! *[Everything disappeared in a flash of brilliant light.]*

Figure 45. An Elder and a group of greys come to Betty and Bob's rescue.

Betty suddenly stopped talking. When she continued, she was once again in the car with Bob driving along the Durham road, only they realized that they were not where they had been a moment ago.

Betty: Bob's driving, and I'm riding, and we're on that highway or road back to Durham. We're coming around the corner and coming up to the lights of Durham, and I say, "Do you remember going...from Lyman's orchard to get to here? I don't recall that whole...length. Do you remember it?" And he says, "No, I...can't recall passing any of that." And I say, "Well, that's weird." And we're going through the lights and around the other lights and we're heading back toward Higganum, riding along and going on that road to get home. And, when we get home, it seems as if we're home much later than when we got out of the movies. It seems like there's 45 minutes to an hour missing, that we should have got home way before now. But, we come in and check the time and get a drink of water and go to the bathroom and get ready for bed.

Fred asked several more questions to clarify what Betty and Bob experienced before proceeding to Betty's next UFO encounter.

Fred: What did he [the being on the roof] look like?

Betty: He looked like one of the [gray] beings , but he was more agile and had sort of an animalistic thing about him. I can't understand...what it was, but it was like animalistic. I think it was because he was on all fours while he was on the roof and was reaching down for whatever that thing was he was after....

Fred: What did he take from the back of the car?

Betty: I don't know what it was. I just saw him take something that was sort of roundish, round, like a ball, but flat on one side like a half a ball.... And it was bright, bright light, and then when he picked it up...it dimmed....

We speculated later that what had hit the car might have been a special tracking device for the alien levitating device to home in on. It could only be seen when Betty was in her half-OBE state. But it must have had mass, for it exhibited both noise and vibration when it was attached to the back of their car. Most likely, Bob's lack of interest in what had hit the car was instigated by the would-be alien kidnappers.

Because time was precious at these hypnosis sessions, it seemed best to continue the probe for similar events in Betty's subconscious. Fred relaxed Betty and directed her attention to the period. Again, Betty's mind drifted quickly to the next encounter. Amazingly, it involved a strange octopus-like object that had entered her bedroom. To those looking on, it was if she had somehow been transported back into the past in a time machine.

Betty: It's 1989...in January, and we're in bed, Bob and I, and we're sleeping. And I suddenly wake up.... I've been tossing and turning—and I see this thing coming through the window, and it's a pale...translucent brown. It has...appendages or something that's…hard to explain. It just comes through the window. [Figure 46]

Figure 46. Betty notices a multi-pronged alien object enter her bedroom through a window.

And all of a sudden, it just sprayed out those fingers, and streaks of light just filled the room. [Figure 47]

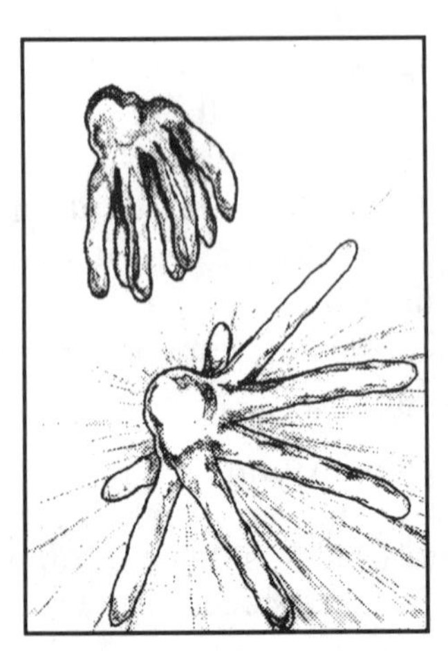

Figure 47. A close-up view of the octopus-like object as it casts out brilliant light.

> And...I feel myself lifting out of my body...and I'm... going out of the trailer, and there's a flash of light, and I'm with...a gray being. He's standing there before me, and he says, "Come along," and I'm moving with him, and we're going into a room. And there's...a blonde girl that is sitting at some screen.

Betty's facial expression appeared to change from...curiosity to puzzlement to astonished recognition.

Betty: It looks like my daughter! One of my daughters.... It's Becky! They have her...sitting at a screen and...she's staring at it and looking at all sorts of symbols. "Becky! Becky! Beckeee!" [Figure 48]

Figure 48. Betty sees her daughter Becky working with symbols on board a spacecraft.

Becky remained totally engrossed with what she was doing as if Betty did not exist. Upset both at her daughter's presence and reaction, Betty reached to grab her attention. Bewildered, she found that her hand passed right through Becky's body! [Figure 49]

Figure 49. Betty tries to touch Becky, but her hand passes right through her.

Betty: I reach out, and my hand just goes through her. She doesn't see or hear me. "Becky!" The being says that she can't see or hear me. I've been taken up in the spirit and she's…flesh, and they're training and teaching her. She's concentrating on the screen and all those symbols.

At this point I must mention that Becky has been able to automatically write in a hieroglyphic-looking script since childhood. The writing has been examined by experts, but thus far, no one knows what it means or how she is able to do it so effortlessly. Becky's experiences and this script will be covered in detail in my next book.

Betty: And one of the beings is going over to her. They're telling her to follow him. And she's moving, getting up and moving with the being. They're going over to another...screen of some kind. And the being and I are going over to watch. "Becky!" I guess she can't hear me. She's stretching both hands and arms outward. She's touching with her fingers, some symbols that are raised on this screen. She's gotta touch each symbol and trace it. [Figure 50]

Figure 50. Becky traces her fingers over raised symbols on a console before her.

That's what she's doing. And, when she does, a ball of light pops out in front of her. And in that ball of light there is some kind of a picture, and I can't see, because *[pause]* she has her hand there, and it goes quick. She's tracing on other raised symbols there. The being says, "Come along now." And I'm wondering why I can't stay and watch what she's doing. And he is saying, "We are training her." And I asked, "Training for what?" And he would not…tell me. We're moving off to the side, and we're into a very narrow hallway off to the right. *[Betty looks back.]* And I see Becky's still there. She's still tracing those raised symbols, and I'm following the being into this narrow hallway. [Figure 51]

Figure 51. A grey leads Betty down a narrow hallway on a space craft.

We're going into a room. We're in that room, and we have to sit in something. There's some kind of a blue machine.

And as we do, the blue machine goes real quick. Whew! We're inside this blue machine, moving along, and it stops abruptly.... [Figure 52]

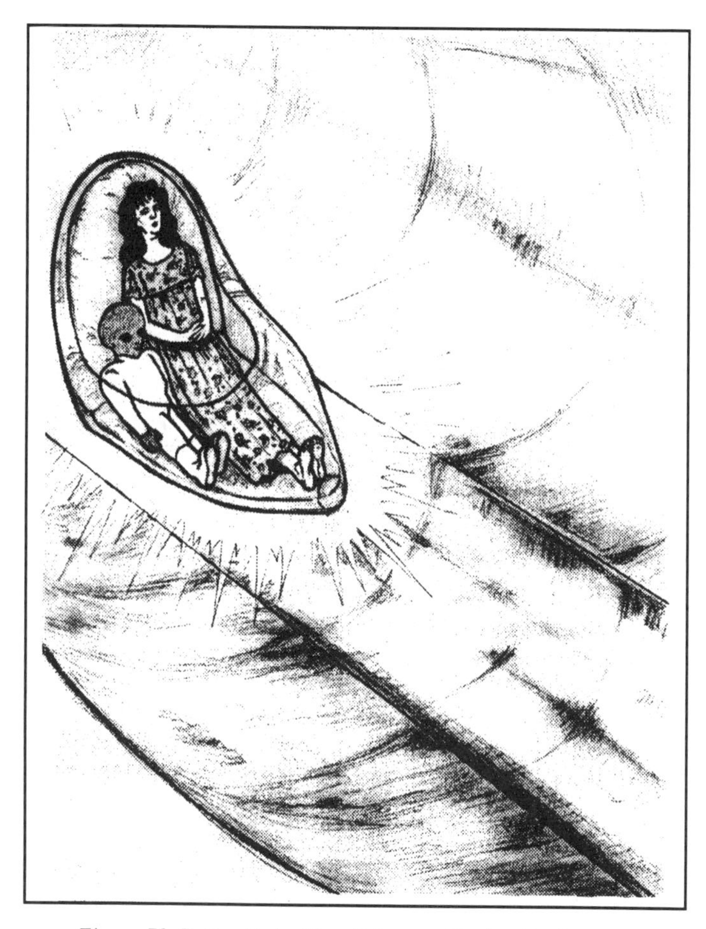

Figure 52. Betty sits inside a "blue machine" with the grey.

It stops because there's a tall being with white hair, white robe, right there. It almost seemed as if we bumped into it. And, off to the side I see a whole bunch of the beings. They're all together, and they're...looking at something. I don't know what it is.... [Figure 53]

Fred: What is this? What year?

Betty: 1989.

Fred: OK.

Betty: And it's January.

Session time was running out. Later, in the comfort of their home, Bob, a skillful hypnotist, placed Betty under hypnosis to find out what happened next. The following are excerpts from our last phase four regression session with Betty. We break in as Betty and the entity are riding along in the blue machine.

Figure 53. Betty is greeted by an Elder as she steps out of the blue machine.

Betty: Whoa, whoa! We're going real fast on this thing. Whoa! And then all of a sudden we're stopping, and we almost bumped into a tall being standing there. He's in a white dress or robe...nightgown and he's—

Bob: Does he look like the greys?

Betty: No, he's got very pale skin and white hair.

Bob: Does he look more like a person?

Betty: Yes, he looks human.

Bob: OK.

Betty: And he summons me to come out...of the machine. And I can see over there...a bunch of the gray beings, and they're around a...cylinder-type thing on the floor with light coming out of it, and they're...studying it real closely with their eyes. They're all bent over looking at it. And...they're looking at it, digesting something about molecular structures. There on the walls...[are] round things that circulate very slowly.... They look like regular type wheels.... I don't know what you would call them. Looks like there's orange wire...probably copper...in there—braided.... It just keeps on circling slowly. All...three of them...on the wall. And the tall being is saying, "Will you follow me, please?" And...I'm really surprised...because he's talking regularly. He's not talking through his mind to me. He's talking with his mouth. Whereas those gray beings, the Watchers, they...always talk to me through their minds.

Bob: And where does he have you follow him?

Betty: He keeps on saying, "Will you please follow me?" And I say, "What is my daughter Becky doing here?" I saw...my daughter in the other room.... And he's saying, "She's being trained in the letters. She's been into training since she was a child," he say. "And her time is soon to come for her to show others those letters." Will I please follow him, he says. And we're just walking over, and I'm following him, and that other Watcher went over and joined the others at that cylinder on the floor...looking at molecular structures. I didn't understand what they meant, but he says, "Come along and follow me please." And we're going to another door off to the left there. These rooms are rounded. This room that we're going in is rounded. I see...two blue cylinders of light.... This is really strange—it's blue light. It's swirling, but on the outside...there's...strips or strings...the width of pencils—strings of light coming down in different sections around this blue thing.... It looks like it's whirling light of some kind inside. It looks like there's something, or someone, inside one of those things, but...it's so whirling and bright that I can't make it out. And then there's also a table...that is sort of in the middle, over to the right part of this room.... It looks like a glasslike table of some sort, and there's also two screens...that come out like a page in a book.... Like a TV screen, but there's nothing in it. It's very, very thin and the second one comes out even further. And then there is a thing on the wall over there. He says, "Come along, please. Follow me." And I'm following him.... We're going through this room and there's another door right down there.... And we're going through that door, and there's...a pie-shaped, funny pie-shaped, little section as we went into the next room.... Right in the center [of this room] there's this thing that comes down from the ceiling and [it] is...part of the floor. It's...a curved thing that goes down and around in part of the floor. And there's a bench that comes right out from the wall to the right here as we enter the door. And...I can see...a big huge screen there.... One of the greys is standing by with something in its hand, some cloth or clothing.... We're just standing there, and *[pause]* all of a sudden that...curved thing that was from the ceiling to the floor—it's splitting in two! And there's bright white light coming from it. Bright, bright light.... The top part is just going up into the ceiling somehow. It's bright, bright light shining down, like on a...lower part of the curved thing. Bright white light. *[gasps]* And there's someone lying down on that...base of it. Oh-h-h! They're naked. Oh, brother. It's such bright light!

Bob: Can you see if it's a young person or old person? A male, a female?

Betty: It looks like a female.... The tall being is saying, "Come along, please," and we're having to go over to...where that woman is lying there like she is...dead...just lying there so still. And he says, "Come along, please." *[pause]* Oh-h-h! That's me that's there! That's me lying there! Oh no, he's saying for me to please enter my form! And I said, "What are you doing? What are you doing? Why am I here *and* there? What are you doing to me?" And he says that my body is being prepared because I will be taken out again very soon, but for me now to enter my form. And I have to step over and step into my form. And I'm going over, and I'm going inside myself.

Bob: Is there any feeling or sensation?

Betty: Oh-h-h! I feel so tired and heavy. *[sighs]* I feel so tired. Oh, I feel just so heavy. He comes over and reaches for my hand. *[sighs]* And I'm being lifted up, but I can barely move. It feels so heavy. I feel exhausted. And he's lifting me up.... As he pulls me upward, I'm...sitting on the edge of this bottom part in the bright light.... That gray being comes over and I'm told to lift my hands—and I do. And the gray being has...my nightgown. And they're putting the nightgown on me as I'm sitting on the side or edge of this thing. I feel so tired and heavy. It's just strange.... They put my nightgown on, but they have it inside out. My nightgown's inside out.... Now he's taking my hands and lifting me up.... We're walking over towards the bench. *[pause]* And we're sitting down, and I'm so tired.... I ask him, "How come I feel so weak and tired?" And he says, "It's part of the process of preparation." He says, "You've been doing very well. You have been very humble and have not been anxious or excited when you speak about our visitations. You are doing very well. You must continue to do this way because no matter what, you must remain calm." And the gray being's coming over to us. And I ask the tall man who is sitting next to me, "Who are these Watchers? What are they doing? What are they about?" *[pause]* He says that "They are our remote imaging surrogates." And they're connected to them in a way with bio-electric mind projections. They serve terrestrial tasks for them. I feel so weak, and he says, "That will clear soon. It will wear off." He says, "Now you must go back." And we're standing up and going over to that thing in the middle of the room. He says, "Get up on the platform once again." And as...I'm on the platform, and lights come down and all of a sudden, I see something whooshing down around me. *[pause]* Ah-h-h! And there's bright light all around. And I'm in bed! I'm [back in the trailer] in bed !

Bob: OK, just relax.

Betty: And Bob is not there!

Bob: What?

Betty: He's not there right now.

Bob: Where is he?

Betty: I don't know. Maybe he's going to the bathroom. I don't know.

This session, apart from Betty and Bob's experiences, again highlighted the fact that their children have also been caught up in the abduction experience. Several of their children were seen being examined by the small gray entities by Betty and Bob during their 1978 OBE abduction experience. Now, during another OBE abduction in 1989, Betty was brought directly to Becky by the entities to share in Becky's abduction. Betty, being in the OBE state, could not communicate with or touch Becky. In retrospect, it appears that the entities wanted Betty to see what they were doing with Becky, but did not want Becky to be aware of Betty's presence. Becky seemed to be undergoing some kind of training on consoles, just as Betty had been during her 1950 abduction.

Based upon the above-mentioned cases and what Betty and Bob have told me about their children, it is quite evident that they have also been caught up in the abduction phenomenon with their parents. Unfortunately, up until this time, none of the children have wished to become involved with the subject.

During our initial investigation in 1967, Becky cooperated and underwent hypnosis to help to confirm details of Betty's experience from her vantage point. Since it was now apparent that Becky had this ongoing experience with the UFO entities, I hoped that she would cooperate once more with us. Betty contacted Becky who lived in another state. She agreed to cooperate, but family responsibilities made it difficult to travel out-of-state for hypnosis sessions with Fred Max. It was decided that Bob, who provided some of the hypnosis for the phase three *[The Watchers]* investigation, would perform hypnosis on Becky during periodic family visits.

During Bob's initial probe, we got more information than we had expected. We discovered that Becky, like her mother, has had UFO encounters and abductions from early childhood. At the time of this writing, hypnosis sessions are being periodically carried out.

These sessions have produced an astounding sequence of provocative interfaces between Becky and the UFO phenomenon. They include Becky's abduction to a craft where Betty, during an abduction, saw her daughter operating an alien console. The results of Becky's sessions will be covered in my next book. As far as this book is concerned, the recording of Betty and Bob's UFO experiences during the phase four hypnosis sessions must now come to an end. It is now time to begin an overall assessment of their content.

PART II
Pertinent Parallels

"Few narrators would have the foresight to organize their stories with all these implications in mind, and no familiar psychological phenomenon installs a multi-faced image of aliens...into many individuals. Reality best explains where this unified picture of purposes and motivations originates."

Dr. Thomas E. Bullard
International UFO Reporter
Vol. 12, No. 4, 1987

This section is an evaluation of the UFO abduction experiences reported by the Lucas in the light of a variety of parallels to their experiences. Along the way we will address types of evidence that, although not physical in nature, are nonetheless often used to establish historical events or to prosecute criminals.

In the first chapter to follow, we will amplify the search for the Watchers that was initiated in my book *The Watchers.* A search of documents old and new will reveal that legends of creatures by that name have existed since the beginning of civilization.

Another chapter will deal with the *possibility* that some of Betty's experiences might have been subconsciously or even deliberately influenced by similar scenarios found in literature and movie sources.

Some experiences that Betty relived under hypnosis are atypical to the general content of UFO abduction reports. An extensive search will be made for reports originating in this country and abroad for precendents to these seemingly incongruous constituents.

Lastly, in our search for pertinent parallels to the Lucas' reported experiences, we will conduct a detailed analysis of Betty and Bob's experiences by comparing them with the results of a landmark comparative study of over 300 cases by Dr. Thomas E. Bullard.

chapter ten

In Search of the Watchers

He says that they are the caretakers of nature and natural forms—the Watchers.... They love the planet Earth, and they have been caring for it and man since man's beginning. They watch the spirit in all things.... Man is destroying much of nature.

Betty Andreasson Luca

In *The Watchers* I alluded to coincidences that exist between the abduction phenomenon and folklore. In such folklore we find dwarflike creatures who abduct human beings to strange timeless worlds of light for reproductive reasons. I also mentioned in passing that ancient writings allude to entities called "Watchers." Although we cannot be sure of a connection between ancient and modern reports of Watchers, we would be negligent not to explore both the origin and use of the name down through the ages in light of Betty Luca's reported revelations.

I feel somewhat qualified to perform such an endeavor, as I have college degrees in both biblical studies and New Testament Greek, as well as some graduate training, including a study of Hebrew.

Biblical writings mention and allude to the Watchers. The first allusion to them is in Genesis, but they are also alluded to in the New Testament books of II Peter and Jude. However, to understand why, we must first turn to books outside of the Biblical canon: the books of Enoch.

The Books of Enoch

The books of Enoch are apocalyptic (containing hidden secrets) in nature. The Secrets of Enoch and I, II, III Enoch belong to a class of writings called the Old Testament Pseudepigrapha (books that were written falsely under someone else's name). This does not necessarily mean, however, that the book's contents do not reflect long-held traditions, perhaps based upon actual historical events.

Enoch, according to Genesis 5:24, did not die, but was taken bodily up to heaven. The description of how this occurred is described in *The Secrets of Enoch,* manuscripts of which were recently found in Russia. Some background follows:

> This new fragment of early literature came to light through certain manuscripts which were recently found in Russia and Servia and, so far as is yet known, has been preserved only in Slavonic. Little is known of its origin except that in its present form it was written somewhere about the beginning of the Christian era. Its final editor was a Greek and the place of its composition Egypt.... Although the very knowledge that such a book ever existed was lost for probably 1200 years, it nevertheless was much used by both Christian and heretic in the early centuries.[1]

The following is the account of Enoch's ascension into heaven. As you will see, it has all the earmarks of a modern UFO abduction experience.

> I was in my house alone and was resting on my couch and slept. And when I was asleep, great distress came up into my ear.... I could not understand what this distress was, or what would happen to me. And there appeared to me two men, exceeding big...their faces were shining like the sun, their eyes too were like a burning light.... They were standing at the head of my couch and began to call me by my name. And I arose from my sleep and saw clearly those two men standing in front of me...and was seized with fear...and those men said...do not fear...thou shalt today ascend with us into heaven...and they placed me on the first heaven.... They brought before my face the elders and rulers of the stellar orders.[2]

I Enoch is the oldest of the four books and consists of five major divisions. Our concern will be the pertinent contents of the first division, entitled The Book of the Watchers; but first, a brief sketch concerning the historical background of I Enoch is in order. [brackets mine]

> I Enoch, also known as the Ethiopic Apocalypse of Enoch, is the oldest of the three pseudepigraphal books attributed to

1. Pratt, 1953, p. 81.
2. Charles, 1896, ch. 1, 3, 4.

> Enoch.... The book was originally written in either Hebrew or Aramaic, perhaps both, but it survives in complete form only in Ethiopia.... The materials in I Enoch range in date from 200 B.C.E [B.C.] to 50 C.E. [A.D.]....[3]

I Enoch was extremely important to early Christianity. It was the contents of the books of Enoch that influenced the Christian Church to include the Book of Revelation in the New Testament canon rather than Enoch. This was done even though I Enoch had been accepted as scripture for several centuries. It was rejected because of the very subject matter under our consideration: The reported sexual activities of the Watchers who copulated with human females.

Although the primitive Christian church and earliest church fathers believed that celestial beings could be physical and sexual in nature, the later church fathers rejected this notion. They decreed that such entities were purely spirit in form, thus what was reported in I Enoch was impossible.

It was believed that a band of evil Watchers landed on earth, led by their leader Azazyel, and mated with human females. This resulted in tall hybrids who terrorized and took advantage of human beings. In order to destroy them, God sent a flood which destroyed both them and mankind except Noah and his family. Pertinent passages from I Enoch are as follows. Such passages, of course, are couched in the theological language and beliefs of the writer's day.

> *Enoch 10:12,18* All the earth has been corrupted by the teaching of the work of Azazyel.... Destroy all the souls addicted to dalliance, and the offspring of the Watchers, for they have tyrannized over mankind.[4]

Because of the unnatural hybridization fostered by this band of evil Watchers, Enoch was reportedly chosen by the good Watchers to bring the evil ones a message of condemnation.

> *Enoch 12:4-7* And behold the Watchers called me Enoch the scribe. Then the Lord said to me: Enoch, scribe of righteousness, go tell the Watchers of heaven, who have deserted the lofty sky...who have been polluted with women and have done as the sons of men do, by taking to themselves wives, and who have been greatly corrupted on the earth, that on the earth, they shall never obtain peace and remission of sin.

---

3. Evans, 1992, p. 23.
4. Laurence, 1882, pp. 11-12.

> *Enoch 15:1, 2, 8* ...Go, say to the Watchers of heaven: Wherefore have you forsaken the lofty and holy heaven...and have lain with women...and have begotten giants?...Now the giants, who have been born of spirit and of flesh, shall be called upon earth evil spirits, and on earth shall be their habitation. Evil spirits shall they be upon earth, and the spirits of the wicked they shall be called.[5]

The Dead Sea Scrolls

The discovery of the Dead Sea Scrolls revealed that more copies of I Enoch and a book entitled Jubilees were present than any other books used by the Essenes (Jewish sect) at Qumran. Both books contain the legend of the Watchers. We will discuss Jubilees later.

> The Book of Enoch provides the calendar...that was followed at Qumran. It talks about the angels of Heaven who descended to earth and mated with the daughters of men before the flood, a very important story in some Qumran literature and other texts.[6]

One example from the Dead Sea Scrolls is the following passage (ii.18) from the Zadokite Document, which had to do with the practical organization of the Essene community at Qumran. [brackets mine]

> For many that be that have strayed thereby from olden times until now, and even strong heroes have stumbled thereby. Because they walked in the stubbornness of their hears, the Watchers of heaven fell.... So to their sons [hybrid offspring], whose height was like the lofty cedars...fell. So too all flesh that was upon the dry land. They also perished [by the flood].[7]

The Bible

Only a few verses in the Bible specifically use the term "Watcher," but others allude to them. The following mentions of the Watchers are found in the Book of Daniel. They are quoted from the Revised Standard Version of the Bible. [italics mine]

> *Daniel 4:13* I saw in the vision of my head as I lay in bed, and behold, a watcher, a holy one, came down from heaven....

---

5. Laurence, 1882, pp. 13-16.
6. Vanderkam, 1992, p. 31.
7. Gaster, 1956, p. 63.

> *Daniel 4:17* The sentence is by the decree of the watchers, the decision by the word of the holy ones....

> *Daniel 4:23* ...The king saw a watcher, a holy one, coming down from heaven....

There are two trains of thought among Biblical scholars concerning the author and origin of the Book of Daniel. Conservative scholars take its contents at face value. They believe that it was written by the Hebrew prophet Daniel around 530 B.C. shortly after the capture of Babylon by Cyrus the Great in 539 B.C. Liberal scholars believe that the Book of Daniel is largely fictional and composed around 167-165 B.C. to encourage Palestinian Jews who were being oppressed by Rome.

Whatever the truth of the matter, the important thing is that the above passages from Daniel tell us that the writer and his readers believed that the Watchers dwell in the heavens and that they have power to influence man, and in this case, to sentence punishment upon the king of Babylon.

Allusions to the Watchers are found in the sixth chapter of Genesis, where they are called "sons of God." This term is often used to describe celestial beings in the Bible. The tall hybrid offsprings are called the Nephilum, which means "fallen ones" (from the Hebrew word *Nephal,* or "to fall"). This was because their fathers fell from the sky. Older translations of the Bible refer to them as giants because of their tall stature. The following are pertinent verses from Genesis, in the New International Version of the Bible. [brackets mine]

> *Genesis 6:1-2* When men began to increase in number on the earth and daughters were born to them, the sons of God saw that the daughters of men were beautiful, and they married any of them they chose....

> *Genesis 6:4* The Nephilum were on the earth in those days—and also afterward [i.e, a second visitation]—when the sons of God went to the daughters of men and had children by them. They were the heroes of old, men of renown.

> *Genesis 6:5* The Lord saw how great man's wickedness on the earth had become....

> *Genesis 6:7* So the Lord said, "I will wipe mankind, whom I have created, from the face of the earth—for I am grieved that I have made them." But Noah found favor in the eyes of the Lord.... Now the earth was corrupt in God's sight and full of violence.... So God said, "...I am going to bring flood waters on the earth."

The most apparent interpretation of this passage is that non-human male celestial beings, genetically compatible with man, mated with human females. The results were hybrid children of large stature who were both renowned and evil. Because of this genetic corruption of mankind's pedigree and its resultant evil, God destroyed by a flood all but Noah and those in the Ark. The passage also mentions a second visitation by these celestial beings after the flood. A Biblical commentary on the Nephilum states that:

> We read of the Nephilum again in Numbers 13:33: "There we saw the Nephilum, the sons of Anak, which come of the Nephilum." How, it may be asked, could this be, if they were all destroyed in the Flood? The answer is contained in Genesis 6:4, where we read: "There were Nephilum in the earth in those days [of Noah]; and also after that, when the sons of God came in unto the daughters of men, and they bare children to them, the same became [the] might men [Hebrew: *gibbor,* the heroes] which were of old men of renown." [literally, "men of the name," men who received a name and were renowned for their ungodliness]
>
> So that "after that," [after the Flood] there was a second irruption [visitation] of these fallen angels, evidently smaller in number and more limited in area, for they were for the most part confined to Canaan.... In Genesis 14:5, they were already known as Rephaim and Emim.... As to their other names, they were called Anakim, from one Anak, who came of the Nephilum [Numbers 13:23], and Rephaim, from Rapha, another notable one among them.
>
> We have in these mighty men, the "men of renown," the explanation of the origin of the Greek mythology. That mythology was no mere invention of the human brain, but it grew out of the traditions, and memories, and legends of the doings of that might[y] race of beings; and was gradually evolved out of the heroes of Genesis 6:4. The fact that they were [thought] supernatural formed an easy step to their being regarded as the demigods of the Greeks.[8]

The above interpretation prevailed within the Christian Church until relatively modern times when man became too sophisticated to believe such things could happen.

So, with the advent of higher Biblical criticism, liberal scholars dismissed this passage as pure myth. It was put on the same par with

8. Companion Bible, Appendix 25: Nephilum.

Greek mythological tales of similar god/man copulation which resulted in the birth of the Greek demigods. Of course, the question remains as to whether this and other similar ancient references have a common origin in an actual historical occurrence.

The conservative wing of the Christian church also found these verses puzzling, so their scholars postulated new alternatives and intellectually more palatable interpretations for modern cultivated minds.

Key to any interpretation of this passage is the meaning of the phrase "sons of God." As we continue to probe the history of the term "Watchers," let us summarize the major alternative interpretations advanced by most conservative Christian scholars.

Theory #1: The "sons of God" were the pious descendants of Seth who intermarried with the ungodly daughters of Cain.

Theory #2: The "sons of God" were simply pious men and the "daughters of men" were simply ungodly people.

Theory #3: The "sons of God" refer to human kings.

In essence, both liberal and conservative scholars dismiss the literal meaning of the Genesis even though it obviously refers to the legend of the Watchers recorded in Enoch and which reportedly reaches back to the dawn of humankind. The following are obvious weaknesses of the above three alternative interpretations.

1. There is no textual evidence that the "daughters of men" were restricted to only the descendants of Cain. The most apparent and logical interpretation is that the whole human family is meant by the term.
2. The theory that "sons of God" means either pious Sethites, godly people or human kings is not supported by the Old Testament's use of the term. It is only applied to humans in the New Testament as referring to those who have become Christians.
3. If the "sons of God" were merely pious or kingly human beings who mated with sinful human beings:
   a. Why would their progeny be nicknamed "giants"?
   b. Why would they be singled out as mighty heroes and men of renown?
   c. Why were they called Nephilum [fallen ones]?
4. The term, "sons of God," in the Old Testament always, except in one instance, refers to celestial—not earthly—beings. (Isaiah 43:6

is the only exception where the term refers to the godly remnant of Israel.) For example, God's council of celestial beings are called "sons of God" in the book of Job 1:6 and 2:1. Even Satan, a fallen angel, is called a "son of God."

5. Both Biblical and extra-Biblical source data that refer to the Genesis 6 passage clearly identify the "sons of God" as being non-human celestial beings. For example, we see the Genesis 6 and Enoch legend alluded to in the books of II Peter and Jude in the New Testament. The following are quotations from the New International Version of the Bible. [brackets mine]

> *II Peter 2:4, 5* For if God did not spare angels when they sinned [mated with human women]…. If he did not spare the ancient world, when he brought the flood…but protected Noah.

Note that this passage and Genesis 6 are both in the context of evil angels [Watchers], the flood and Noah. Jude is even more specific:

> *Jude 6* And the angels [Watchers] who did not keep their position of authority but abandoned their home [the heavens].

It is apparent that Jude is alluding to passages from Enoch because several verses later, verse 14 quotes from another section of the book of I Enoch: "Enoch, the seventh from Adam, prophesied…."

Other Apocryphal Books

Another extra-Biblical apocryphal work dating from about 192 A.D. was respected and quoted by the early church fathers Tertullian and Origen.[9] It also alludes to the Genesis 6 passage. The Testament of the Twelve Patriarchs reads: [italics mine]

> *Chapter 1:5* …Command your wives and daughters that they adorn not their heads and their faces…. For thus they allured the Watchers before the flood…and they…gave birth to *giants* [Nephilum], for the *Watchers* appeared to them as reaching even unto heaven.

> *Chapter 8:3* …In like manner also the *Watchers* changed the order of their nature, whom also the Lord cursed at the *flood*.[10]

As mentioned, the apocryphal book of Jubilees also contains a reference to the Watchers. It too found wide acceptance in early Judaism.

9. Coxe, 1951, p. 3.
10. Coxe, 1951, pp. 10, 27.

> Jubilees [was] written in Hebrew by a Pharisee [a Jewish Sect] between 135 and 105 B.C.E. [B.C.] It is a midrashic rewriting of Genesis-Exodus from creation to the giving of the law on Sinai, given to Moses on the Mount.[11]

The by-now familiar legend of the Watchers appears in chapters 4 and 5 of Jubilees.

> *Jubilees 4:22* And he [Enoch] testified to the Watchers, who had sinned with the daughters of men, for those had begun to unite themselves, so as to be defiled, with the daughters of men, and Enoch testified against [them] all.

> *Jubilees 5:1-5* And it came to pass when the children of men began to multiply on the face of the earth and daughters were born unto them, that the angels of God saw them on a certain year of this jubilee, that they were beautiful to look upon; and they took themselves wives of all whom they chose, and they are unto them sons, and they were giants. And lawlessness increased on the earth...and God...said: I shall destroy man and all flesh upon the face of the earth.... But Noah found grace before the eyes of the Lord.[12]

What is the origin of the Watchers? Who were they in the minds of ancient peoples? And what correlations exist between these legends and the entities reported in the abduction accounts of Betty and Bob Luca? Let us examine these questions one at a time.

The Watchers' Origin

The origin of the Watchers stretches all the way back to the dawn of civilization in Babylonia at Sumer. In fact, the very word for Sumer (Shumer) means literally, the "Land of the Watchers"![13] The existence of Sumer is an enigma. Carl Sagan states that:

> Sumer was an early—perhaps the first—civilization in the contemporary sense on the planet Earth. It was founded in the fourth millennium B.C. or earlier. We do not know where the Sumerians came from. Their language was strange; it had no cognates with any known Indo-European, Semitic, or other language, and is understood only because a later people, the Akkadians, compiled extensive Sumerian-Akkadian dictionaries.[14]

---

11. Evans, 1992, p. 31.
12. Prophet, 1983, pp. 420-423.
13. Sitchin, 1980, p. 86.

As mentioned in *The Watchers,* Carl Sagan postulated that extraterrestrial entities were responsible for Sumerian civilization. For the sake of continuity, I will now summarize his statement and reasoning for it.

> Some years ago, I came upon a legend which more nearly fulfills some of our criteria for a genuine contact myth. It is of special interest because it relates to the origin of Sumerian civilization.... Taken at face value, the legend suggests that contact occurred between human beings and a non-human civilization of immense powers on the shores of the Persian Gulf, perhaps near the site of the ancient Sumerian city of Eridu [Biblical Eden].[15]

Sagan references three different but cross-referenced accounts of such a contact that date from classical times: the accounts of Alexander Polyhistor, Abydenus and Apollodorus. He states that:

> Each can be traced back to Berosus, a priest of Bel-Marduk, the city of Babylon, at the time of Alexander the Great. Berosus, in turn, had access to cuneiform and pictographic records dating back several thousand years before his time.[16]

Rather than repeat these accounts again in this book, I will merely quote Sagan's summary of the matter.

> [These] ancient writers present an account of a remarkable sequence of events. Sumerian civilization is depicted by the descendants of the Sumerians themselves to be of non-human origin. A succession of strange creatures appears over the course of several generations. Their only apparent purpose is to instruct mankind. Each knows of the mission and accomplishments of his predecessors. When a great inundation [the Flood] threatens the survival of the newly introduced knowledge among men, steps are taken to insure its preservation. Thereby, the access of Berosus to antediluvian records is formally explained. The straightforward nature of this account of contact with superior beings is notable.... [They] are described as "beings," "semi-daemons," and as "personages." They are never described as gods.[17]

As time went on, it would appear that these non-human entities became the gods of a rather complex Sumerian extraterrestrial mythology. Sagan writes that:

---

14. Sagan, 1966, p. 456.
15. Sagan, 1966, pp. 455, 456.
16. Sagan, 1966, p. 456.
17. Sagan, 1966, p. 459.

> The gods are characterized by a variety of forms, not all human. They are celestial in origin. In general, each is associated with a different star. In fact, in the earlier Sumerian pictographs, which preceded cuneiform writing, the symbols of god and for star are identical. The cosmos is conceived as a state governed by an apparently representative and democratic assembly of the gods, which made the great decisions on the fates of all beings.... Such a picture is not altogether different from what we might expect if a network of confederated civilizations interlaced the Galaxy. [18]

It is interesting to note that the accounts quoted by Sagan also associate the arrival of these celestial beings before the Flood. Appolodorus refers to the "Great Flood" as does Alexander Polyhistor, who refers to it as the great "Deluge."[19] Note that the later legends discussed earlier equate the evil Watchers mating with human beings in context with Noah and the flood story. Polyhistor does the same thing within his account of human contact with human beings at Sumer. He speaks of a Noah-type personage who is told by a god to:

> build a vessel, and take with him into it his friends and relations; and to convey on board everything necessary to sustain life, and to take in also all species of animals.... Having asked the deity whither he was to sail, he was answered, "To the Gods...."[20]

Thus, it would appear the legend of the Watchers finds its origin as far back as the beginning of civilization!

It is interesting to note that Sagan's seemingly novel hypothesis was also advanced over a century ago by Malbim, a noted Jewish biblical commentator of his day. He wrote that:

> In ancient times the rulers of countries were the sons of the deities who arrived upon the Earth from the Heavens, and ruled the Earth, and married wives from among the daughters of Man; and their offspring included heroes and mighty ones, princes and sovereigns....[21]

Malbim equated these entities with the Watchers and the pagan gods of Classical times as corruptions of earlier legends.[22] He states that the pagan gods were:

---

18. Sagan, 1966, p. 460.
19. Sagan, 1966, p. 459.
20. Sagan, 1966, p. 459.
21. Sitchin, 1976, p. 172.
22. Sitchin, 1976, p. 172.

> Sons of the deities, who in earliest times fell down from the Heavens upon the Earth.... That is why they called themselves "Nephilum," [or "Those who Fell Down"].[23]

Concerning the possible Extraterrestrial/Sumer connection, Sagan concludes that:

> In any event, a completely convincing demonstration of past contact with an extraterrestrial civilization will always be difficult to provide on textual grounds alone, but stories...and representations, especially of the earliest civilizations on Earth, deserve much more critical studies than have been performed heretofore.[24]

As some readers already know, Zecharia Sitchin has taken up Sagan's challenge and has published a number of books on the possible connection between Sumerian and other ancient writings with extraterrestrial contact.[25]

Watchers' Identity

Who were the Watchers in the minds of the most ancient peoples? Again, return to the region of Sumer in Babylonia to find the answer to this question.

> The Chaldeans, an ancient and dominant people in Babylonia, believed that these entities were responsible for watching over the affairs of mankind on earth. Their name for this class of celestial entity was "Ir" which translated means "Watcher."[26]

Still later, another great civilization, the Egyptians, used the very same term "neter" [Watcher] for their gods. And, as we have seen, the legend became part of the Judeo-Christian tradition. Rejected and largely forgotten, the legend of the Watchers has now been revived—on one hand by scholars like Sitchin and on the other by a modern-day female Enoch named Betty, who, like Enoch of old, has been taken up in the heavens to converse with the Watchers!

---

23. Sitchin, 1976, p. 172.
24. Sagan, 1966, p. 461.
25. Sitchin, 1976, 1980, 1985, 1990a, 1990b.
26. Companion Bible, Notes: Daniel 4:13, p. 1186.

Ancient/Modern Connections?

What connections exist between these legends and the entities reported in the abduction accounts of Betty and Bob Luca?

Betty's abductors called themselves the Watchers and Caretakers of Earth's life-forms, therefore equating themselves with the Watchers of antiquity who claimed to fulfill this very function. Indeed, they told her that they have been on Earth since humankind's beginning.

The gray entities, like the ancient Watchers, have used surrogate human mothers to assist in the propagation of their offspring. Indeed, they claimed to be mature human fetuses themselves!

But, who or what are the tall beings, who look like us and call themselves our Elders? Where do they come from? Most scientists believe it most unlikely that humanoid creatures like us could evolve elsewhere. Their human appearance indicates some genetic or other kind of relation to humankind. Were they among the types of entities who influenced Sumer and initiated civilization on Earth? Did they alter primate life forms to create *Homo sapiens sapiens* as suggested in The Watchers. But, how could this be if they, too, are a form of *Homo sapiens sapiens?* If they are, how can we explain their paraphysical nature? Answers to these questions will be attempted later. But now let us play the devil's advocate as we explore the possibility of more mundane stimuli for the Lucas' UFO experiences.

chapter eleven

Memories or Mirages?

The witness somehow combines...abduction constants with data from the imagination, memory, and known UFO information to create a real UFO encounter. The subjective intensity of the witness's interpretation of the sequential experience convinces him/her that the entire experience is a physical event.[1]

Alvin H. Lawson, Ph.D.

During my analysis of the overall experiences of Betty and Bob Luca, I came across a number of uncanny parallels to things mentioned in several of their accounts that may be significant. Some seem near replicas of what Betty reported to have seen or experienced.

One instance that struck me rather forcibly was a device shown on an episode of *Star Trek.* It bore a near-exact likeness to a device that Betty had reportedly seen during her 1973 abduction. This information was retrieved during hypnosis sessions conducted by Bob in December 1987 and January 1988. Betty reported that some of these devices had been placed around a landed craft. Interestingly enough, a similar device was used to offset the effects of a fiery storm in the *Star Trek* episode.

When I queried Betty about these similarities, she admitted seeing things on TV that remind her of what she has reported. She has even suggested that script writers may have got their ideas from her experiences. What is going on here?

These déjà vu-like impressions remind me of my pre-military induction physical taken long ago. I and others were subjected to psychological tests. One of these was the Rorschach Test. This involved my

1. Lawson, 1980, p. 205.

looking at ten inkblot designs. As the inkblots were displayed, I was asked to give my first impression of what they represented. What I associated each blot with was supposed to reveal the underlying structure of my personality.

Now what about the parallels to Betty's experiences that I have observed from time to time? Are some caused by the same psychological forces at work during a Rorschach Test? Are Betty and I so familiar with her experiences that we tend to see what we want to see? Perhaps, but there are several important alternatives that need to be discussed:

1. Some parallels may be due to deliberate deception by Betty and Bob to make their abductions accounts seem authentic.

2. Some may be non-deliberate assimilations of irrelevant data subconsciously added to real memories.

3. Some parallels may be real and supportive of their experiences.

The first alternative is possible. But, if I believed that these parallels reflected a deliberate hoax by the Lucas, I would be the first to expose them as such. However, it is safe to say that those who have met and/or investigated the Lucas would reject such an assertion. Both appear to be sincere persons. Character reference checks, lie detector tests and the complementary consistency of their testimony over a decade of intensive investigation make a hoax possible, but highly improbable. This chapter deals with the second alternative—that some of these parallels to Betty's experiences are there because Betty is unknowingly assimilating irrelevant data from the outside world and subconsciously adding them to her already real memories. The third one will be dealt with thoroughly in the next chapter.

The Theological Element

In the pre-teen and teen UFO abduction experiences of the then-Betty Aho, her accounts are essentially non-theological in nature. Even when Betty meets the One and the robed entities as a teen in 1950, neither she nor the entities identify themselves as divine or angelic in nature. The first theological element appeared in 1961 when Betty, age 24, was drawn from her home by an outside force to rendezvous with a tall gray alien in the woods. This entity explicitly identified himself and his mission in the context of Betty's Christian beliefs.

The Sent One

The Andreasson Affair Phase Two	Fowler	phase two
Betty: He has been sent, and I am not to fear. The Lord is with me and not to be afraid.... They are pleased because I have accepted [Christianity] on my own.... I am to go through many things and...love will show me the answers because I have given my heart over to love the Son.... Many things shall be revealed to me. Things that I have not seen...ears have not heard.... I shall suffer many things...but will overcome them through the Son.... I have been watched since my beginning. I shall grow naturally and my faith in the Light will bring many others to the Light and Salvation because many will understand and see.... The negative voices don't like it.... [They] are against man...bad angels that wanted to devour man...hurt man...because they are jealous...of the love that is upon man.... [The aliens are] telling me strange things.... I don't know what they're about...that for every place there is an existence...that everything has been formed to unite.... [He says] Jesus is with me...that I will understand as time goes by...for me not to be anxious.... They want me to grow and live naturally...that I am blessed and that I will forget, and I am now to go back to my house, and I will not remember.... He says, "Peace be with you as it is."		

In 1967, when entities invaded the home of Betty Luca (age 30) at South Ashburnham, MA, Betty assumed that they were angels. If you recall, the entities passed right through the closed wooden door of the house as they seemed to fade in and out of physical reality.

Betty's Angel Interpretation

The Andreasson Affair	Fowler	phase one
Betty: They came in like follow-the-leader...right through the wood, one right after the other. It's amazing! Coming through! And I stood back a little. Was it real? I was wondering. How did they ever do that? How did they get in here like that? I'm thinking they must be angels, because Jesus was able to walk through doors and walls and walk on water. Must be angels.		

Then, at the apex of her 1967 experience, Betty was brought before what appeared to be a holographic display of the death and rebirth of the legendary Phoenix. Immediately after this experience, she heard what sounded like many voices blended into one great booming voice. Again, note the explicit allusions to Betty's Christian faith as we listen in on Betty's conversation with the voice.

The Phoenix Experience

The Andreasson Affair	Fowler	phase one
Betty: I hear somebody speaking in a loud voice. **Voice[s]:** You have seen, and you have heard. Do you understand? **Betty:** They called my name, and repeated it again in a louder voice. I said, "No, I don't understand what this is all about, why I'm even here." **Voice[s]:** I have chosen you. **Betty:** For what have you chosen me? **Voice[s]:** I have chosen you to show the world. **Betty:** Are you God? Are you the Lord God? **Voice[s]:** I will show you as your time goes by. **Betty:** Are you my Lord Jesus? I would recognize my Lord Jesus. **Voice[s]:** God is love, and I love you. **Betty:** Why was I brought here? **Voice[s]:** Because I have chosen you. **Betty:** Why won't you tell me why and what for? **Voice[s]:** The time is not yet. It shall come, that which you have faith in, that which you trust.		

At this juncture, Betty defensively proclaimed her Christian faith to whomever was speaking to her.

The Andreasson Affair	Fowler	phase one
Betty: It is true. I have faith in God, and I have faith in Jesus Christ. Praise God, praise God, praise God. There is nothing that can harm me. There is nothing that can make me fear. I have faith in Jesus Christ! **Voice[s]:** We *[note plural]* know, child. We know, child, that you do. That is why you have been chosen. I am sending you back now. Fear not.... Be of comfort. Your own fear makes you feel these things. I *[note singular]* would never harm you. It is your fear that you draw to your body, that cause you to feel these things. I can release you, but you must release yourself of that fear through my son.		

As mentioned in *The Andreasson Affair,* the words "through my son" instantly became the catalyst for the most intense religious experience that I have ever witnessed. Betty's face literally shone with unrestrained joy as tears streamed down her beaming face.

The Andreasson Affair	Fowler	phase one
Betty: Oh, praise God, praise God, praise God! *[crying, sobbing]* I know...I am not worthy. Thank you for your Son. *[uncontrollable sobbing]* Thank you for your Son!		

At the time, looks of puzzlement and alarm were expressed on the faces of the investigators. At this point, a religious connotation to Betty's hitherto relatively typical but detailed abduction experience caused great consternation among us.

Mere words, even the above excerpts from transcriptions, cannot convey what Betty had relived before us. To have both seen and heard Betty was a profoundly unique experience. Listening to the tape recordings still provoke deep emotions within those who listen.

Betty herself, after being brought out of hypnosis, feared for her sanity as memories of this experience were now part of her conscious mind. It was the Phoenix episode that convinced her to undergo a psychiatric examination. To her relief and ours, she was told that she appeared to be in good mental health.

Betty's two meetings with the One in 1950 and 1989 caused extraordinary feelings of joy and excitement similar to her reaction to the voice she heard after the Phoenix experience. We wondered if she equated the One with God, but we could neither get an answer from Betty nor persuade her to describe the One and what she saw behind the Great Door that led there.

Fred: Would you say that the One was God?

Betty: Do you really know what God is?

Fred: I don't know. I was hoping that you had seen Him and could therefore tell me.

Betty: I can't tell you about that.

The Watchers

Betty referred to this term long before I wrote the book by this title. Shortly after *The Andreasson Affair* was published in 1980, she believed that the entities that had entered her house were angels. She also wondered if they were entities called Watchers in the Bible and the non-canonical book, I Enoch, as discussed in the last chapter.

Although Betty did not remember it in 1980, the entities reportedly had identified themselves as the watchers and caretakers of Earth's life forms during her 1973 abduction. Was the name "Watcher" a bleed-through memory from her unsuspected 1973 experience? Or, did she use the name "Watcher" during the 1973 experience deliberately or subconsciously because of her knowledge of the Bible and Enoch? These are questions for which we have no firm answers.

The Elders

Betty, being intimately acquainted with the contents of the Bible, would certainly be acquainted with the Elders mentioned in the New Testament book of Revelations. There, we find reference to entities called Elders, mentioned several times in Revelations chapters 4:4,10; 5:5,6,11,14; 7;11,13; 11:16, 14:3 and 19:4. Only chapter four of Revelations describes their appearance, which is similar to Betty's description of them. In addition, it also contains other pertinent parallels contained within the circumstances under which they reportedly were seen by the author of the book of Revelation. The following quote is from Revelations 4:1-5 of the New International Version of the Bible. I have italicized key words that may parallel terms used within certain segments of Betty's experiences.

> After this, I looked. There before me was a *door* standing open in heaven. And the *voice* I had first heard speaking to me like a trumpet said, "Come up here, and I will show you what must take place after this." At once, I was in the *spirit,* and there before me was a throne in heaven with someone sitting on it. And the one who sat there had the appearance of jasper and carnelian. A rainbow, resembling an emerald, encircled the throne. Surrounding the throne were twenty-four elders. They were *dressed in white* and had crowns of gold on their heads. From the throne came flashes of *lightning,* rumblings and peals of thunder.

Could this intense visual imagery, which was very familiar to Betty, have deliberately or subconsciously influenced the reliving of her abduction experience under hypnosis? Let's examine these references, one by one.

1. The author, like Betty, speaks of a door in heaven being opened.

2. The author heard himself being called by a booming voice. In verse 19:6 he writes that it sounded like "like a great multitude." This is analogous to the voice that told Betty after witnessing the Phoenix that she was chosen to show the world. If you recall, Betty described this voice as a chorus of voices. She had also

heard this chorus of voices speaking as one as a seven-year old when a marble-sized ball of light attached itself to her forehead. I might interject here that Daniel 19:6 also describes a voice speaking as "the sound of a multitude."

3. The author of Daniel states that when he witnessed the open door, he was at once in the spirit form. Betty, too, when standing before the great door, immediately came out of her body to visit the One in an OBE state.

4. The author described the Elders as being dressed in white. Betty described them as wearing white robes.

5. The author describes flashes of lightning from the throne that the Elders encircled. Betty reported that "a strike of lightning" coincided with the appearance of the Elder that rescued her and Bob from entities that abducted them in their car in 1988.

Another Biblical parallel worth mentioning concerns Betty's reporting beautiful music after revisiting the One in 1989. The author of Revelation, during his experience, also reported hearing beautiful music. "The sound I heard was like that of harpists playing their harps."

There are other instances in the Bible where entities looking like the Elders figure prominently in Betty's Christian belief system. They appear in passages from the New Testament Gospels and the book of Acts that would be extremely important to Betty. They would be intimately familiar to her:

> *Matthew 28:2,3* An angel of the Lord came down from heaven.... His appearance was like lightning, and his clothes were white as snow.
>
> *Mark 16:5* As they entered the tomb, they saw a young man dressed in a white robe sitting on the right side, and they were alarmed.
>
> *Luke 24:4,5* While they were wondering about this, two men in clothes that gleamed like lightning stood beside them. In their fright, the women bowed down with their faces to the ground.
>
> *John 20:11,12* Mary...bent over to look into the tomb and saw two angels in white.
>
> *Acts 1:10* They were looking intently up into the sky as he was going, when suddenly two men dressed in white stood beside them.

As mentioned in the previous chapter, Betty is also familiar with extra-Biblical literature. Such literature also contains imagery that Betty's subconscious mind could have drawn upon. One such example would be from the Protevangelion. This document is an alleged historical account of the birth of Christ reportedly written by James, the brother of Jesus and first bishop of the early Christian church. Although it is considered now to be apocryphal by Biblical scholars, the early Church fathers alluded to it frequently. It was publicly read in the eastern churches as canonical for a time.

The Protevangelion describes an instance where persons (and animals) had been placed in a state of suspended animation around the immediate area of Jesus' birth. It is reminiscent of Betty's description of her family having been placed in this state when she was abducted from her home at South Ashburnham, MA in 1967. The following excerpt describes what Joseph reportedly witnessed while hurrying to find a midwife for Mary, who rested in an animal stall located in a cave.

> *Protevangelion 2* But as I was going, I looked up into the air, and I saw the clouds astonished and the fowls of the air stopping in the midst of their flight.
>
> *Protevangelion 3* And I...saw a table spread, and working people sitting around it, but their hands were upon the table, and they did not move to eat.
>
> *Protevangelion 4* They who had meat in their mouths did not eat.
>
> *Protevangelion 5* They who lifted their hands up to their heads did not draw them back.
>
> *Protevangelion 6* And they who lifted them up to their mouths did not put anything in;
>
> *Protevangelion 7* But all their faces were fixed upwards.
>
> *Protevangelion 8* And I beheld the sheep dispersed, and yet the sheep stood still.
>
> *Protevangelion 9* And the shepherd lifted up his hand to smite them, and his hand continued up.
>
> *Protevangelion 10* And I looked unto a river and saw the kids with their mouths close to the water and touching it, but they did not drink.[2]

---

2. Crane, 1879, p. 33.

Joseph, like Betty, describes a situation where time had seemed to have stood still in the area around him. However, neither he nor the midwife were affected. An interesting aside is the UFO-like description of what happened when they reached Mary in the cave. The midwife found that her services were not needed. Something extraordinary allegedly occurred.

> *Protevangelion 13* And the midwife went along with, and stood in the cave. Then a bright cloud overshadowed the cave....
>
> *Protevangelion 14* On a sudden the cloud became a great light in the cave, so that the eyes could not bear it. But the light gradually decreased, until the infant appeared, and sucked the breast of Mary.[3]

The last and crowning theological element came to the surface when the tall white-robed entities called Elders seemed to ascribe divine attributes to someone or something called "Oh." This elicited a quick response in the form of a defensive question from Betty concerning the personage of Jesus Christ.

Jesus

Betty: This tall person with white hair...said they were ambassadors of "Oh."

Ray: Who is "Oh"?

Betty: *[pause]* The tall one said that "Oh"is the external internal, eternal presence. What we know is omnipotence, omnipresent. And when I asked them, "Do you know Jesus? Do you know who Jesus is? Jesus Christ, do you know?" And the tall one said "Yes, he is the hypostasis." *[Betty answers]* "He's my savior." And he says, "Yes, I know."

I phoned Betty after transcribing the tape of this particular session and asked her if she knew the definition of the word, "hypostasis." She told me that after the session, she and Bob looked the word up in the dictionary and that its theological meaning had to do with the Christian concept of a triune God. She assured me that as far as she could remember, she had not known the word or its meaning prior to reliving this particular episode under hypnosis.

---

3. Crane, 1879, pp. 33-34.

I referred to *The Random House Dictionary of the English Language,* 2nd Edition, Unabridged, which gives several meanings of this rather specialized term. They are as follows.

1. Metaphysics
   - a. Something that stands under and supports foundation.
   - b. The underlying or essential part of anything as distinguished from attributes; substance, essence, or essential principle.

2. Theological
   - a. One of the three real and distinct substances in the one individual substance or essence of God.
   - b. A person of the Trinity.
   - c. The one personality of Christ in which His two natures, human and divine, are united.

3. Medieval
   - a.The accumulation of blood or its solid components in parts of an organ or body due to poor circulation.
   - b. Such sedimentation, as in a test tube. Greek: That which settles at the bottom, a substance, essence, equivalent to Hypo + stasis [standing].

What is alarming is that if we take this conversation between Betty and the aliens at full face value, then they are not only cognizant of Betty's Christian beliefs—they are part of them as well! Thus, it is no wonder that UFO investigators, especially those who write serious, well-documented books on the physical side of the UFO abduction phenomenon, are so reluctant to deal with the paraphysical and especially theological element in abductee experiences.

What can we make of such accounts? Their content may offend not only persons of other religions, but those who hold to some aspect of the Judeo-Christian tradition. Most such adherents could not easily accept any connection between the UFO phenomena and their particular well-defined set of religious beliefs. Many times during a personal conversation or questions after a UFO lecture, I am asked, "What does this do to *religion?"*

The Religion Question

"What does this do to religion?" is a question that no one person should answer for another. It is a question that must be resolved individually.

My retort to such a question would be, "What religion?" and what do you mean by "What does this do?" This could mean any number of hypotheses suggested for the nature and origin of UFOs.

Each individual has the responsibility for personally evaluating their belief system in the light of their preferred hypothesis. Both religion and UFO hypotheses are mostly based upon anecdotal data and personal experience. Both have a starting point requiring faith. Thus, any answer to such a question must be based on a "what if" premise. In short, there is yet to be a final answer for this innocent, yet obviously sincere, question.

Having escaped a definitive answer, the question still begs some comment in the light of the experiences recorded in this book. Betty Andreasson Luca has maintained from the very beginning that her UFO experiences have an integral connection with the Judeo-Christian tradition. This notion comes not only from her own interpretation of the phenomenon, but reportedly from the UFO entities themselves.

This being the case, I feel somewhat justified in providing some comment on this aspect of Betty's experiences. But, in doing so, I will remain neutral as regarding its validity. First, I shall assume for argument's sake that Biblical reports of aerial phenomena and entities actually occurred as recorded. Secondly, I will only discuss her belief in the light of the UFO/afterlife hypothesis. Humans will be portrayed as a larval life form being carefully raised and bred for their future in the next world. Having set the stage for comment, let us move on.

The Old and New Testaments, accompanied by tradition, have provided the foundation for the Judeo-Christian heritage for centuries. For the purpose at hand, it matters not whether the aerial phenomena and entities from the sky recorded in the Bible have a divine or other origin. In either case, religion can be used as a system of control over the behavior of humankind.

On earth, humans control the behavior of lower life forms in a number of ways. These include the use of fences, buildings and punishment and reward training. Whether angel, theophany or other, the entities in the Bible have used religious teachings backed up by the demonstration of paranormal displays as a form of physical and moral control over the form of human—the very source of their survival.

This type of control would be a relatively simple thing to accomplish with a non-technical culture. Just the sight of a huge cylindrical craft would cause reverence and awe by those who witnessed it. Entities from such an object that exhibited such supernatural-like powers could easily convince such a culture to believe anything.

If we accept Israel's tradition of the cloud cigar and heavenly entities recorded in the Old Testament at face value, we already have an example of the above scenario. I might add that Israel is not exceptional in this respect. Christianity and Islam also have a tradition of heavenly entities intermediate between God and humankind.

In addition to the religious and moral teachings given the Israelites, directives analogous to breeding methodology were also imposed upon them. This is significant in the light of the breeding programs implied in UFO abduction reports today and in light of the UFO/afterlife hypothesis. The UFO entities exhibit an inordinate amount of interest to maintaining the form which becomes them!

The Israelites were told, like some abductees today, that they were chosen. Heavenly entities, whether angel, theophany or other, commanded then to separate themselves from the rest of the nations living about them. Breeding (inter-marriage) with other peoples was utterly forbidden. Strict health rules and food diet were imposed upon them. These directives, in turn, were governed by a form of strict reward and punishment training.

The above scenario is analogous to modern breeding programs. In order to produce a certain form of animal, a modern breeder would separate a number of animals from the main herd. The chosen animals would be segregated in order to prevent interbreeding with outsiders. They, like the Israelites, would be subjected to rigid sanitary conditions and restricted to a special food diet.

From time to time, chosen members of the selected herd would receive physical examinations, including inoculations, blood sampling, biopsies, extraction of sperm and ova and other operations very much analogous to what is being experienced by human UFO abductees. Later, the offspring of the herd would be segregated and bred in an ongoing attempt to produce certain types of progeny: race horses, show dogs, beef steers, etc. The long- term breeding program would be the same type family affair that we find in UFO abduction reports today. It is quite apparent that this religious control system has continued into modern times. Lest you doubt the possibility of modern human being influenced by such, consider the following.

> It resembled a plate of silver.... It made strange and abrupt movements, outside of all cosmic laws.... A very clear disc, which gleamed.... It...stood out clearly in the sky, with a sharp edge, like a large gamin table.... It looked like a plate of dull silver.... It began to...shake with abrupt movements, and finally to turn on itself at a dizzying speed while throwing out rays of light.... The pearllike disc had a giddy movement.... It turned on itself with impetuous speed...took on all the colors of the rainbow...[then] blood-red...plunged towards the earth threatening to crush us.[4]

Is the above a witness's descriptions of a flying saucer from the latest issue of the *MUFON UFO Journal?* No. The above was published in the Roman Catholic magazine, *The Fatima Crusader.* It records witnesses' descriptions of the Miracle of Fatima, which took place in six increments at Fatima, Portugal, between March 13 and October 13, 1917. Included in this miracle was the appearance of a shining woman dressed in white that ascended out of the sky in a path (beam?) of light. The entity identified herself as the Virgin Mary and brought a reward and punishment type message for humankind. The entity also foretold the death of one of the three witnesses chosen to hear the message. The prophetic segment of the message of a "catastrophic change" has received high attention by Pope John Paul II. This in turn is having a great impact upon the theology and policies of the Roman Catholic Church.

History has recorded a number of such appearances. Such apparitions have affected the belief systems and behaviors of millions of people. For example, the National Shrine of Our Lady of LaSalette is located just a few miles down the road from me. It is the center of a great religious order. How was it founded? A paragraph from a brochure obtained at the Shrine reads: [italics mine]

> On September 19, 1846, a "Beautiful Lady" appeared to [shepherds]...watching their herds on a mountain side in the French Alps, near the town of LaSalette. A *globe* of *blinding light* opened to reveal a woman.[5]

A national example is the Church of Latter Day Saints, or Mormon Church, which is now established all over the world. How did it originate? Its catalyst can be traced to the reported appearances of an unearthly entity to a young man named Joseph Smith at Manchester, NY,

4. The Fatima Crusader.
5. Brochure, The National Shrine of Our Lady of LaSalette.

in the spring of 1820. Excerpts from his descriptions of these visits are quoted below. [italics mine]

> A *pillar of light*...above the brightness of the sun...descended gradually until it fell upon me.... When the light fell on me, I saw two personages, whose brightness and glory defy all descriptions, standing above me in the air.
>
> I discovered a light appearing in my room, which continued, to increase...when immediately a personage appeared beside my bedside, standing in the air, for his feet did not touch the floor. He had on a *loose robe of most exquisite whiteness.*[6]

The entities identified themselves as "God," "God's Son" and "the angel Moroni." The messages and teachings reportedly given Smith were the basis for the founding of the Mormon Church, whose influence and membership is international in scope.

If one removed the religious trappings of the entities at Fatima, LaSalette and Manchester, the accounts would read like modern CE-III UFO reports! These events occurred in a simple rural cultural setting, far removed from the high tech society in which we live today. They appeared within the context of the simple religious belief system of the local peoples. I suppose that if a given culture's belief system included Dumbo, the powers behind UFOs could easily produce an apparition of a flying elephant as well! Humankind's modern technology would be capable of doing the same to an aboriginal culture.

Although not equating it with the religion question, UFO researcher Linda Moulton Howe and others have nonetheless speculated along these same lines of reasoning:

> Some researchers are convinced that humanity is property—that we belong to something else that...tests us like lab animals, communicating and controlling us.... The implication is that the chronic harvest of genetic material from earth life, both humans and animals...[dates] back to mankind's origins.[7]

Please be assured, I do not mean to denigrate the religious faith of anyone. I am neither denying nor advancing the possibility that the phenomena reported in the Bible, Fatima or LaSalette had a divine origin. The above examples are used merely to illustrate how God, God's agents or other beings could exert control over the human form. Such

---

6. *Joseph Smith's Testimony.*
7. Moulton Howe, 1993, p. 39.

interpretations are pure conjecture on my part. They need not discount the religious message of the heavenly entities. Reports of Biblical aerial phenomena and entities as well as their religious message could be equally valid. Evidences for either are of the same nature. Whether the Lord, angels or others shepherd the human form on Earth still remains a matter of faith!

Mirror or Mirage?

As an investigator and reporter, I will endeavor to put my own religious beliefs aside and concentrate primarily on the recording and evaluation of the Lucas' experiences. In essence, my evaluation boils down to just four major possibilities. The reader can take their pick. I remain neutral!

1. *Accommodation:* Betty and other abductees are deliberately introducing the theological element and using their abduction accounts as a vehicle to promulgate their religious beliefs. A number of so-called New Age groups use the UFO phenomena and other anomalous experiences to do very same thing.

2. *Superposition:* Betty and other abductees are subconsciously overlaying their religious beliefs onto their UFO abduction experiences to help them cope with what appears to be an insurmountable challenge to their religious belief system.

3. *Deception:* The alien entities are using the religious beliefs of abductees as part of their control system over the mind and emotions of the abductees.

4. *Connection:* The UFO phenomena with its abduction component is somehow connected to Judeo-Christian tradition.

Microamnesia

In a report to the Smithsonian Institute, Dr. Wilbur Penfield, director of the Montreal Neurological Institute, stated:

> Your brain contains a permanent record of your past that is like a single continuous film, complete with sound track. The film library records your whole waking life from childhood on. You can live again those scenes from the past, one at a time, when a surgeon places a gentle electric current and applies it to a certain point on the temporal cortex of your brain.

> As you relive the scenes from your past, you feel exactly the same emotions you did during the original experience.[8]

Adherents of hypnotic regression would say that the same results, relatively speaking, can be obtained using hypnosis. Others would insist that hypnotic regression is not reliable. Still others would deny that hypnosis is real! We have discussed these arguments in *The Watchers.* I proposed that hypnotic regression is efficacious in recalling and/or reliving past memories provided that a candidate is sane, honest and a good hypnosis subject. However, if we take Dr. Penfield's statement at face value, our subconscious minds hold much data long forgotten by our conscious mind. Such data may consist of what we glanced at while passing a store window, or an item on a magazine cover that we briefly noticed while waiting at a check-out counter, etc.

Such things are not considered worthy to remember and they are stored with lots of other things we do not remember somewhere in the dark recesses of the brain. This is called microamnesia.

Some researchers have hypothesized that abductees, while under hypnosis, might be tapping on such memories and subconsciously weaving them into their accounts. Some go so far as to say that many if not all abductees make up the whole abduction scenario from bits and pieces that they have read of the abduction phenomenon in the past. It is possible that the Lucas have been influenced by microamnesia? It is impossible to know for sure. Certain parallels to their accounts suggest a possibility, but only a *possibility.* It is not hard to find parallels to most detailed accounts on any subject. In any event, let's examine a few that came to my mind during my evaluation of their experiences.

Betty and Oz?

During some of the phase two hypnosis sessions, a woman who was both a professional hypnotherapist and stress therapist was invited to observe. She took it upon herself to get to know Betty and Bob very well outside of the sessions. We were especially interested in her comments on the conduct of the sessions and on Betty's UFO experience itself. In her written evaluation concerning Betty, she later stated:

> Meeting Betty Luca for the first time on May 10, 1980, was rather like meeting the grown-up Dorothy from *The Wizard of Oz.* So pure of heart, so innocent and incorruptible that it was difficult to understand how this [could be] possible.

---

8. Swindoll, 1985, p. 373.

Betty might have reminded the therapist of Dorothy, but segments of her 1950 experience reminded me of Dorothy's adventures in the fabled land of Oz. I pointed this out in *The Watchers.*

> Both were whisked to a strange place in the sky, populated by small creatures who stood in awe of a powerful being. In Dorothy's case, it turned out to be a charlatan who posed as a wizard. Betty, on the other hand, was taken to meet the One, but was prevented from telling us about her rapturous meeting.[9]

I recently borrowed and studied certain portions of the movie, *The Wizard of Oz,* and found several striking visual parallels in addition to this general story. One clip from this film pictures Dorothy standing transfixed as a big bubble-like object approaches her. A comparison of Betty's drawing of the same type of object approaching her in 1950 with this clip reveals a remarkable similarity between the two.

Another visual parallel involves the good witch arriving in Oz within this same transparent bubble. As you know, Betty on several occasions was also transported in a transparent bubble similar to that which carried the good witch.

Another extraordinary visual parallel is a comparison of Betty's drawing of the glasslike Great Door that she entered to meet the One with a clip of the glasslike door that Dorothy entered to visit the Wizard. Also, both Betty and Dorothy wore glass shoes. Both were told that they were "going home."

The Wizard of Oz is a classic. Its imagery must lie dormant in millions of minds. Could it be that this imagery contaminated Betty's testimony? Betty was born in 1937, the movie was released in 1939, and her teenage experience took place in 1950. Thus, it would be her adult memories being superimposed back over a childhood experience, rather than a childhood experience affected by the movie.

Betty through the Looking Glass?

Lewis Carroll's *Alice in Wonderland* and *Through the Looking Glass* are also well read classics. In the latter, we find Alice walking in a beautiful garden with the Queen when suddenly she began to run.

> Just at this moment, somehow or other, they began to run. Alice could never quite make out, in thinking about it after-

9. Fowler, 1990, p. 110.

> wards, how it was that they began: all she remembers is that they were running hand in hand, and the Queen went so fast that it was all she could do to keep up with her. And still the Queen kept crying, "Faster! Faster!" And they went so fast that at last they seemed to skim through the air hardly touching the ground with their feet.[10]

We found Betty in a strange glasslike wonderland containing trees, butterflies, flowers and birds. She is walking with one of the Watchers when all of a sudden he tells her to run.

Betty: He's telling me to run! *[panicky voice]* I've gotta run! *[shouts in terror]* I've gotta run.... I don't know why I'm running on that path, and I keep on running and running.

Both Alice and Betty are in a strange garden-like place accompanied by an entity. Both suddenly break into a tremendously fast run although neither is sure why they are doing so.

Was Betty's experience intentionally or subconsciously influenced by Alice's experience in a garden?

Betty and the Djed Festival

One of the readers of *The Watchers* wrote and told me that he had found a remarkable parallel relating to Betty and Bob's dual OBE abduction experience from their home in 1978. He referred me to a book entitled *America B.C.* by Barry Fell. It dealt with alleged archaeological anomalies that indicated the presence of ancient settlers in America. One of the alleged ancient finds was what is known as the Davenport Calendar. It was excavated from an apparent Indian burial mound near Davenport, IA, in 1874, by an amateur archaeologist, Rev. M. Gass. Nearby, lay two adult skeletons, and a third skeleton of child placed between them.

I immediately bought a copy of the book and was amazed to find a drawing almost identical to Betty's drawings and paintings of the place she and Bob had been taken in an OBE state in 1978. Through the cooperation of the Putnam Museum at Davenport, IA, I was able to get an excellent photograph of the item in question. [Photo 3]

Basically, the Davenport Calendar is a piece of slate with a picture and lettering etched onto its surface. The picture depicts a group of peo-

10. Carroll, 1946, pp. 30-31.

ple gathered together at a burial ceremony. Barry Fell, professor emeritus of biology at Harvard University identifies the drawing as that of an ancient Egyptian celebration of the New Year on the morning of the Spring Equinox:

> This festival consists in the ceremonial erection, by parties of worshipers pulling on ropes, of a special New Year Pillar called the Djed. It is made of bundles of reeds, surmounted by four or five rings. It represents the backbone of the god Osiris.[11]

Photo 3. Stone carving depicting the Djed Festival.

According to Fell, the inscriptions above the drawing are in Egyptian, Iberian Punic and Libyan. Fell translates the Egyptian as follows, which prescribes how the Djed festival should be held. I mention this because of a curious synchronistic mention of the term "The Watcher" is part of the translation!

11. Fell, 1979, 1989, pp. 265-266.

> To a pillar attach a mirror in such manner that when the sun rises on New Year's day it will cast a reflection on to the stone called "The Watcher." New Year's day occurs when the sun is in conjunction with the zodiacal constellation Aries, in the House of the Ram, the balance of night and day being about to reverse. At this time [the spring equinox] hold the Festival of the New Year, and the Religious Rite of the New Year.[12]

Before continuing, I will add here that there is and has been a controversy over the authenticity of the Davenport Calendar and Barry Fell's translation of the writings inscribed on it. Putnam Museum informed me that professional archaeologists believe it to be a fake. For those interested in examining the pros and cons of this matter, I would recommend reading Fell's book and a book by Marshall McKusick, a research archaeologist who teaches at the University of Iowa.[13]

McKusick claims that the Davenport Calendar and other items found in the burial mounds were placed there by hoaxers who belonged to a local amateur archaeological society. They sought to embarrass Reverend Gass because he had insulted them. Their plan was to expose them as fakes at a later date. However, they waited too long. The hoax got out of control. Articles appeared in leading scientific journals in the United States and abroad. The hoaxers kept silent because of fear of losing their reputations. Fell counters such claims in his book.

Fell maintains that the drawing depicts the ancient Djed Festival of Osiris. He bases this on accepted archaeological evidence yielded by a tomb excavated in Thebes, Egypt. McKusick claims that they are a fake drawing of a Indian mound burial service. For our main purpose, it matters not who is right on this matter. One pertinent fact remains: Whatever the drawing represents, it still bears a striking resemblance to Betty's drawings.

After seeing the drawing in Fell's book, I phoned Betty and asked her if she had ever read the book. She said that she neither owned the book nor could she remember ever reading it. I then sent her photocopies of the drawings in the book and asked her to comment upon them.

---

12. Fell, 1979, 1989, pp. 265.
13. McKusick, 1970.

Betty sketched the drawing and made annotated comparisons with her own drawing for me. [Figure 54] I have also included a collage of the drawings from *The Watchers* for the reader's comparison. [Figure 55]

Again, we are faced with some interesting questions. Are the similarities between the two drawings due to deliberate copying by Betty? Had Betty seen the book at sometime and forgotten it? That being the case, are the similarities a non-deliberate assimilation of irrelevant data subconsciously added to real memories?

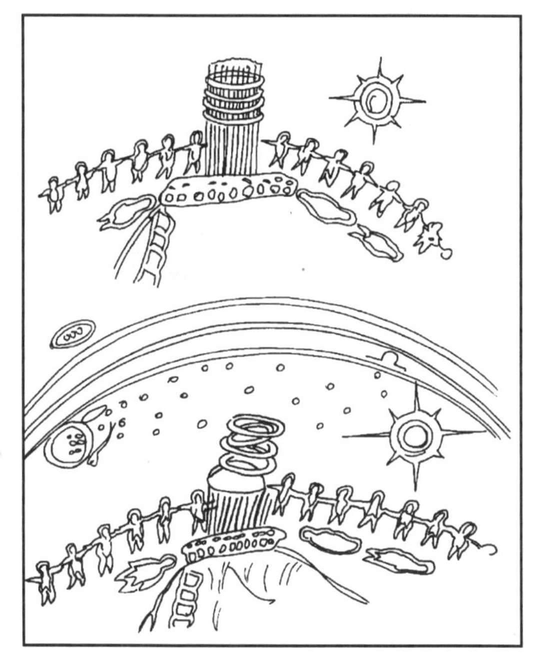

Figure 54. Betty's sketches of drawings from Barry Fell's book, America B.C.

Of course, neither of the above hypotheses may be the case. We may be just dealing with an interesting coincidence. Yet, still another possibility exists. It is very speculative, but nonetheless is the most intriguing of all. What if the drawing accurately depicts the Djed Festival? For the purpose of argument, it matters not if a hoaxer copied a real description of the Festival onto the tablet or if it was done by an ancient settler of the Americas.

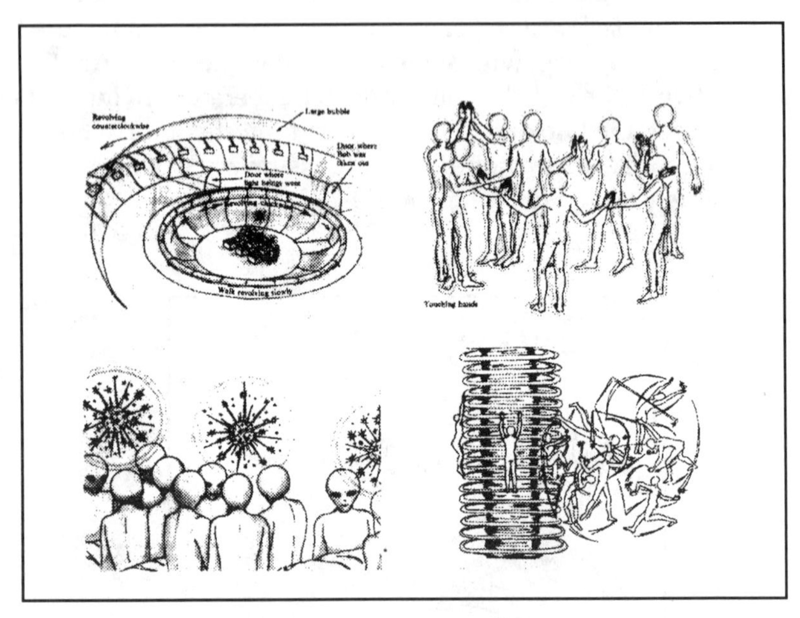

Figure 55. A collage of Betty's drawing from The Watchers.

What if the ceremony Betty actually experienced was a facsimile of the Djed Festival? This would mean that the origin of the festival was linked to ancient human contact with the Watchers. Thus, the Djed Festival would be a corrupted version of the same ceremony that Betty and Bob Luca witnessed in modern times!

Betty and The Hermit

I received letters on July 20 and August 16, 1993, from Mr. G. R. Muller of Port Elizabeth, South Africa, who informed me that a book entitled *The Hermit* contained some amazing similarities to the Lucas' experiences. Muller kindly summarized these as follows:

1. A Tibetan monk is somehow induced to go to a remote location by UFO occupants who proceed to abduct him.
2. He undergoes an OBE induced by the UFO occupants.
3. During this OBE, he is taken "somewhere" and is shown by means of alien technology the evolution of our planet from its birth to the current time and beyond.

4. These UFO occupants called themselves "The Gardeners of the Universe," stating that they have been the "Caretakers" of Earth from its birth to the present.... In one of the chapters...one of the "Gardeners"...actually uses these words, "but the Watchers were not satisfied...."
5. They stated that there will be a problem with humanity's ability to reproduce.
6. They mention a plan to help humankind, which was, however, not revealed to the monk. The experiences that the monk underwent were apparently the first phase of their plan.... I would estimate that the monk underwent his experience between 100 and 150 years ago....
7. The monk was conditioned to reveal his experiences at some predetermined future date only.
8. They told the monk that the reason for his abduction and the subsequent experiences that he underwent were all part of their "plan to help mankind and his world."

I was intrigued with what Muller described. Betty's abductors also identified themselves as "Caretakers of nature and natural forms"—the Watchers. Betty, too, was part of their plan to help humankind. She, too, was told that "They love the planet Earth, and they have been caring for it and man since man's beginning."

They also told Betty that "Mankind will become sterile. They will not be able to reproduce." Betty, too, was taken to strange places and shown earthly events on a screen. I wondered if this allegedly abducted monk's account mirrored any other of Betty's experiences that had been recorded for *Watchers II.* My next step was to obtain this out-of-print book. While I was going to England in September of 1993, I had a specialist find the book and ship it to me. When I returned home a remarkable synchronism occurred regarding this book. As I prepared to give a lecture on UFOs, a young lady sat in the front row on purpose to urge me to read none other than *The Hermit!*

I finally received the book by mail from England. Its preface said that it contained "A story that was the foundation of all religions, all fairy tales, and all legends upon the world."[14]

I read the book very carefully. Amazingly, it did contain a number of fascinating similarities to Betty's recorded experiences. Excerpts from *The Hermit* follow.

---

14. Rampa, 1971, p. 11.

We are the Gardeners of the Earth.... We travel in universe putting people and animals on many different worlds. You Earthlings have your legends about us, you refer to us as the Gods of the Sky, you talk of our flaming chariots. Now we are to give you information as to the origin of Life on Earth so that you can pass on the knowledge to one who shall come after and shall go into the world and write of these things, for it is time that the people knew the Truth of their Gods before we initiate the second stage. *[Betty was told by her abductors that she was chosen to give a message to the world.]*[15]

We, by our science, sent for you. *[The monk who was abducted was, like Betty, drawn by a mysterious force to the place of his abduction.]*[16]

Our tests show that you have a most eidetic [i.e., photographic] memory, so you are going to have information—which you will never forget—and which you will much later pass on to another who will come your way. *[Betty also has a near photographic memory.]*[17]

There I saw a most extraordinary thing a dwarf...a body like that of a five-year-old child.... The head was immense, a great dome of a skull, hairless.... The chin was small...the mouth was not a mouth the same as we have, but seemed to be more of a triangular orifice. The nose was slight, not a protuberance so much as a ridge.... Very, very small humanoids busied themselves with things which I dimly understood to be instruments. *[Betty described similar creatures as her abductors.]*[18]

This rocky plateau upon which the vessel rests was formerly a volcano. There are deep passages and immense chambers through which, in ages long gone, molten lava flowed and spewed forth. We...have increased the volume of those chambers for our own purposes.... You were taken from the ship and into a rock chamber.... Here was a vast cavern some two hundred or more feet high. Its length and breadth were beyond my comprehension. *[In 1967, Betty was brought through a tunnel carved out of rock into an immense area.]*[19]

Throne of the Great One...Great One's talk...to the Great One. *[Betty was taken to see someone or something called the One.]*[20]

---

15. Rampa, 1971, p. 14.
16. Rampa, 1971.
17. Rampa, 1971, p. 23.
18. Rampa, 1971, p. 26, 120.
19. Rampa, 1971, p. 61, 81.
20. Rampa, 1971, p. 62-63.

At the end of my life a young man would come to take all the knowledge I had and to carry it on and eventually place it before an unbelieving world. *[Betty was given messages to carry in her mind for release at the appointed times.]*[21]

The table rose into the air and men guided it through the doorway and into the corridor beyond. *[Betty, too, experienced such levitations.]*[22]

The females of the species are faulty. Their fertility mechanism is at fault.... We inserted a probe into her body to analyze her secretions.... The people of this world are developing a technology which, unless checked, may well destroy them.... We must prevent that. As you well know, this world and others are our testing grounds for different types of creatures. *[Betty's abductors were also concerned with humankind's infertility. They, too, inserted a probe through her naval for tests dealing with procreation.]*[23]

We [aliens] tried it with fair success with a man whom the earthlings named Moses.... The man Moses would then ascend the mountain...leaving with...Tablets of the Commandments which we had prepared for him.... The woman was visited by one of us whom she took to be an angel and told that she was to...bear a male child who was to found a new religion. *[Betty also equates her experiences with Judeo-Christian traditions.]*[24]

As I approached, I discovered the whole area seemed to be made of glass, and upon its surface there were strange metal craft...like two metal bowls stuck rim to rim. *[Betty, too, was brought to a place made of glass and saw metal disc-shaped crafts there.]*[25]

But the Watchers were not satisfied.... We are the Gardeners, and a gardener has to remove dead wood, he has to pluck unwanted weeds.... Our history goes back billions of years of Earth time.... Man is so new upon the Earth that no human has the right to even attempt to judge what we do.... We must ensure that the works of Man do not pollute Space and endanger people of other worlds.... Our purpose is to save your world. To save it from what threatens to be suicide. To save it from the utter pollution.... New weapons will be developed. Man will enter space within the next hundred years. Thus it is that we are interested. *[Betty's abductors called them-*

21. Rampa, 1971, p. 67.
22. Rampa, 1971, p. 86, 89.
23. Rampa, 1971, p. 90-91.
24. Rampa, 1971, p. 92, 151.
25. Rampa, 1971, p. 107.

selves Watchers. They were also concerned with man's pollution of the earth. They, too, told Betty that they had been on earth since humankind's beginning. They told Betty that it was better to lose some than lose all.][26]

"Your disembodied spirit, only temporarily detached from your body, has journeyed beyond the further reaches of your universe, to the center city of the chief planet. We have much to show you, and your journey, your experiences, are just beginning. Be assured, however, that what you are seeing is that world as it is now, as it is at this moment, because in the spirit time and distance mean nothing." *[Both Betty and Bob had a shared OBE/"disembodied" abduction. The aliens told them that time did not exist for them, that what we call time was localized and that they could travel in what we call time.]*[27]

I glanced at the screen as the Gorgeous one did.... The tube building, which I now knew to be a spaceship, stopped, and much activity took place. Then from the bottom of the ship there appeared a great number of small ships circular in shape. They scattered hither and thither, and with their departure life aboard the great vessel resumed the even tenor of a well-ordered existence. Time passed, and eventually all the small discs returned to their parent ship and were taken aboard. Slowly the massive tube turned and sped off like an affrighted animal through the reeling heavens."[28] *[Betty, too, witnessed a huge cylindrical or tube-shaped mother ship that contained, released and took on board small circular craft.]*

Please understand that I do not blindly accept what is recorded by T. Lobsang Rampa in his book as reality. I only recognized parallels to Betty's experiences within it. Most likely it is fiction presented in the guise of truth. The events portrayed in *The Hermit* supposedly took place over 100 years ago, yet modern terms such as "spaceship" and "mother ship" are used by the alleged monk abductee!

Our first investigation of Betty took place in 1977 and my first book relating her experiences was published in 1979. Thus, it's author could not have been influenced by Betty's experiences. Was Betty influenced by this book? Betty claims that she had neither heard of the author nor the title of this interesting book. *The Hermit*—mirror or mirage? The answer to this question depends ultimately upon the memory or honesty of Betty Ann Luca.

---

26. Rampa, 1971, p. 110, 123, 140.
27. Rampa, 1971, p. 111.
28. Rampa, 1971, p. 127.

Conclusion

We have touched upon just a few examples of material that I have noted which may have subliminally influenced Betty and Bob's memories of their experiences relived under hypnosis. Whether or not they have done so remains an open question. We may be just dealing with interesting coincidences or even astounding connections in some cases. Now it is time to address some analogous precedents that tend to support their experiences.

chapter twelve

Plausible Precedents

In the last chapter, we examined the possibility that some of the atypical experiences of the Lucas might be non-deliberate assimilations of irrelevant data subconsciously added to real memories.

In this chapter, we will examine modern parallels that appear to be analogous to the Lucas' UFO experiences. We shall also explore ancient parallels which, like the legend of the Watchers, may or may not be based on historical events.

Let us first examine several examples of modern parallels which are supportive of the Lucas' UFO experiences.

Modern Parallels

Aliens' Prediction of Sterility

During Betty's 1973 abduction, she witnessed two fetuses being taken from a surrogate human mother by alien entities. Alarmed, she asked them, "Why do you have to do such a terrible thing?" They answered, "We have to because as time goes by, mankind will become sterile. They will not be able to produce."[1] They explained to Betty that "The human race will become sterile by the pollution and the bacteria...that are on the Earth."[2]

The above conversation between Betty and the entities was retrieved via a hypnosis session recorded on December 8, 1987. It was quoted in my book, *The Watchers,* which was published in hardcover in July 1990. On March 8, 1992, the Associated Press released a story from London, England, that appeared in newspapers all over the world. Excerpts from this story are as follows: [italics mine]

1. Fowler, 1990, p. 25.
2. Fowler, 1990, p. 48.

London (A.P.)—Scientists Note Dramatic Decline in Sperm Count

The sperm count of Western men has fallen dramatically over the past 50 years, and *pollution* is the most likely culprit, Danish scientists say.... "I don't think anyone went away thinking that this work was invalid," said Richard Sharpe, a researcher at the Medical Research Council's Reproductive Biology Unit in Edinburgh, Scotland. "I have seen the research and I know several other colleagues have seen it who are well qualified to judge its merits, and you've got to say you can't think what things they have not covered and what allowances they have not made. So you've got to believe that there is probably something in it." Skakkebaek said that he could not give a firm explanation for the decline in sperm counts, but there were signs it could be the result of a *buildup of toxins* in the environment that disrupt the function of the testes. He declined to comment in detail on his work until it is published in a scientific journal.[3]

Six months later, Skakkebaek did publish the results of the landmark study in the prestigious British Medical Journal. The Associated Press again released news on its findings on September 11, 1992.

London (A.P.)—Sperm Counts Are Way Down

Sperm may be a casualty of pollution, according to a new report that the average sperm count in healthy men has dropped by half in the past 50 years.

Dr. Neils E. Skakkebaek of the University of Copenhagen directed the review of 61 studies around the world that looked a 14,947 men. His findings are published in the Sep. 12 issue of the British Medical Journal. Experts say the study lends credence to speculation that environmental pollutants may damage production of sperm cells.

"I think there is cause for concern," said Dr. Richard Sharpe, a respected reproductive biologist at the University of Edinburgh. "If there is something in our environment having an effect that is drastic enough to decrease sperm count by 50 percent, we should know what this factor is...." Skakkebaek said his review was the first to collect worldwide statistics and limit the analysis to healthy men.

"It would have to be something in the environment or life-style," said Skakkebaek. ...Changes that occur within a generation could hardly be due to a change in genetic background.... Investigators reviewed all international scientific

3. Connor, March 8, 1992, p. A-1.

> studies on semen analysis of healthy men from 1938 to 1990, Skakkebaek said. They found average sperm count declined from 133 million sperm per milliliter in the 1940s to 60 milliliter in the 1990s.
>
> Men who have less than 20 million sperm per milli liter are considered infertile, although they may be able to father children through test-tube fertilization. [4]

The results reached by the study quoted above represents yet another possible verification for the reality of Betty Andreasson Luca's extraordinary UFO experiences. If correct, they confirm the chilling prediction given Betty by the alien entities. They also show reason for the entities great concern in this matter if they are symbiotically dependent upon us for their own survival.

OBE Abductions

For years, mainstream UFO researchers advocated a "nuts-and-bolts" approach to the UFO phenomenon. Reports of any paranormal phenomena associated with any given UFO report automatically disqualified both witness and the report immediate suspect.

However, in the early days of UFO research, it was hard for some of us to come to accept the ever-escalating types of UFO activity which had started as simple flybys.

Its progression through close encounters of the first, second and third kinds preceded our progression through rejection, doubt, curiosity, investigation, validation and final acceptance of these types of reports.

Close encounters of the fourth kind in the early days were routinely equated with the contactee movement of the 1950s. This movement involved mentally unbalanced people and charlatans claiming contact with extraterrestrials. The contactee movement inadvertently provided a smoke screen of ridicule that effectively prevented recognition and investigation of early abduction cases.

We appear to have been going through a conditioning or learning process either as a matter of course or one that is directed by the alien entities themselves. Paraphysical happenings that have been considered atypical to the overall abduction phenomena may have always existed. Prejudice and prejudice alone may have kept them in that category.

---

4. Associated Press, September 11, 1992, p. 10B.

Thus, now, we are faced with the prospects of accepting the escalating types of paraphysical activities that are being exhibited directly and indirectly by the UFO phenomenon. One of these types are reports of OBE Abductions. These reports provide supporting evidence for the Lucas' reports of such experiences. Some summarized examples follow.

Houston, TX	Moulton Howe	May 1973

...A family was returning home from a bingo game in Houston Texas when they sighted a bright light hovering in the sky. They stopped the car beside a pasture. Judy Doraty stepped out to get a better look at the light. At that point the family experienced a period of missing time.

Later, during an investigation, hypnosis revealed that an abduction had taken place during this missing period of time. A beam of light shot down from the object and lifted a calf from the pasture adjoining the car. Judy and her daughter were then lifted up the beam into the object. Family members remaining in the car were placed in a state of suspended animation.

Both Judy and her daughter relived complementary accounts of an abduction/examination scenario on board a craft. While on board, Judy also observed the typical small entities [greys] operating on the calf before lowering its remains back to the ground.

The pertinent segment of her testimony given under hypnosis indicates an OBE abduction because Judy described a bilocation of her body. She experienced standing by the car in suspended animation watching the hovering object and being aboard the craft simultaneously!

> I feel in two places at once. I feel like...I was able to see what was going on in the craft, but I was also standing beside the road.[a]

a. Moulton Howe, 1988, video.

Near Grapevine, CA	Rogo	spring 1956

...Two women were returning from vacation in their car. It was night and traffic was heavy, so they pulled into a rest stop to sleep awhile until the traffic was lighter. Later, a yellowish light flooded their car. The car vibrated. They became paralyzed. A glowing object hung over the trees near the car. A UFO OBE abduction took place.

The following excerpt from a hypnosis session involving one of the abductees is extremely interesting. It not only is a parallel to the Lucas' experience, but [it] is almost a carbon copy of what Judy Doraty described in the above account.

Hypnotist: You're in the car?

Abductee: Not in the car. But I am in the car. It's silly.... You can't be in the car and out of the car, too. That's silly. *[laughing]* But I am.... I can see me...in the car. I'm asleep—I'm asleep in the car.[a]

a. Rogo, 1980, pp. 64-65.

Avely, Essex, England	Randles	October 27, 1974
This case also involved persons in a car. Again, note the striking similarity to the last two discussed cases. They were driving home from visiting relatives when they saw a blue light in the sky. Rounding a bend, they encountered and drove through a green mist. Sparks flew from their radio and they felt a slight bump. When they arrived home, they found that they could not account for 2 1/2 hours of missing time. An investigation ensued using hypnosis to probe into what occurred during the strange time lapse. British researcher and author Jenny Randles commented that during hypnosis: ...a very long account emerged, wherein the family were drawn out of their car. Sue [a witness] described it to me in detail, and it struck me that she was relating an out-of-the-body experience. The floating sensation and hazy memory of entry into the UFO again featured [the Oz factor], but there was a puzzling period where they saw themselves and the car...floating about the UFO.[a]		

a. Randles, 1988, p. 80.

West Yorkshire, England	Randles	1976
Randles tells of another case involving an OBE.... The witness reported that an entity with a gray face and cat-like eyes appeared in his bedroom one night. He was told to lie flat on his bed with his arms folded across his chest and his toes pointing upwards. He felt a numbness come over his body and then found himself floating upwards out of his body.... Mr. L. now found himself entering a craft.[a]		

a. Randles, 1979, p. 162.

An American researcher, Dr. Edith Fiore, has been a clinical psychologist for twenty-five years. Using hypnosis as a therapeutic tool, she has found some of her patients remembering what seem to be UFO abductions. Some of these were OBE abductions! Let us now examine two pertinent excerpts from her hypnotic regression sessions. [italics and brackets mine]

not recorded	Fiore	1973

The encounter took place around 1973. Sandi, 12 years of age, was watching television when she noticed a bright light shining through her window.... She became totally paralyzed. Then, the next thing she knew was that the ten o'clock news was on and she could move, but she felt tingly. Years later, at age twenty-seven, she then described [while under hypnosis] what happened during this period of paralysis and missing time. I will only quote from excerpts pertaining to the OBE segment of her experience.

> There is a light.... It got brighter.... I looked at the light a long time.... I feel my body is...rising up. It's raising up higher and higher out into the night.... My other body is still in the chair.... I'm going up...higher...higher.... I'm in a large room.... I see a head.... It's got big *wings* for eyes [large and slanted]—dark black.[a]

a. Fiore, 1989, pp. 12-14.

not recorded	Fiore	1973

In this case, the witness experienced an OBE UFO abduction from his bed around 1973. Something awakened him. He thought somebody was in the room, but he saw no one. As soon as he woke up, he experienced an OBE abduction to a craft where he was examined and returned to bed. Excerpts of the hypnosis session follow:

> I'm looking down at everything. I'm looking at me. I'm looking at me lying in bed...going through those Venetian blinds.... I'm scared to death. I'm floating.... I'm inside.... I'm on the table. [a]

a. Fiore, 1989, p. 309.

The North Atlantic	Fowler	1978

A sailor wrote to me and told me about the following experience. His name and letter are in my personal files.

> In 1978...I was at sea in the North Atlantic on the way to Scotland on a merchant ship when I had an out-of-body experience.... I recall looking down at myself in bed. I was hovering over myself.... Moments later I was summoned to a white room, fluorescent white.... In the room was a table with people [entities] around it.... They, too, were radiant white.... I can't remember anything after that until I was back on the ship looking at my body again.... I then laid down into myself. I, again, haven't had the experience since.[a]

a. Personal Files.

Another atypical component of the Lucas' experiences is the appearance of the "Elders." Human-looking entities have cropped up from time to time in abduction reports. Most were dressed in coveralls like the smaller greys, not in the flowing white gowns that Betty described. In other words, they looked the part of spacemen. These beings have been dubbed "Nordics" by some UFO researchers.

Elders?

Ranton, Staffordshire, England	Randles	October 21, 1954
British researcher Jenny Randles described the witness as being in her late twenties. She had experienced a tingling feel prior to her experience. Late in the afternoon, she heard a strange hissing sound and went outside of her isolated farmhouse to investigate. There she was confronted by an unearthly sight. It was a disc with a flat base, shiny, like aluminum, and with a large transparent window on top. Through this, two figures were staring down as if observing.... They wore blue "ski-suits" and had long blond hair. Their skins were very white and their chins were pointed, but they seemed otherwise human.[a]		

a. Randles, 1988, pp. 68-69.

Birmingham, England	Randles	November 18, 1957
Randles reports that this case was thoroughly investigated by a doctor. A pertinent excerpt from Randles' description of the event follows. At 3 P.M....a rose color appeared in the sky outside.... There was a whistling sound and from nowhere a figure materialized in the living-room.... The figure was more than six feet tall and had very long blond hair. He...wore a dark suit and old-fashioned hat.[a]		

a. Randles, 1988, pp. 70-71.

Venezuela	Randles	August 7, 1965
Two businessmen and a respected medical doctor were startled to see a glowing sphere descending. Amazed, they watched a beam shoot out of the hovering object. Inside of and floating down within the beam they sighted: ...two very strange beings, seven-feet tall with long, golden-blond hair.... Their suits shine as if made of metal.[a]		

a. Randles, 1988, p. 134.

My Father

As mentioned in *The Watchers*, my father had a number of UFO and paranormal experiences, including many OBEs. He claimed that he was being taken in this state of being by white-robed entities. I wondered if their appearance matched that of the Elders reported by Betty. To find out, we brought him from the nursing home to our house for dinner. After dinner, I showed him Betty's drawings and asked for his comments. Excerpts from our recorded conversation follows:

Ray: These entities you say that you met. What did they look like?

Dad: They were beautiful. Noble looking.

Ray: What did they wear?

Dad: Robes in golden-white rays of light.

Ray: What color were their eyes?

Dad: Mostly beautiful blue eyes.

Ray: What color was their hair?

Dad: Some are blond and some are white, almost white.

Ray: What did they wear on their feet?

Dad: Some had bare feet and others had sandals. But they radiate so much light, that...you can be with them for quite a while before you get acclimated to the light they're in.

At this juncture, I showed Dad the sketches that Betty had drawn of the Elders.

Ray: Did they look anything like those tall beings there?

Dad: Just like these.

Ray: Just like those? Were they dressed the same?

Dad: Yeah, they generally wore a robe-like affair.

It is fair to say that tall blue-eyed men with blond or white hair wearing white robes and bare feet certainly do not appear within most abduction reports. Similar entities do appear during NDEs. Later on, we shall see that this fact is of extreme significance. Such entities are also reported in Biblical texts. In fact, entities of this description and ability appear more like Biblical figures than alien entities from outer space!

I could only find one case in which both Elders and greys were seen together. It was mentioned in *The Watchers* and quoted from the

November 1980 issue of the *MUFON UFO Journal*. A summary follows. [italics and brackets mine]

> On July 4, military personnel from the Navy Air Base at Cantania felt a *compulsion* to ascend the slopes of Mt. Aetna, and there saw three red pulsating UFOs, one of which landed. It was a domed disk about 12 meters [40 feet] in diameter with red and yellow body lights. The group then encountered two *tall* golden-haired, *white-robed* beings accompanied by three or four *shorter* beings.

This is the only reference that I could find that described tall white-robed entities and the smaller greys together during a UFO encounter, despite the fact that I have access to hundreds of UFO reports.

The same applies to the next topic: mother ships. I have never heard or read about an abductee being taken to a huge cylindrical craft in space such as Betty described. However, there are plausible parallels for the type of craft that she described. Let us now examine them.

Mother Ships

Type II Cloud Cigars

It should be noted that these giant mother ships and their brood of smaller craft reported by Betty have been sighted by other witnesses from the ground. However, they seem to rarely leave the reaches of outer space to enter earth's atmosphere. This is apparent from the relatively scarce number of reports we have received of this type of object.

When they do enter the atmosphere, they sometimes appear to be swathed in cloud-like vapor by day and are seen to glow at night. Some significant reports of this type of craft occurred during a huge wave of UFO sightings in Europe in 1954. Relatively few sightings of this nature, however, have occurred in the United States. It is no wonder that the government has shown particular interest in receiving the rare reports that exist for this type of craft.

This intent became apparent to me during the late 1960s when I served as an early warning coordinator to an Air Force-contracted UFO project conducted by the University of Colorado. I was told by the team that sightings involving cigar-shaped craft releasing and/or taking on board smaller objects were a major concern.

Our government's interest in this type of vehicle is also indicated within official documents. Some of these consist of formerly restricted and classified memos acquired from the Central Intelligence Agency

(CIA) via the Freedom of Information Act (FOIA). The following three sightings were extracted from news clips for subsequent analysis by the CIA. They were used within an appendix to a restricted CIA document that described procedures for the analysis of UFO reports.[5] Note that the news clip extracts pertain to the same type of craft that Betty witnessed. [italics mine]

> On 2 October 1952, at about 2000 hours, several people in Corsica observed a *spindle-shaped,* luminous object traveling noiselessly in the sky....
>
> On 6 October 1952, at 1830 hours, a luminous object was seen flying for several seconds along the western coastline of Algeria.... Witnesses described it as *cigar-shaped* and enveloped in orange flames.
>
> About 100 inhabitants of Gaillac (Department of Tarn, France) reported witnessing a "flying saucer" formation at about 1600 hours on 27 October 1952.... The spectators said they also saw a kind of *elongated cylinder,* a "flying cigar," traveling in the center of the saucer formation.

In the mid 1960s, former Air Force UFO consultant Dr. Jacques Vallée invented a coding system that broke UFO sightings down into specific types and categories for comparative analysis. The type of UFO that Betty saw orbiting in space is designated as Type II. Vallée defined Type II as follows:

Type II: the observation of an "unusual object," with vertical cylindrical formation in the sky, associated with a diffuse cloud. This phenomenon has been given various names, such as "cloud cigar" and "cloud sphere."[6]

Vallée then broke down Type II into three separate categories that I have summarized below.

IIA: slow, sometimes erratic flight

IIB: stationary: absorbing/ejecting smaller objects

IIC: accompanied by smaller objects

Vallée's analysis of Type II cases in Air Force and civilian files revealed the following data. Common descriptions: "cigar," "cylinder," "pencil," "tube," "strange elongated cloud," "cigar-shaped cloud formation"; altitude: a few miles; sighting duration: at least several minutes, commonly in excess of ten minutes; cloud characteristics: boiling

5. Personal Files.
6. Vallée, 1966, p.54.

motion, "wisps of smoke streaming out"; and generation of secondary phenomena.[7] Of the latter, Vallée writes:

> Objects smaller and more sharply defined than the main "cloud" are seen emerging from it.... In some cases the witness describes their return to the main object.[8]

The Corsican sightings mentioned in the above CIA document falls into the Type IIA category, whereas the French sighting would be categorized as a Type IIC. Betty's sighting would be classified as Type IIB, as would her husband's UFO sighting and abduction from his car in 1967.

Those who have read the earlier books concerning Betty and Bob will remember that just prior to his abduction, Bob and a group of railroad workers had watched two cylindrical objects in the sky. One of these objects released two small disc-shaped objects, which flew off in different directions. It is assumed that soon after, one of them approached Bob's car, effecting his abduction.

Let us now examine several summarized examples of Type II sightings from my own files. Such reports not only add substance to the reality of Betty's sighting, but they lay the groundwork for a later examination of ancient Type II UFO sightings. We shall then see that ancient sightings of this type may shed further light upon the paraphysical relationship that exists between alien entities and humanity, especially in light of what Betty experienced while aboard their giant celestial space-shuttle carrier. But now, let us compare Betty's description of this huge cylindrical ship with several more incidents that parallel her own observations. We'll start with an event that took place almost in my own back yard. (My backyard sighting will come later!)

I was fortunate to have first-hand exposure in investigating a Type IIB event which took place just several miles from my home. It occurred just prior to my involvement as an early warning coordinator for the Air Force-sponsored UFO Study at the University of Colorado. Needless to say, it was of great interest to the project. The following is a summary of the report.

---

7. Vallée, 1966,pp. 175-176.
8. Vallée, 1966, p. 176.

Ipswich, MA	Fowler	September 17, 1966
Type IIB: Observation was from a house that overlooked a private reservation bordered by miles of beach.... Susan awoke...at 4:45 A.M. She got out of bed to get a drink of water.... She noticed a strange glow coming through the window from the beach. Startled, she shouted for her husband to come quickly. Both were transfixed at the sight of a huge yellowish-glowing cigar-shaped object hovering vertically over the deserted beach.... Two small, glowing, ringed oval objects appeared...toward the giant glowing cylinder with an up-and-down skipping motion. Amazed, they watched them enter the upper end of the hovering cylinder.... They watched in amazement as similar smaller glowing objects entered and left the immense cylinder.[a]		

a. Personal File #66-42.

Homer, NY	Vallée	April 11, 1964
Type IIA: A New York physiotherapist and his family watched...a dark oblong object which assumed a vertical position in the sky. Boiling wisps of smoke streamed out of its main body.[a]		

a. Vallée, 1966, p. 34.

Trenton, NJ	Vallée	August 19, 1959
Type IIC: The witness...described this object as an elongated, vertical cigar...surrounded by five shining objects which regrouped with the larger object and moved out of sight to the northeast.[a]		

a. Vallée, 1966, p. 178.

Offut AFB, Omaha, NE	Hall	September 8, 1958
Type IIB: A group of officers, airmen, and missile engineers observed an elongated UFO with satellite objects for about 20 minutes at 1840 hours. It...glowed and dimmed to reveal the distinct shape of a...cigar standing on end[a]		

a. Hall, 1964, pp. 25, 27.

100 miles NW of Las Vegas, NV	Hall	November 1, 1955
Type IIC: Frank Halstead, Curator of Darling Observatory at the University of Minnesota, and his wife sighted an object which they first thought was a blimp.... Halstead stated that "It was about 800 feet long.... We noticed that another object had joined it...very suddenly. It was a disc-shaped thing...about 100 feet in diameter, flat on the bottom with a shallow dome on top."[a]		

a. Hall, 1964, pp. 52-53.

Vernon, France 40 miles NW of Paris	Vallée	August 23, 1954
Type IIB: At 1:00 A.M., businessman Bernard Miserey saw a...huge...luminous mass...like a gigantic cigar standing on end.... He reported: "Suddenly from the bottom of the cigar...a horizontal disk...dived horizontally across the river.... A similar object came from the cigar.... A third object came, then a fourth...finally a fifth disk detached itself from the cigar."[a]		

a. Vallée, 1965, p. 66.

Danvers, MA	Fowler	Summer 1947
Type IIA: I [author] spotted a strange elongated cloud shaped like a dash hovering extremely high in the sky almost directly above our house. Curious, I called my brothers, sister and mother out to see it. It remained there hanging in the sky all morning long.... It must have moved off around noon because it was no longer there when we came outdoors to look for it after lunch.		

Was this a Type IIA UFO?

The question might be asked if such craft have been tracked by our deep-space radar tracking systems. Surely Betty's rendezvous with the huge cylindrical craft would have not gone by unnoticed. My answer would be that it probably was noticed. It would have been classified as a unknown satellite. Let us now examine such mystery satellites as other plausible parallels to Betty's experiences upon an orbiting alien craft.

Mystery Satellites

It might surprise the reader to know that mysterious objects were tracked by radar soon after its early inception. They were dubbed "angels" in those early days. UFO researchers have since collected many instances of radar/visual sightings from government files through the Freedom of Information Act (FOIA).

Actually, the very first case of a mystery satellite involved a visual sighting of an orbiting object. It was sighted in April 1949. Rocket expert, Naval Commander Robert B. McLaughlin, leaked the sighting to the press in 1950. He stated that the object was about 105 feet in diameter and was flying at an altitude of approximately 56 miles.[9]

9. McLaughlin, March 1950, p. 26.

As radar systems advanced in power and range, anomalous objects outside of the earth's atmosphere were also tracked by radar. The earliest references that I could find to them comes from the early 1950s.

> When radio waves are sent out into cosmic space, faint echoes return from spheres that are far above the earth's atmosphere. Some come back from "mirrors" that must be even farther than the orbit of the moon. Nothing is known about these mysterious spheres and speculation about them is premature.[10]

Another report came from aviation writer and UFO researcher Major Donald E. Keyhoe, USMC, Ret. Keyhoe was director of the National Investigations Committee on Aerial Phenomena (NICAP). He also had served as Chief of Information, Civil Aeronautics, Department of Commerce (now the Federal Aviation Administration, or FAA).

It was September, 1953. Keyhoe had just completed an interview on national defense with Admiral Arthur W. Radford, Chairman of the Joint Chiefs of Staff for *This Week* magazine. Keyhoe related that a naval Captain who knew of his interest in UFOs asked to speak with him after his interview with the Admiral. Later, he paraphrased the conversation that ensued.

> When I came back, he got me to one side.
>
> "I should have known you'd be in on it.... You certainly turned out to be a prophet. Is it a fact that one of the big ones is orbiting us?" he asked.
>
> "Orbiting? You mean a space base?"
>
> He stared at me.
>
> "If it's true, I should think Admiral Radford would know. Didn't he tell you?"
>
> "We weren't talking about UFOs," I said.
>
> A stunned look came over his face.
>
> "Good God, I thought they'd decided to reveal—" He broke off. "Forget what I said. It was all just a crazy rumor."[11]

This apparent leak sent Keyhoe scurrying to dig out the truth of the matter. He went straight to one of his many trusted contacts, who told him:

> They've spotted a satellite between 400 and 600 miles out...big enough for a mother ship.... An experimental long-

---

10. Kahn, 1954, p. 306.
11. Keyhoe, 1955, p. 33.

> range radar caught it the first time. It seems to be circling at about 18,000 miles an hour, in orbit near the equator.[12]

This was just the first of many leaks about mysterious objects orbiting our earth. In 1952, astronomer Dr. Clyde Tombaugh was commissioned by the department of defense to initiate a systematic sky search by telescope and camera for such objects.

> In 1953, it leaked out that two unknowns had been spied far out in space, circling the earth. They were called "moonlets." ...Other astronomers failed to verify any such permanent and age-old bodies. This put the Pentagon in a hole, and they never officially admitted that two satellites had been observed.... The mere fact that they later disappeared proved they had moved out of orbit and were therefore powered craft.[13]

Then, a year later, the Associated Press carried a story on two more unidentified satellites.

> Mystery Satellites #5 and #6, 1954. On Aug. 23, 1954, the Associated Press quoted *Aviation Week* magazine in revealing that Dr. Lincoln La Paz, government authority on meteoric phenomena, had announced the sighting of two mystery satellites orbiting at 400 miles and 600 miles, respectively.[14]

The August 23, 1954, issue of *Aviation Week* magazine, under the caption "Satellite Scare," stated:

> Pentagon scare over the observance of two previously unobserved satellites orbiting the earth has dissipated with the identification of the objects as natural, not artificial, satellites. Dr. Lincoln La Paz, expert on extraterrestrial bodies from the University of New Mexico, headed the identification project. One satellite is orbiting at about 400 miles out, while the other track is 600 miles from the earth....
>
> Dr. La Paz later denied this.... *Aviation Week* was not asked to make a retraction. The matter dropped into the Obscurity Bin of the Pentagon, a fate that all such question-mark satellite discoveries were doomed to suffer.[15]

However, an independent satellite search by the Adler Planetarium in Chicago on February 18, 1955, tracked at least one and possibly more tiny "moonlets."[16] Then, in 1957, Italian astronomers tracked a

---

12. Keyhoe, 1955, p. 67.
13. Binder, December 1967, p. 36.
14. Binder, December 1967, p. 36.
15. Binder, December 1967, p. 36.

huge mystery satellite orbiting earth three months before Sputnik I. Another unknown satellite was photographed in 1957 by Dr. Luis Corrales of Venezuela while tracking Sputnik 2. The object paralleled it partway around the earth, veered away and then trailed the Russian satellite once again.[17] On November 7, 1957, the Commonwealth Observatory near Canberra, Australia, tracked a similar object that trailed both Sputnik I and II.[18]

In 1960, reporters unearthed yet another unknown satellite that had been orbiting earth since 1959. It was tracked by the Navy's Space Surveillance Radars in a polar orbit never used by either Russia or the United States. Hastily, the Pentagon squelched the story, stating that it was the capsule of the U.S. Discover-5 capsule that somehow shifted orbit to cross over the pole! But on August 23, 1960, a tracking camera of the Grumman Aircraft Company obtained its own photos and estimated the object's weight as at least 15 tons! The Discoverer-5 capsule weighed only 1200 pounds.

It is important to note that at this time there were only a dozen man-made satellites in orbit, and the heaviest was a Soviet vehicle weighing about 3000 pounds.

The February 22, 1960, issue of *Life* magazine carried a story of the polar orbiting object, complete with Grumman Aircraft Company's photographs on its tracking camera. It also obtained photographs of its radar image on the Navy's Space Surveillance Radar.

> The U.S. was trying to unravel a mystery which involved everybody in the world. A satellite, clearly spotted on radar, was circling the earth every 104 minutes, but no one claimed it.... The object has the brightness and the speed of a satellite. But it travels westwardly, whereas other satellites are launched eastwardly to take advantage of the earth's spin.

Suffice it to say, such unknown satellites have continued to appear and disappear. News reporters from time to time would investigate leaks and publish material such as the dispatch from Washington in the *Boston Herald*, dated January 20, 1967, via the New York Times News Service.

> Three objects are still in orbit and are still listed as "unknowns." ...Secrecy policies prohibit government officials from discussing the sizes of the objects....

---

16. Binder, December 1967, p. 37.
17. Binder, December 1967, p. 37.
18. Binder, December 1967, p. 37.

How and by whom are UFOs detected at the present time? Today, tracking systems are even more sophisticated. In addition to the already mentioned Navy Deep Space Surveillance Radars, there are four huge deep-space radar systems named PAVE PAWS. These are designed to track sea-launched ballistic missiles. They also support the United States Space Command's (USSPACECOMM) space surveillance mission to track known and unknown objects in space.

The North American Aerospace Command's (NORAD) localized airborne/ground radar networks are supported by larger systems such as the Ballistic Missile Early Warning System (BMEWS) that is designed to track land-launched ballistic missiles. These systems in turn are supported with data gathered by Defense Support Program satellites. Even the FAA's radar network is part of this country's air defense network.

Government documents state that UFOs within the earth's near envelope or in deep space fall under the general category of Unknown Observations (UOs). Those recorded on tracking equipment (radar, photographic and other) are referred to as Uncorrelated Targets (UCTs).

The tracking capabilities of the overall detection systems mentioned above are fantastic. Just one PAVE PAW's site can track any of the more than 7000 man-made objects in space. These include everything from satellites and the space shuttle to a drifting camera lost by an astronaut. Many of the objects tracked remain unknown.

According to USSPACECOMM publications I have obtained, UCTs now average about 70 per day.[19] Most may eventually be identified as space junk, but some display characteristics that keep them in the unknown category.

In the 1960s, while working on the Minuteman Missile project for GTE Government Systems, I was given confidential information from a trusted source. He told me that a deep space radar system at Westford, Massachusetts, was tracking unknown objects entering and leaving earth orbit. When I queried the station's public information director about it, he was upset and told me that some people don't know how to keep their mouths shut.

During my last assignment with GTE government systems, I worked on a project to update the computer system that integrates all missile, air and space surveillance information to USSPACECOMM Space Surveillance Center and the 73rd Space Group's 1st Command

---

19. Love, August 1992, p. 5.

and Control Squadron at Cheyenne Mountain. The data is used to identify objects and continually update an electronic catalog listing human-made and unknown objects. A retired Air Force Colonel working at GTE leaked some fascinating information about such surveillance data.

The retired Colonel commanded one of five United States Air Force Ground-Based Electro-Optical Deep Space Surveillance (GEODSS) tracking stations. He told me that the station would optically track and record unknown objects entering and leaving orbit from space. This data was relayed to the USSPACECOM in Cheyenne Mountain. When he asked what was being done with the data, he was told (and I quote him) that "A Blue Ribbon Panel was studying the data," and that he should just let the matter go and do his job. I was determined to look into this fascinating story.

Much later, through the help of Armen Victorian, I was able to obtain a number of documents released through the FOIA that confirmed the retired Colonel's account.

Two of these documents were the GEODSS Phase I Training Handbook and the GEODSS Specifications Sheets. These state that each site has three telescopes, two mains and one auxiliary. The main telescopes have a 40-inch aperture, and a two-degree field of view. The auxiliary has a 15-inch aperture and a six-degree field of view. The system only operates at night when the telescopes are able to detect objects 10,000 times dimmer than the human eye can detect. It can track objects as small as a basketball more than 20,000 miles out in space.

GEODSS cameras take very rapid electronic snapshots of the field of view. Data collected is sent almost instantaneously to the North American Aerospace Defense Command's (NORAD) huge underground facilities in Cheyenne Mountain in Colorado. One wonders if the craft containing Betty that rendezvoused with the huge mother ship was recorded on NORAD's candid camera!

What if it were? You certainly would not hear about it because of the directives contained within USSPACECOM Regulation 55-12. An amplification of this USAF regulation is found in a document, entitled *Uncorrelated Target Processing Handbook,* which is used to direct the activities of personnel serving in USSPACECOM Space Surveillance Network (SSN) Sites.

In summary, the handbook states that the 1st Command and Control Squadron (1 CACS) is responsible for processing all UOs that are reported to the Cheyenne Mountain Space Surveillance Center (SSC) from the worldwide Space Surveillance Network (SSN).

This includes UCTs.

When a sensor site acquires an object, the site will compare the observations (OBS) on the object against all satellites maintained in its database. The object is given a special tag and is initially subjected to a detailed attempt at identification. If the object does not associate with a satellite in its database, the site will treat the object as a UO. It then will be retagged and placed on file with other UOs, which are tagged sequentially with a 9XXXX number. From this juncture, all UOs are routed to a Retag program which compares the OBS against the entire SSC satellite catalog database. If the object still remains unknown, it retains the 9XXXX number and is sent to what is called an unassociated observation file.

In essence, 9XXXX tagged observations that do not associate to satellites in the Cheyenne Mountain SSC's database, represent true UOs. They are then given special attention and tracked manually by orbital analysts. The *Uncorrelated Target Processing Handbook* states that:

> All DS UCTs (Deep Space Uncorrelated Targets) are classified SECRET (per existing directives).[20]

I might add that I have in my possession computer printouts from Space Surveillance Squadrons (SSNs) that contain *secret* UCTs.

All of them bear a Priority One designator, the highest priority that can be assigned in rank of importance to the government.

If such deep space objects do not belong to any government on earth, then they obviously belong to somebody not of this earth. Betty's mother ship, if detected, would have fallen into the UCT category. It is no wonder that the public only hears about unidentified satellites and deep space objects through rare leaks to newspapers. Such objects, especially those that enter and orbit under intelligent control, are among the highest classified subjects in the United States.

This ends our brief summary of modern parallels. With a little imagination, one can recognize such parallels as being highly pertinent to the validity of the Lucas' experiences. We now turn to possible parallels that may have occurred in ancient literature.

Ancient Parallels

Our first topic concerns possible sightings of Type II mother ships in ancient times, all cloud cigar types.

---

20. Wilson, February 16, 1993, Par. 2.0.1, p. 8.

Mother Ships

Vence, France	Vallée	March 23, 1877
Fiery spheres, extremely luminous, came out of a cloud of a peculiar shape and went slowly toward the north for one hour.[a]		

a. Vallée, 1965, p. 12.

London, England	Vallée	August 10, 1809
I saw many meteors moving around the edge of a black cloud.... For at least an hour, these lights...played in and out of this black cloud.[a]		

a. Vallée, 1965, p. 10.

Augermanland, Sweden	Vallée	1752
Luminous spheres coming out of a bright cylinder.[a]		

a. Vallée, 1965, p. 9.

Nuremburg, Germany	Vallée	April 14, 1661
Large tubes shown in inclined positions from which spheres originate. [Drawings are preserved in Zurich, Switzerland.][a]		

a. Vallée, 1965, p. 8.

At Sea	Vallée	July 29/30, 966
A luminous vertical cylinder was seen.[a]		

a. Vallée, 1965, p. 6.

We find identical descriptions of the Type II Cloud Cigar in Biblical texts. Observed objects were cylindrical-shaped; they glowed when observed at night and looked like cloudy pillars by day. The Israelites called such an object the *Shekinah Glory* or "Glory of the Lord." They believed that it contained the Angel of the Lord. Of this and other objects and celestial entities reported within the Bible, Marcia Smith, Analyst in Science and Technology, Science Policy Research Division at the Library of Congress, writes in a report for Congress, entitled "The UFO Enigma" that:

It is difficult to assess what import stories from the Bible really have for the study of UFOs since the book concerns itself with powers from the heavens that can visit Earth and perform remarkable feats. Opinions vary on how much of this is actual factual reporting and how much is symbolic interpretation. Some ufologists, however, seem to claim that most of the references to the Lord and his angels are in fact references to extraterrestrial visitation misunderstood by the people of those times.[21]

Whether or not this is true, one fact certainly remains. If mechanical aerial devices were reported in ancient times, they would be described in a non-technical manner in the terms and language limitations of those times. Most likely, both aerial objects and the entities associated with them would be given a religious or supernatural interpretation. Having said this, let us look at references to the Glory of the Lord.

Bethlehem (6-4 B.C.?)

The author of the Gospel of Luke writes that an angel of the Lord appeared to shepherds and announced Jesus' birth as "the Glory of the Lord shone around them."[22]

Babylonia (586 B.C.)

This involves the well-known story of Ezekiel and the chariot wheels, which often has been given a UFO interpretation. I include it here not only because of the account's similarity to the modern Type II Cloud Cigar sightings, but as a description of an abduction as well! Let's briefly summarize what Ezekiel reportedly observed. Excerpts are from the King James Version of the Bible. [brackets mine]

1. "A whirlwind came out of the north." [rushing sound?]
2. "A great cloud, and a fire infolding itself," [literally, 'flashing continually,' without the application of external fire] "and a brightness was about it" [surrounded by a brilliant light].
3. "And out of the midst thereof as the color of amber [something with the color of glowing metal came out of the huge cloud].

21. Smith, March 9, 1976, p. CRS-37.
22. Luke 2:9, New International Version.

4. "Also out of the midst thereof came the likeness of four living creatures.... They had the likeness of a man. [Out of the glowing metal thing came four humanoid entities.] ...Now as I beheld the living creatures, behold one wheel [disk-shaped object?] upon the earth by the living creatures."

5. "The appearance of the wheels and their work was like unto the color of a beryl" [sparkled like chrysolite, a silicate of magnesium and iron/a gray-green mineral].

6. "Their appearance and their work was as it were a wheel in the middle of a wheel." [A disc or saucer inverted upon another disk or saucer?]

7. "When they went, they went upon their four sides and they turned not when they went." [They were able to go move in any one of the four directions, perhaps describing the ability to turn at right angles without a curve radius.]

8. "And their rings [rims] were full of eyes." [Perhaps these were orifices or round windows?]

9. "And when the living creatures went, the wheels went by them: and when the living creatures were lifted up from the earth, the wheels were lifted up...for the spirit of the living creature was in the wheels." [The wheels were under control of the entities.]

10. "And when they went, I heard the noise...like the noise of great waters" [a rushing sound].

Ezekiel may be describing a typical cloud cigar releasing four glowing objects which land and fade to four sparkling grayish-green disks. They look like the typical modern UFO (a saucer inverted upon a saucer joined by a rim with glowing orifices). They appear to be under control of the entities and are able to move by making right-angle turns.

Ezekiel compared the strange entities in terms of man and familiar animals. He believed that they must be the legendary Cherubim, which had the face of a man, lion, ox and an eagle. He described something that joined them together as "wings" because somehow they were able to float above the ground when the disks rose into the air and moved above them.

1. "And their feet were straight feet [rigid]; and the sole of their feet was like the sole of a calf's foot." [Were these boots?]

2. "...And they sparkled like the color of burnished brass." [They wore shiny suits.]

3. "...And the likeness of the firmament [expanse, sky-like hemisphere] over their heads was as the color of the terrible crystal [ice], stretched forth over their heads above."

Ezekiel could very well be describing humanlike humanoid creatures in stiff booted shiny suits with transparent ice or glassy-like helmets over their heads! What he describes next is a bit harder to put into modern language.

> And above the firmament that was over their heads was the likeness of a throne [a chair] as the appearance of a sapphire stone, and...the appearance of a man above upon it. And I saw as the color of amber [glowing metal], as the appearance of fire round about within it...and it had brightness round about. As the appearance of the bow that is in the cloud...so was the appearance of the brightness round about. This was appearance of the likeness of the glory of the Lord [a glowing pillar or cylinder].

Ezekiel's words are his attempt to describe a sight beyond his vocabulary and understanding. It is hard to visualize what he is seeing except for his recognition of the object in the sky as the Shekinah glory!

What happened next again typifies segments of Betty's experiences within the huge cylindrical mother ship.

1. "I heard a voice of one that spake...and the spirit entered into me when he spake unto me...that I heard him that spake unto me." [mental telepathy?]

2. "Then the spirit took me up...and took me away...to them of the captivity at Tel-abib. "

Although set in an ancient culture and language far from our own, the elements of a typical Type II Cloud Cigar sighting, the generation of disks, the appearance of entities, telepathy and the abduction and transfer of Ezekiel to another place with a message to Israel shine clearly through to those who are acquainted with the modern UFO phenomenon.

Egypt to Mt. Sinai (1450-1200 B.C.?)

One sixth of the Old Testament is devoted to Israel's emancipation from Egypt to its establishment as an independent nation. The prophets and psalmists acclaim this deliverance as the most significant happening in Israel's history. It is not surprising that this remarkable experience was retold and relived annually from then to today in the observance of the Passover.

Taking the story at full face value, we find that their successful emancipation was due to a pillar-shaped object enveloped with vapor by day and glowing with light at night, which they called "the glory of the Lord." Its description tallies with the Type II Cloud Cigar sightings observed today, including the huge cylindrical object that Betty was brought to somewhere in outer space.

Reportedly, this object took part in some of the greatest events of Judaism and Christianity. It laid down the equivalent of a smoke screen to slow down the pursuing Egyptian army.[23] It hovered over and perhaps parted the waters of the Sea of Reeds allowing passage by the Israelites who were fleeing from Egypt.[24] It threw the Egyptian army into a state of confusion and caused wheels to come off their chariots.[25] It may have caused the walls of water on either side of the path through it to fall back and flood the pursuing Egyptian army. It dropped food to the Israelites as it led them through the desert.[26] The Israelites called it manna and referred to it as the "food of the angels."[27] It reportedly hovered over Mt. Sinai when angels gave Moses the Ten Commandments.[28,29] It reportedly hovered over Bethlehem at Jesus' birth and may have been responsible for the "star" of Bethlehem. It may also have been associated with the bright cloud reported to have hovered over the cave where Jesus was brought after he died on the cross. Such a cloud hovered over Jesus and several disciples at Jesus' transfiguration.[30] Also, it was a "cloud" that bore Jesus away at the ascension.[31]

However we may interpret these Biblical texts, we must at least conclude that the stories may possibly be based upon actual sightings of a strange pillar-shaped aerial object. Rather then quote the many references to this aerial object, I will use just one typical excerpt from the book of Exodus in the Pentateuch.

> And the Lord went before them by day in a pillar of a cloud, to lead them the way; and by night in a pillar of fire.[32]

---

23. Exodus 14:20
24. Exodus 14:21,22
25. Exodus 14:24,25
26. Exodus 16:4
27. Psalms 70:25
28. Acts 7:53
29. Exodus 20:9, 16, 20
30. Matthew 17:5
31. Acts 1:9

Needless to say, if people today saw such a sight over their home town, it would most certainly be reported as a UFO! If such was reported to Dr. Jacques Vallée, he would classify the report as that of a Type II UFO sighting.

Elders?

Since we have already discussed a number of incidents in the Bible involving entities that looked like the Elders in Betty's accounts, they will not be repeated here. However, these also could fall under the category of ancient parallels. There are other ancient records that also fall into this category. Let us examine several examples.

In the ancient historian Julius Obsequens' book, *Prodigiorum Liber,* as well as in Livy's writings, it is said that in many places there appeared men in white clothing coming from very far away; in the city of Arpi a shield flew through the sky; luminous lamps were seen at Praeneste—all this is 218 B.C. In 213 B.C. in Hadria, an "alter" was seen in the sky, accompanied by the form of a man in white clothing. A total of a dozen such observations between 222 and 90 B.C. can be listed.[33]

Finding plausible parallels to the Lucas' experiences may or may not provide credibility to their accounts. One could say that such could have influenced their testimony rather than support their claims. On the other hand, if there were none, one could equally state that their unique claims are false because they do not correspond to the typical abduction scenario.

Regardless of either of the above assertions, I felt strongly that such parallel data should be fully examined as part of my evaluation of the Lucas' experience. Such a study, at the very least, indicates that even the atypical segments of the Lucas' experiences, though rare, do have some known precedents. This fact itself provides strong circumstantial evidence for the authenticity of these aspects of Betty and Bob Luca's experiences.

How then can we continue to evaluate the credibility of their overall accounts? One way would be to conduct a detailed comparative analysis of their reported experiences with several hundred other abduction cases. Strong correlations between them would further undergird the reality of their relived accounts as retrieved through hypnosis. We will search for such correlations in the chapter that now follows.

---

32. Exodus 13:21
33. Vallée, 1965, p. 3.

chapter thirteen

Correlations

A landmark comparative study of more than 300 UFO abduction reports was published in 1988. The 642-page, two-volume work is entitled *UFO Abductions: The Measure of A Mystery.*[1] It was commissioned by the Fund for UFO Research.[2] The author is Dr. Thomas E. Bullard, a folklorist, who wrote his doctoral thesis at Indiana University on UFOs and their correlates as a folkloric theme.

Geographically, 142 of Bullard's cases occurred in North America. A total of 51 cases took place in European countries. South America hosted 66 cases, and the rest took place in other parts of the world. It is apparent that the location of the abductions in his sample is directly related to the availability of such cases through known investigative sources. Thus, no accurate distribution pattern can be accurately extracted from his listing.

Volume One analyzes the sequence of events in abduction stories from capture to aftermath. It categorizes the mental and physical effects associated with the experience, explores the various descriptions of the aliens and their craft, and examines the validity of the extraterrestrial and psychological interpretations. Volume Two is a catalog and summary of each case used in Bullard's analysis. Each is rated according to the reliability of the witness and the investigation. In summary, Bullard writes that the reports, which he calls "stories," show a great number of similarities, both major and minor—too many in fact for them all to be hoaxes or random fantasies. Bullard cannot explain why they are so similar, but notes that his study is:

> ...an act of literary criticism, an effort to reconcile an adverse collection of details into a hypothetical unity. Making sense of such different parts of the story requires many assumptions and oversimplifies the evidence, but one inescapable conclu-

1. Bullard, 1987.
2. P. O. Box 277, Mount Rainier, MD 20712.

> sion is this: Clues of many kinds from all through the story converge on one general interpretation. Dissimilar parts of the story interlock into the same meaning. Few narrators would have the foresight to organize their stories with all these implications in mind, and no familiar psychological phenomenon installs a multifaced image of aliens...into many individuals. Reality best explains where this unified picture of purposes and motivations originates.[3]

It is not my intent to attempt a summary of Bullard's massive work in this chapter. However, his study affords a unique opportunity to compare the story content of the Luca's experiences with several hundred other UFO abduction reports. Thus, in this chapter, the many faceted and intriguing elements of the events experienced by the Luca's will be the catalyst for a correlation with the benchmarks arrived upon by Dr. Bullard's thorough survey of the UFO abduction phenomenon. In order to accomplish this, we shall use a general outline of the Bullard study as our template for comparison.

Concerning the witnesses' recall of the abduction event, Dr. Bullard states:

> Hypnosis has become a recognized tool to unlock the memory of a witness, but also a controversial issue in the investigation of abductions. In 97 cases [31%], the investigators used hypnosis at some point. At no time in any of the reports on record has an abduction appeared out of nowhere to someone undergoing hypnosis for unrelated reasons. All abductees have some inkling of a disturbing event or else they would not submit to further investigation. The degree of awareness an individual may have varies greatly from case to case: Steven Kilburn felt a nagging uneasiness for years.... Sara Shaw knows of a light outside followed by an inexplicable time loss.... Patty Roach...and Betty Andreasson...retained vague but unusual memories from the peripheries of their experiences.... The Hills maintained a state of mental and emotional upset and Betty [Hill] relived the abduction in a series of nightmares.... In cases where some sign of the experience lingers on...hypnosis serves to recover the hidden abduction. In other cases, the witness may recall some or even a great deal of the abduction proper and hypnosis serves only to firm up those memories and clarify occasional vague points.... Only a minority of cases include hypnosis in their discovery and investigation. For 212

3. Bullard, 1987, p. 17.

cases [69%], the reports include no mention of hypnotic probes.[4]

The Lucas' experiences reflect all of the above patterns. They both have experienced UFO sighting, unexplained time loss and nagging uneasiness. Both have relived segments of their encounters in nightmares. They also reflected subsequent episodes through vivid dreams. At one time, Betty's mental and emotional reactions led to psychiatric counseling, as she feared for her sanity.

The Bullard study revealed that the ages of abductees ranged throughout the course of their lifetimes. Statistically, abductions reach a peak in the twenties and drop drastically beyond the age of 40. Some witnesses experienced abductions from childhood to adulthood as if being monitored by the aliens over a period of time. Both Betty and Bob have experienced UFO encounters since childhood.

But, let us now turn to the heart of the Bullard study, which deals with the types of UFO abduction. His definition of "story type" is as follows. [italics mine]

> Story type refers to a recognizable pattern of events recurring among different narrative texts. The names and places may change, details may differ; but whoever the actors may be, if they perform the same actions or experience the same events in the same order in two different narratives, these narratives tell the same story. Both stories belong to the same type.... The abduction report...tells a story of action and events, often several episodes long, and offers a narrative pattern with enough complexity to identify a kind of story as *uniquely as a fingerprint* identifies its owner.... If two complex narratives bear extensive resemblance of form and content, *change becomes implausible* and only an origin shared in common explains the resemblances in a convincing way. Extensive similarities among abduction reports would force a conclusion that diverse witnesses were telling the same story.
>
> All true abduction stories fit within a single type. One conclusion follows from this fact alone—abduction stories are remarkably consistent. That is not to say that they are all alike...but rather, each story corresponds to an ideal pattern or portion of it with little or nothing left over.[5]

Dr. Bullard discovered that the ideal pattern for UFO abductions breaks down into eight parts. He emphasizes that not every story con-

4. Bullard, 1987, p. 35.
5. Bullard, 1987, pp. 47-48.

tains all possible parts. In fact, the only account in his sample that contains all eight parts is the Andreasson case, which I have been investigating for over a decade. This is highly significant in that Betty reportedly has been specially chosen by the alien entities to deliver their message to the world.

The eight parts are:

1. *Capture.* Witness is caught and taken aboard a UFO.

2. *Examination.* Witness subjected to an examination.

3. *Conference.* Witness talks with aliens for a period of time.

4. *Tour.* Aliens allow witness to see parts of the ship.

5. *Otherworldly Journey.* Witness visits strange place.

6. *Theophany.* Witness has a religious experience.

7. *Return.* Witness returns and departs from ship.

8. *Aftermath.* Aftereffects and other unusual events.

Concerning the above eight parts, Dr. Bullard states the following:

> A narrative counts as true to form if episodes follow the order of the prescribed pattern; that is, the conference follows the examination, the tour follows the conference, and so on. Not every potential episode has to be present, but an episode present must take its proper place in the sequence. To show significant relationships, a narrative must contain at least two episodes.... An impressive majority of abduction stories [72%] describes the same order of events.
>
> The greatest number of orthodox narratives consist of just two episodes, usually Capture and Examination...Capture and Aftermath...or Capture and Return.... Three-episode cases comprise nearly one third of the total, four episodes [18%], and five episodes [10%], while even six and seven-episode cases are present, all true to the same pattern.[6]

The abductions of Betty and Bob Luca echo the content of the greatest number of orthodox narratives in the Bullard study. Both experienced the most common four of the eight episodes: Capture, Examination, Return and Aftermath. Of these four, Bob experienced the Conference. Betty, as mentioned, experienced all eight, including the Tour, Other-Worldly Journey and Theophany.

---

6. Bullard, 1987, p. 52.

Let us examine each of them in the light of Dr. Bullard's findings. The excerpts are from hypnotic regression sessions during the phase one, two, three and four sessions.

Capture

The typical sequence reported during the Capture consists of the following four specific events. Each will be defined and then a correlation made with the Lucas' experiences.

Alien Intrusion

An initial observation of a UFO is the common denominator for 71% of the cases in the study.

Obviously, some of the Lucas' incidents correlate perfectly with this subset of Capture. Both have sighted a UFO at the onset of an abduction experience.

The Andreasson Affair	Fowler	phase one
Betty [1967]: I then see the ship.		

The Andreasson Affair Phase Two	Fowler	phase two
Betty [1950]: It looks like a big bubble. Bob [1967]: The round one...comes down.		

Zone of Strangeness

Prior to entering the craft, the witness seems to enter a twilight zone where natural laws fail to work or work in unnatural ways.

The Andreasson Affair	Fowler	phase one
Betty [1967]: I was going through...the wood [door].... My legs feel very strange. My whole body does. It feels like it's weightless.		

The Watchers	Fowler	phase three
Betty [1978]: He [Bob] came out of his body.... I see myself coming [out] of myself, too!		

Seventy-seven cases include the zone of strangeness incident. Of these, 66 cases locate the incident at a point following the initial intrusion.[7]

Time Lapse

The third subevent during the capture represents a change in the relationship of the witness with the abductors. Bullard writes:

> So far the witness has merely observed external happenings. Now he exchanges his seat in the audience for a part in the action—and a key part it is, because the action focuses on the witness from this point onward. Where before the witness has kept control of his mind and body, his mental and physical states now change. Conscious memory of a period of time may lapse and be recovered only under hypnosis. Physical paralysis or lethargy may set in, actions may become involuntary or uncharacteristic and the witness has no idea why. One of these possibilities, or several, may cluster together as the witness loses his will to escape and memory of what happens.[8]

Dr. Bullard elaborates further concerning this typical time lapse that occurs during the capture phase of a UFO abduction.

> What the time lapse amounts to then is a period of memory excised from consciousness and the two ends of normal recall sutured together to give the appearance of a normal continuum, often with dubious success. The time lapse does not mean actual unconsciousness or semi-consciousness, because the witness remains more or less aware of what happens.... Dreams, spontaneous recall or hypnosis later demonstrate that the memories were present in the unconscious all along, even if inaccessible to conscious recall. Time lapse acts to blanket the whole experience as a retroactive effect, a gradual fading of recollection.[9]

This, of course, is exactly what happened to the Lucas. Memories of their UFO abduction experience were mostly blocked from their con-

---

7. Bullard, 1987, p. 60.
8. Bullard, 1987, p. 60.
9. Bullard, 1987, p. 178.

scious minds except for flashbacks and dreams. It took hypnotic regression to break through these mental blocks.

A total of 188 cases in the Bullard study contain the time-lapse phenomenon. The fact that 177 cases and 94% of narratives contain this incident and locate it in the prescribed place affirms that events in the capture episode are consistent to a high degree.

Procurement

The final sequenced subevent of the capture episode is the actual acquisition of a human being by the aliens. A total of 185 cases in the Bullard study reflect the event of procurement. Dr. Bullard states that:

> In the previous parts of the capture episode, a single event often represents the recurrent element, but procurement events are likely to be several in number and successive in relationship, so that this portion of the story lengthens into its own sub-episode. Some 16 events with fixed positions recur among the procurement accounts though the frequency varies considerably. The truly common elements reduce to eight.

1. A beam of light strikes the witness,
2. a drawing force pulls him toward
3. beings who then appear, and
4. converse with the witness, usually to reassure or instruct him.
5. Physical and mental controls follow, as the witness feels pacified or paralyzed, loses his will or lapses into an unconscious or semi-conscious state.
6. The beings escort the witness, often touching or holding him,
7. so that he floats toward the craft, and then
8. enters with a temporary memory lapse, or doorway amnesia. [10]

Let us examine several of the Lucas' experiences in light of each of these eight sub-episodes of procurement.

The Beam

Dr. Bullard states the following concerning the beam.

---

10. Bullard, 1987, p. 61.

> In 61 cases, the witness reports that a light strikes or engulfs his person, car or bedroom. This light may beam directly from the craft or from a being.... The usual position of the light incident is early in the story during capture, where a beam functions to deprive the witness of mental and physical freedom. The witness loses consciousness as soon as the light strikes or soon thereafter.[11]

Here are some examples from Betty and Bob's UFO abduction experiences.

The Andreasson Affair Phase Two	Fowler	phase two
Bob [1967]: This red light shines on me...and then I'm inside this room.		

The Watchers	Fowler	phase three
Betty [1973]: And a light is coming out of the bottom of the craft and we're standing in that light—and we're in the craft!		

The Watchers II	Fowler	phase four
Betty [1988]: And we're going down the highway.... Whew! What a bright light! He's [Bob] staring straight ahead, not moving. And I'm not moving either.... Those beings...have taken us [with the car] into a craft.		
Betty [1989]: That ball of light shot out a light toward me.... Oh-h-h! I'm in another room [in the UFO].		

Again we see a perfect correlation between these abduction incidents and the statistics reflected in the Bullard study. When the beam hit the Lucas, they were suddenly transported into an alien craft and indeed deprived of their mental and physical freedom.

The Drawing Force

Dr. Bullard states the following concerning the drawing force associated with the acquisition of the abductees by aliens.

> In 40 cases, some sort of force draws the witness toward the UFO or beings. This element holds the same relative position in 32 cases and initiates procurement in 25 cases. In 5 in-

11. Bullard, 1987, p. 199.

> stances, the force follows or has some connection with the beam.... Beams of light may serve other functions, most notably to float or draw the witness toward the craft.[12]

The drawing force is also mirrored within two of Betty's encounters.

The Andreasson Affair	Fowler	phase one
Betty [1961]: I feel strange, like something is pulling me along.		

The Watchers II	Fowler	phase four
Betty [1989]: I'm getting a strange drawing feeling, like I have to get up.... I've got to go outdoors.		

The Beings Appear

Under this episode, we find a typical deviation which also shows up in the Bullard study. A number of abductions have the beam of light strike the abductee and draw the victim towards the beings, who then escort the abductee to the waiting UFO. This is not so within the framework of the Lucas' encounters.

Bullard states that:

> A far more common course of events has the beings appear at the *end* of the capture sequence, after the UFO brings them and various changes in the outer world and the witness's consciousness prepare the way.... Sometimes the account may be fragmentary or the witness may awaken to find beings already in the room. [italics mine][13]

The latter scenarios has been experienced by the Lucas over the course of their abductions.

The Andreasson Affair	Fowler	phase one
Betty [1967]: There are beings...starting to come through the door now... *right through* the wood, one right after the other.... It's amazing!		
Bob [1967]: Something in the red light [beam].... I can see the person...and then I'm inside this room.		

12. Bullard, 1987, pp.51, 62.
13. Bullard, 1987, p. 62

The Andreasson Affair Phase Two	Fowler	phase two
Betty [1950]: Oh-h-h, I'm standing in some kind of a room…and Oh! There's little people coming in the room toward me!		

The Watchers	Fowler	phase three
Betty [1973]: There's light coming in the window…. Something's in the bedroom…those strange beings.		
Betty [1978]: We're both being lifted up somehow…There is a very tall—looks like men in white robes.		
Betty [1986]: I'm in the trailer all by myself…. Oh! There's a being…standing next to me.		

The Watchers II	Fowler	phase four
Betty [1989]: Oh-h-h! I'm in another room…. That blue light is pouring off me, and I can see a little person, a little being there.		
Betty [1989]: There's a bright, bright light here and…I'm like half in me and half out of me…. I hear something on the roof. Oh, it's one of those beings.		
Betty [1989]: Streaks of light just filled the room…. I feel myself lifting out of my body…out of the trailer. And there's a flash of light and I'm with a being, a gray being…and I'm moving with him and we're going into a room.		
Bob [1989]: Betty's sleeping over there and I wake up and there's one of those beings, the gray beings with the bluish, the blue uniform.		
Bob [1992]: I wake up and…something woke me up and I looked straight downstairs. There's one of the gray beings.		

Let us now examine the fourth segment of the sequence of events involved in procurement.

The Beings Converse

The first communication from the aliens takes place soon after the first confrontation with their captors. In some cases, this takes place when the abductee is first confronted by the aliens outside the craft. When this is so, the aliens usually reassure the witness and ask that the witness come away with them. The following excerpts reflect this particular scenario from the Bullard study.

The Andreasson Affair	Fowler	phase one
Betty [1967]: We will not harm you.... Would you follow us? *[Aliens speaking to Betty.]*		

The Watchers	Fowler	phase three
Betty [1978]: Those strange beings...one is still pulling at my arm and telling me to get up...and they are leading me out.		
Betty [1986]: The being...put a small box or some thing on the couch.... We're fad[ing] away.... We're coming to a ball-shaped craft.		

The Watchers II	Fowler	phase four
Bob [1989]: I wake up and there's one of those beings. And he wants me to go.... He tells me again, he wants me to go with him and I'm saying, "I don't want to go!"		

When the witness is drawn directly into the UFO first, the communication takes place soon after the first confrontation with the aliens on board the craft. Again, some of the incidents relived under hypnosis by the Lucas follow this sequence of events. In either case, the conversation is usually one-way and consists of either reassuring or instructing the witness.

The Andreasson Affair Phase Two	Fowler	phase two
Betty [1950]: I'm standing in some kind of a room.... There [are] three little people standing there. And they are funny.... They say not to be afraid...and they said, "We're going to take you someplace."		
Bob [1967]: I'm inside this room...all of a sudden.... He [alien entity] told me to take my clothes off...tells me I should not be afraid.		

Of 124 cases with the means of communication specified, 98 [79%] involve telepathy, thought transference, or the witness being able to understand or hear the beings without their mouths moving or any apparent auditory input.[14]

The Andreasson Affair	Fowler	phase one
Betty [1967]: It seemed like an oral sound, but I think it was a transformation of thought.		

The Andreasson Affair Phase Two	Fowler	phase two
Betty [1961]: He told me…through his eyes or his head. I don't hear him talking.		
Bob [1967]: It's just like a voice inside…myself.		

The Watchers	Fowler	phase three
Betty [1973]: And that one being is communicating to me through the mind.... They are talking among themselves, but not by their mouths, just with their minds.		
Betty [1975]: They are standing there communicating with me [by telepathy].		

The Watchers II	Fowler	phase four
Betty [1989]: They don't talk with their mouth, they just communicate through their eyes or something, I don't know. Mental telepathy or something,		
Bob [1967]: I knew what they wanted me to do.		
Bob [1978]: I don't think they are talking. I think, I think it's just thought. I'm not sure.		
Bob [1989]: I just knew what their thoughts were—that I was supposed to know, I guess. I can hear them in my head, but it's not like anyone's talking.		

Once more we note the fascinating affinity that exists between Betty and Bob's experiences and other abduction reports on record. The harmony continues as we move to the fifth aspect of human acquisition by the aliens.

14. Bullard, 1987, p. 109.

Physical and Mental Controls

As we have seen, the Bullard study reveals that an abductee usually suffers debilitating effects before their direct confrontation with the beings. However, once on board the UFO, the aliens exert further physical and mental influences in order to make the abductee acquiesce to their every demand. The techniques used are often ascribed to the aliens' hypnotic eyes or to actual physical contact with them.

In 71 cases from the Bullard study, the aliens make some effort to control the witness. Pacification, paralysis, rendering the abductee unconscious or semi-conscious and somehow taking control of the will and behavior of the victim are the techniques usually employed by the aliens. Such control was certainly exerted by the aliens upon the Lucas. The following excerpts from their hypnosis sessions demonstrates this quite convincingly.

The Andreasson Affair	Fowler	phase one
Betty [1967]: There was something that they had—power that I automatically went.... I was held somehow [on a table], because I didn't want that examination.		

The Andreasson Affair Phase Two	Fowler	phase two
Betty [1950]: I don't know what is happening, but I seem to be going...along with them. Bob [1967]: I just had to sit on the bench.... I'm just stuck on this table.		

The Watchers	Fowler	phase three
Betty [1973]: They are coming over to me, and...one is standing still and the other one's getting in front of me, and I'm moving [floating] along with them. Betty [1978]: They are moving and I'm moving with them. We're floating across, one in front of me and one in back of me.		

The Watchers II	Fowler	phase four
Betty [1988]: He [Bob] looks stiff. His hands are like on the wheel, gripped to the wheel. His eyes are wide.... We're still. We're just still.		
Betty [1989]: He's moving a little bit, and I'm moving around with him, but I feel top heavy. Phew! Through their mind, I guess, their eyes and their mind, they move me somehow.		
Betty [1989]: And I'm with a being, a gray being. He's standing there before me and he says, "Come along," and I'm moving with him, and we're going into a room.		
Bob [1978]: And they are telling me to sit down...and to relax. Yeah, I'm relaxed.		
Bob [1989]: I don't want them to put me on that table! They do! They do! They put me on that table again!		

Floating Effect

Soon after a witness is confronted by aliens outside a UFO, he or she is often then floated up to the hovering craft.

The Andreasson Affair	Fowler	phase one
Betty [1967]: And...that door is opening...and we are getting all lined up. And he swoops right up...! Soon as he goes up, I'm swooped up, and the others are following.		

The Andreasson Affair Phase Two	Fowler	phase two
Betty [1987]: I don't know, I just floated [into the UFO] from my car.		

The Watchers	Fowler	phase three
Betty[1973]: And a light is coming out of the bottom of the craft and we're standing in that light [floating upwards]. And we're in the craft!		
Betty [1978]: We're both being lifted up somehow...into a room.		

The Watchers II	Fowler	phase four
Betty [1989]: I'm in that ball of light now.... I'm up, I'm up so high.... Oh-h-h! I'm in another room.		
Bob [1989]: And the same one that takes me in grabs my arm, my left arm, and we go...back down...where the windows are to the bed, and I go back in bed.		

Doorway Amnesia

Dr. Bullard explains this last event of the procurement cycle as follows:

> A funny thing happens on the way to the spaceship. The witness undergoes a memory lapse as he enters the ship, then recovers consciousness once inside. Why or how this brief hiatus takes place remains unknown, but it appears in 32 cases and 28 of them station this incident as the last significant event of the procurement sequence.[15]

This is exactly what Betty as a teenager experienced. As far as she could remember, she was climbing steps to a field and sighted an approaching UFO. She became paralyzed and suddenly found herself on board the craft without any memory of how she got there.

The Andreasson Affair Phase Two	Fowler	phase two
Betty [1950]: It's [UFO] coming closer.... I can't move! Oh-h-h, I'm standing in some kind of a room.		

The Watchers II	Fowler	phase four
Betty [1988]: We're going on into Durham.... Whew! What a bright light! Those beings must have taken us [with the car] into a craft.		
Betty [1989]: I'm inside...the blue light.... Oh! I'm in another room.		

Before we move on to the second episode of the typical abduction, it is worth mentioning one more event that sometimes takes place dur-

15. Bullard, 1987, p. 63.

ing the procurement cycle of capture. Dr. Bullard lists several less common events that recur. He states:

> The most memorable of these scarcer incidents occurs when the witness resists his captors. Fourteen cases contain this occurrence. The witness feels an ambivalence about his situation, or more properly, the controlling effect temporarily wears off...and the witness grows anxious over his predicament.... Then the witness's anxieties boil over into action, and the beings suddenly have a fight on their hands.[16]

Bob's anxieties certainly "boiled over" at the onset of his 1989 abduction in Florida. It occurred when an alien entered the bedroom and asked Bob to come away with him. Bob's resistance against the alien's mental control process caused the alien to take additional control measures.

The Watchers II	Fowler	phase four
Bob [1989]: I'm not going to go, I'm not going to go, I'm not going to go! Oh, my will is strong. I won't go, I won't go, I won't go! They can't make me. He puts his hand on my forehead.... He's pouring that liquid in my mouth....		
Fred: What are the immediate physiological effects you feel after having ingested it?		
Bob: I just felt kinda more relaxed....		
Fred: Why did you take the liquid?		
Bob: Because I couldn't move.		

For most abductees, the next major episode of the abduction story type appears to be the very reason for their capture.

Examinations

Dr. Bullard makes the following opening statement in the section of his study that deals with what he refers to as the "heart of the matter."

> A bizarre and unpleasant ordeal awaits the captive once he enters the ship. Beings usher the witness into an inner room of uniform lighting and hospital cleanliness, then subject him to a systematic, thorough and often painful medical examination....

16. Bullard, 1987, p. 63.

The examination events follow a regular course of action with the following steps:

1. *Preparation.* The beings make the witness ready for examination.
2. *Manual Examination.* The beings touch or manipulate the witness's body by hand or use handheld instruments.
3. *Scanning.* An eyelike device scans the witness's body.
4. *Instrumental Examination.* Instruments probe the witness body.
5. *Samples.* The beings take samples of blood or other body materials.
6. *Reproductive Examination.* Tests concerned with reproduction or genital organs follow.
7. *Neurological Examination.* Attention turns to the head, brain and nervous system as the beings explore the mind, brain and nerves of the witness.
8. *Behavioral Examination.* The beings test behavior and ask questions of the witness.[17]

A number of cases in the Bullard study contain one or more elements of the manual examination. Twenty-four provide only one event. Forty-one cases show two events. Fifteen have three events. Seven reflect four events and one has five events. The study reveals that:

> Examination episodes are little better ordered than capture episodes.... The beings can resort to as full a repertoire of techniques as the job demands.... If one examination event changes place with another, it never strays far from its place or loses meaning in the context of associated events.
>
> Taking sperm, for example, relates to the reproduction exam, but may fall more conveniently within the activities of sample taking. For the beings to rearrange the order of events to take advantage of this opportunity simply demonstrates that the course of events is flexible in favor of efficiency, rather than mechanically rigid.[18]

Generally speaking, the examinations of Betty and Bob Luca seem to have involved at least five of the typical examination events as far as it is known.

---

17. Bullard, 1987, p. 82.
18. Bullard, 1987, p. 90.

Preparation

Eighty percent of the cases analyzed in the Bullard study describe some form of preparation comprised of three constituents. The most common element [57%] is a table on which the witness lies or finds himself lying. The second most common element [26%] is the removal of all or part of the abductee's clothing. Only 7% of the cases describe a third constituent that involves the cleansing of the abductee.

Bullard states that there is no strong pattern of order among these three constituents. Sometimes the witness may simply stand for a brief examination. The witness may undress or be undressed before lying on a table. Conversely, the witness may lie on the table before undressing. The Lucas' examinations reflect all three elements of preparation.

The Table

The Andreasson Affair	Fowler	phase one
Betty [1967]: Here's something like a desk or boxlike thing...and somehow they've got me—they are putting me on that flat center thing.... It seemed like I floated up there somehow.... I was held somehow, because I didn't want that examination.		

The Andreasson Affair Phase Two	Fowler	phase two
Betty [1950]: And in the middle of this bright room, there's a box [table].... I'm floating up and lying on it, and I feel like I'm stuck to it.		
Bob [1950]: They put me over on that big table. I don't like it, because I can't move.		

Watchers II	Fowler	phase four
Bob [1989]: And I saw the table. Oh-h-h, they want me on that table.... Oh-h-h, they want me on that table—don't want them to put me on that table...! They do! They do!		

Undressed

The Andreasson Affair	Fowler	phase one
Betty [1967]: And so I took off the first thing of my clothing, and I wondered if they've got something looking in there. And so I took that white garment, and I put it around me while I took off the rest of my [under clothes].		

The Andreasson Affair Phase Two	Fowler	phase two
Betty [1950]: And they are undoing my dungarees and they are taking them off.... I want my mother! Bob [1967]: He told me to take my clothes off.... It's just like a voice inside myself.... I do what they told me.		

Cleansing

The Andreasson Affair	Fowler	phase one
Betty [1967]: "Would you get under that please?" the entities asked. "Well, what is it first?" I asked. "It is just a cleansing thing."		

Manual Examination

According to Dr. Bullard's analysis of this early phase of the alien examination:

> The beings touch, feel or use handheld instruments to inspect the witness in a general, apparently preliminary, way in 16 cases.... In other cases, the beings simply touch the witness, poke at some point like the base of the spine, or feel the head or some other part of the body. Handheld instruments independent of connection to any larger device may play a part in this examination...like a pen-like device or chrome pencil. The small device may emit a beam of light to illuminate or probe somehow the witness's body....
>
> An offshoot of the manual examination involves more vigorous experiments with the witness's body, where the beings flex or twist limbs to the point of causing pain.[19]

19. Bullard, 1987, p. 84.

Both Betty and Bob were subjected to this same type of preliminary manual examination. However, only Bob had his limbs flexed and twisted.

The Andreasson Affair	Fowler	phase one
Betty [1967]: He's taking an instrument and.... Why do you have to put that thing in my nose?		

The Andreasson Affair Phase Two	Fowler	phase two
Betty [1950]: They took a long, long needle.... They put that needle in my head.		
Bob [1967]: It looks like a little chrome pencil or dentist's tool.		

The Watchers II	Fowler	phase four
Bob [1989]: One of the little gray guys is looking into my right eye, and he's got a strange light. It looks like—It's bigger than a pencil.... And it looks like it's chrome or something polished. And it emits a...bright light.		

Flexure

The Andreasson Affair Phase Two	Fowler	phase two
Bob [1967]: They move my head back and forth; and they move my ankles.		

Scan

Dr. Bullard states the following concerning scanning devices reported by abductees:

> Witnesses have reported an optical or X-ray scanner passing over them with systematic movements in 31 cases.... Often the scanner descends from the ceiling on an arm or rod.[20]

Both Betty and Bob described such a device during an examination.

20. Bullard, 1987, p. 85.

The Andreasson Affair	Fowler	phase one
Betty [1967]: Something up in the center of the ceiling—coming down! It's like a big eye of some kind.... I don't know, maybe like a lens.... And it's moving down, all the way down—by my stomach! And they are bringing it real close!		

The Andreasson Affair Phase Two	Fowler	phase two
Bob [1967]: Something's coming down, an arm. There's a light inside it, like a tube, a fluorescent or something. It goes to my feet up to my head [i.e., back and forth].		

Instrumental Examination

A number of instruments are often described by witnesses. Abductees are sometimes connected to machinery by wires or electrodes. Others report being touched or probed with needles wired to machinery. A few examples from Betty's examination follow.

The Andreasson Affair	Fowler	phase one
Betty [1967]: They took those long silver needles—they were bendable—and they stuck one up my nose and into my head...! And he has...this thing...two bars in the side, and like a fan and tulips on the end. And...he's waving it over me.		

The Andreasson Affair Phase Two	Fowler	phase two
Betty [1950]: They got some long steel needles that they are holding toward my head.		

Specimen Taking

Concerning this phase of the alien examination of human beings, Bullard writes the following:

> In the course of an examination, the beings collect specimens of bodily materials from the witness in 29 cases.... The favorite material is blood, gathered in at least 16 cases.... Other bodily fluids like...eye fluid...sperm...urine...gastric juices

> and spinal fluid.... Solid as well as liquid materials attract attention...hair... nails...ear wax.... Scraping provides the skin.[21]
>
> This procedure was employed by the aliens with Bob.

The Andreasson Affair Phase Two	Fowler	phase two
Bob: And they are scraping my skin. They scrape my toenails.... They put a cuplike device on me while I was on that table, and they took sperm from me. And I'm on that table, and I want to get out of there!		

Reproductive Examination

This phase of the examination involves the aliens' specific interest and examination of the genital area. In the case of female abductees, a needle is often inserted into the naval to examine her reproductive system and remove ova. Other cases allegedly involve male abductees forced to have sexual intercourse with alien beings.

The Andreasson Affair	Fowler	phase one
Betty [1967]: Now they are looking over at me.... And they are saying they have to measure me for procreation.... Now they are pulling...that needle again with a tube.... He's going to put that in my navel!		

Neurological Examination

The Bullard report states that:

> The beings next move on to investigate the nervous system, brain and mind of the witness. Two main parts make up this examination. One is a mental probe present in 18 cases...in which the beings read the mind, take the thoughts or examine the brain of the witness. The other has the beings implant a small device in the body of the witness, usually in the head or spine, or remove such an implant. Thirteen cases include this element.[22]

---

21. Bullard, 1987, p. 86.
22. Bullard, 1987, p. 87.

The Andreasson Affair Phase Two	Fowler	phase two
Betty [1950]: And they pulled down my underpants, and...he shot something that felt like needles up my spine...a bright, white, light needle. And they had one of those tiny little glass things on the end of it. They put that needle in my head through where they took out my eye.... There's a square black thing in front of me. And he told me to put my fingers on those things. I did and they lit up. [A machine seemed to be testing coordination and displaying symbols and pictures.]		

The Watchers II	Fowler	phase four
Bob [1989]: They are putting something on my head. They are putting something on my head like a metal strap.... It doesn't hurt.... It's making me see all kinds of sparkling things inside my eyes. It's...like a sparkler, like a fourth of July sparkler. I can see. My eyes are closed. And there's little symbols—there's circles and they are little triangles. There's—butterflies? There's butterflies. There's white light. Oh, oh, I see the Earth. I see the whole planet. There's dark spots on some parts of the planet. And they ask me if I know, if I understand. I have no idea.... They say, I will...in time.		

The four episodes that follow the examination are conference, tour, otherworldly journey and theophany. These episodes seem to be reserved for specially-chosen abductees like Betty Andreasson. Betty was given preferential treatment and a message to give humankind. Dr. Bullard reiterates that these internal episodes are rare in occurrence.[23]

Conference

Betty experienced conference during all of her abductions. Bob did only once during the shared OBE with Betty in 1978. If you recall, he had a long discourse with an Elder while waiting for Betty.

Tour

Betty was taken on a tour by the aliens during all of her abduction experiences.

---

23. Bullard, 1987, p. 104.

Otherworldly Journey

Betty's otherworldly journeys include her 1950 journey to the underground base and Crystal Forest, her 1967 time through the landscape where she experienced the Phoenix, her 1978 visit to the Crystal Forest and her 1986 experience with the strange, indescribable landscape.

Theophany

Dr. Bullard describes a theophany as:

> A meeting with a divine being or a sacred experience of some other sort. With only six cases [in his study] to represent this episode, it qualifies as the rarest part of the abduction story, and yet a distinctive part....[24]

According to this definition, Betty's experience with the Phoenix in 1967 and her meetings with the One in 1950 and 1989 all would be considered theophanies.

We now move on to the third major episode highlighted by the Bullard study. It involves when and how the abductees are released by their captors.

The Return

The abduction experience ends with the abductee being brought back to familiar surroundings and the normal activities being pursued at the time of the abduction. Bullard recounts it this way:

> How the witness reenters the everyday world rounds off the abduction story with a necessary episode. It often reflects a mirror image of capture.... 111 cases refer to it...fewer still detail the experience in any clear and substantial way. The distinctive consistencies of the episode are as follows.

1. *Farewell.* The beings give their captive some final messages and bid him farewell.
2. *Exit.* Doorway amnesia returns as the beings escort the witness and he floats out of the craft.
3. *Departure.* The craft takes off while the witness watches.

---

24. Bullard, 1987, p. 106.

4. *Reentry.* The witness takes up normal activities while memory of the abduction fades out.[25]

The events comprising the return of the Lucas correlate well with each of the above consistencies. A few sample excerpts for each of the above categories from hypnotic regression sessions follow. First, the farewell.

Farewell

In the preamble to this section, Dr. Bullard makes the following introductory remarks:

> Indistinctiveness, rather than a clear-cut boundary, marks the beginning of return. Redressing after an examination...may provide a point of departure. Not long before the witness leaves the craft occurs the first distinctive event—the beings, or a least one of them...bids the witness farewell...and leaves the witness with positive impressions.... A compromise version begins when the beings say that now is the time for the witness to leave...and finally the beings ask, advise or admonish the witness to forget, at least for now, about the abduction.[26]

The Andreasson Affair	Fowler	phase one
Betty [1967]: Quazgaa's in that silver suit.... He's putting both hands on my shoulders and is looking at me. And he says, "Child, you must forget for awhile."...And he's saying, "Go, child, now, and rest."		

Exit

During exit, a phenomenon called "doorway amnesia" sometimes takes effect. Dr. Bullard states the following about this mental lapse. [italics mine]

> A reversal of procurement accounts for most of the action in the return episode. As the witness leaves the ship he experiences a mental lapse in 55 cases...the highest proportion of any event in the episode.... In 25 cases, a period of amnesia at the end of the abduction provides a narrative with its only point of contact with the return episode.... Even when the be-

25. Bullard, 1987, p. 64.
26. Bullard, 1987, p. 64.

> ings plant a seed of forgetfulness as the witness leaves the craft, their influence sometimes grows to full effectiveness only after he experiences several other events. Most common are the alien escort to the door of the ship and sometimes beyond [24 cases], and floatation from the ship to the ground [22 cases]. In six cases, a beam of light also takes part in the process.[27]

After Bob's abduction from his car in 1967 and from his bed in Florida in 1989, the aliens placed him in exactly the same circumstances from which he was taken. Doorway amnesia immediately took effect and he had no conscious memory of the abductions.

The Andreasson Affair Phase Two	Fowler	phase two
Hypnotist [1967]: How did you get back in the vehicle? Bob: I floated back, and then I was there.		

The Watchers II	Fowler	phase four
Bob [1989]: And we came back down. I go in back into the bedroom with him...and I go back to bed.		

Departure

The Bullard study contains 20 cases that describe the UFO taking off from the ground or flying away after dropping off the captive. All cases insert this event between the time witnesses were returned to earth and before they resumed normal activities. Neither Betty nor Bob ever watched the departure of a UFO after being returned. Their return always mirrored their capture. Typically, they were placed in exactly the same situation that they were in just prior to their capture. As mentioned, the abduction experience was no longer part of their conscious memory.

Reentry

Dr. Bullard gives the following description of this facet of the return:

---

27. Bullard, 1987, p. 64.

> Once back on earth the witness resumes his normal activities, but sometimes unusual effects shadow the return. Drivers recover in a particularly notable way. Their car may lower to the highway and drive itself for a while, or the witness may drive in a state of unawareness until he passes some barrier and becomes conscious of what he is doing once again. Ten cases include this element.... Once the driver or other witness recovers normal consciousness, all memory of an abduction may have disappeared, so only discovery of missing time clues him that something extraordinary happened to him.
>
> Comparison of capture and return affirms a general symmetry between the two episodes, since the UFO comes and goes, vehicle effects set in and leave off, the witness loses mental control then regains it, and the beings take him in and turn him out.
>
> The message which accompanies the farewell often enlists the witness into a sort of cooperative relationship with the beings. They may entrust the witness with secrets or promise him important work to do. He has to forget, but only for a while, only with regret and for his own good.[28]

The factor of missing time was realized by the Lucas after having been abducted with their car after watching a drive-in movie in 1988.

The Watchers II	Fowler	phase four
Betty: We're coming around the corner and coming up to the lights of Durham, and I said, "Do you remember going...from Lyman's orchard to get to here?" And he says, "No, I can't recall passing any of that."...And, when we get home, it seems like there's forty-five minutes to an hour missing.		

The factor of being entrusted with secrets and being told to forget for awhile is an intricate component of Betty Luca's abduction in 1967.

The Andreasson Affair	Fowler	phase one
Betty [1967]: He says that he has had others here.... Many others have locked within their minds—secrets.... He is locking within my mind certain secrets.... They will be revealed when the time is right.		

28. Bullard, 1987, p. 66.

Aftermath

The Bullard study breaks down this episode into three categories: immediate, intermediate and long-term aftereffects.

Immediate Aftereffects

Twenty cases recorded in the Bullard study involve cuts, scrapes and punctures. Betty, if you recall from *The Watchers,* has had several anomalous scars appear overnight that resemble punch biopsies. This type of scar is typical of others reported in UFO abduction cases.

Intermediate Aftereffects

In the mental realm, the study lists 42 examples in which the nightmare or abduction dream counts as one of the most common of all aftereffects. The Lucas have had such dreams.

Long Term Aftereffects

Dr. Bullard lists a number of happenings that have been reported by abductees over the long term. Those applicable to some members of the Allagash four concern the "Men in Black," instances of phone tapping, mystery helicopters, apparitions, personality changes and, last but not least, subsequent UFO experiences.

Men in Black

Betty and her daughter Becky witnessed what could be categorized as men in black observing their house in Ashburnham, Massachusetts, in 1977.

The Andreasson Affair Phase Two	Fowler	phase two
Betty: One was very tall and stiff. He was dressed in black and sort of looked like somebody from a funeral home that has a real smooth pressed suit. He had black hair, but the forehead was very, very high and the skin very pale. He stood very stiffly.... The tall man in black raised his hand as if to point, but without bending his elbow. It just swung up and out.		

Phone Tapping

The Lucas have had a history of strange things going on with their phone wherever they lived. This started when Betty first began to be investigated and has continued since. Clicks heard during conversations, strange noises, and the phone going dead for days without satisfactory explanations from the phone company may indicate phone tapping.

Apparitions/Subsequent UFO Experiences

Needless to say, the Lucas have had their share of both of these aspects of the aftermath episode in the form of bedtime visitations and subsequent abductions. There is no need to repeat them here.

This completes the correlation of the Lucas' abduction experiences with the eighth and final episode of the typical abduction story type in the Bullard study. However, one more set of striking correlations needs to be examined before bringing this chapter to a close. These relate to the abductee's description of the alien occupants in the Bullard study.

The Occupants: The Head Region

Shape and Size

Dr. Bullard makes the following summary regarding the most typical descriptions given to this area of the alien's body.

> A standard humanoid possesses a large hairless cranium and narrow chin.... Witnesses use metaphors like "egg," "light bulb" or "pear" to portray the general effect.... In overall effect, the being looks fetal.[29]

Eyes

The Bullard study reveals that the alien's eyes capture the attention of the abductee like no other bodily feature. Almost half of its cases refer to the eyes. They are described as large in 42 cases. Words used to describe their shape include elongated, almond, walnut, slanted, teardrop, wraparound and cat-like. References to eye color in the sample

29. Bullard, 1987, p. 242.

are scarce but, when present, describe them as unusually dark and uniform.

Mouth, Nose And Ears

In striking contrast to the aliens' eyes, one finds that the abductees in the Bullard study describe almost non-existent features in these three areas. Adjectives like small, lipless, hole and slit mouths predominate. The aliens' noses are so diminutive that witnesses often report that the nose is practically not there. This is also true of the ears, which are tiny or simply holes in the head.

Body Build

Bullard remarks that 25 out of 39 given descriptions of standard humanoid aliens describe them as frail, thin, without muscle-tone or definition, sickly, thin necked, narrow-shouldered, and like a skeleton. He states that sketches made by abductees often confirm these descriptions.

> Illustrations often confirm this...by making the beings look top heavy and precarious with the huge heads balanced on thin necks and the rest of the body all out of proportion with skinny limbs and sunken chests.[30]

Clothing

The following is a composite description of the clothing worn by alien beings from the Bullard Study.

> The...alien wears a one-piece suit of some kind in 82 out of 105 cases. These suits usually cover the entire body except for the hands and face, and show no signs [of] buttons, zippers, seams or separation into pants and shirt.... The [most] common adjective used to describe these suits is "tight" or "close-fitting...."
>
> Sometimes the clothing is so tight the beings seem naked.[31]

The reader will immediately recognize the occupants that the Bullard report describes to be the same as what Betty refers to as the Watch-

30. Bullard, 1987, p. 246.
31. Bullard, 1987, p. 246.

ers. The tall human-like beings or Elders are less commonly reported by abductees. Bullard states that:

> Humans come as no surprise in abduction accounts, making up a sizable fraction of the crews and even appearing on the otherworld as the angel-like beings Betty Aho [Andreasson Luca] reported.... But these humans maintain an air of alieness despite their appearance.[32]

This chapter has dealt essentially with the remarkable similarities that exist between the data elements in the UFO abductions of Betty and Bob Luca and those contained within the sample of abduction reports in the study prepared by Dr. Bullard.

These extraordinary correlations provide overwhelming circumstantial evidence for the reality of the Lucas' experiences, thus providing support for the startling hypothesis that will appear later in the conclusion of this book.

---

32. Bullard, 1987, p. 255.

PART III

Phenomenon Prognosis

"Whatever else be certain, this at least is certain: that the world of our present natural knowledge is enveloped in a larger world of some sort of whose residual properties we at present can frame no positive idea."

William James
International UFO Reporter
July/August 1984, vol. 9, no. 4

This section deals primarily with the paraphysical components culled from eighteen years of investigating Betty and Bob Luca's UFO abduction experiences. Along the way, the experiences of others, including myself, family members and members of Betty's family, have contributed to this unearthly data base.

The question posed in the following chapters is: "What are these ultra-bizarre constituents telling us if taken at full face value?" The answer coincided with an underlying intuition that I had kept to myself for many years because of its incredulous nature. Little did I know that I would someday offer it as the prognosis for the UFO phenomenon in the concluding pages of a book.

I am sure that both peer and reader alike will think that the author has been mentally affected from years of UFO research. I trust that this is not the case. However, years ago I myself would have thought the same of anyone who dared to propose such a seemingly unrelated and preposterous hypothesis; namely, a paraphysical connection between the UFO abduction phenomenon and human existence after physical death!

chapter fourteen

UFOs & NDEs

> *"Could it be that the world of the NDE and that of the UFO abductions, for all their differences, are not, after all, universes apart, but a part of the same universe? Could it be that NDErs and UFO experiences have more in common with one another than we have heretofore suspected?"*[1]
>
> *Kenneth Ring, Ph.D.*
> The Omega Project

The above quote comes from a book that I casually picked up in a local book shop. What attracted me was its subtitle: *Near-Death Experiences, UFO Encounters and Mind at Large.* I had heard of its author, Dr. Kenneth Ring, during my studies of the near-death experience (NDE) when writing *The Watchers.* If you recall, I briefly alluded to my suspicions that somehow the NDE and UFO experience were intimately related. This was founded on the basis that Betty's paraphysical experiences in some ways mirrored NDE and reports in my files that equated UFOs with human death.

Betty's and Bob's experiences during this latest phase of my investigation have served to solidify my suspicions. Thus, in this chapter, I will further develop the UFO/NDE connection to bolster a daring hypothesis that before now I dared only share with one person for fear of ridicule and rejection by my peers. It has remained a secret until the publication of this book, and it will be revealed in the next chapter. The latest experiences of the Lucas were the catalyst for keeping silent no longer. But first, let us turn our attention to the UFO/NDE connection as a preface to the astonishing conclusion to this book.

---

1. Ring, 1992, p. 110.

Betty had mentioned to me that she and Bob had met Dr. Ring, who was interested in their experiences, but I had no idea that he, at the time, had begun to suspect that a connection between these two unearthly experiences existed. In any event, I turned to his book's index and found my name and that of the Lucas' listed. Turning to the referenced pages, I found Dr. Ring's description of his meeting with Betty and Bob and a reference to my suspected UFO/NDE connection mentioned in *The Watchers*. The following are excerpts from these sections. They will serve to introduce the subject matter of this chapter.

Dr. Ring met the Lucas at a local restaurant where he and his wife listened to their stories. He stated that:

> I would soon enough hear and read the claims of many such events in the lives of those who have had UFO encounters, but listening to them that day from Bob and Betty, two obviously sincere and thoughtful persons who were as puzzled by what had happened to them as my wife and I were, had a particularly strong impact on me.... Something indeed very strange—and strangely wonderful in her case—had happened to her, and...furthermore, for her at least, there was no question of its reality.[2]

Concerning my treatise on the UFO/NDE connection in *The Watchers*, Dr. Ring commented that:

> Fowler...makes a major effort in his book to point out, as [Micheal] Grosso[3] does, the connections between NDEs and UFOs, and arrives at similar conclusions concerning the importance of considering the implications of both phenomena together. In this respect, at least, their views—and mine, too—tend to converge.[4]

I thought it quite significant that Dr. Ring, one of the leading authorities on NDEs, should find his studies leading to similar conclusions as those of mine from my studies of the UFO abduction experience. It was as if both of us, tunneling through our mountain of anecdotal data had suddenly converged in the middle of the mountain!

Needless to say, I immediately bought the book and read it as part of the research for the preparation of this chapter. How and what did Dr. Ring conclude about the similarities between UFOs and NDEs?

---

2. Ring, 1992, pp. 36-37.
3. Author of *The Final Choice*. Walpole, NH: Stillpoint Publishing, 1985.—Ed.
4. Ring, 1992, pp. 232-233.

It started when Dr. Ring received a copy of Whitley Strieber's book, *Communion*, from their common publisher. Ring's editor urged him to read the book as it might have commonalties with his studies of NDEs. At first, Ring was repulsed by the idea of any such connection, but after reading *Communion*, interviewing Betty and Bob, and researching the literature, he began to see similarities not usually seen between the experiences themselves, but between the people reporting the experiences—the experiencers.

To test this suspected connection, Ring and his associates prepared a battery of questions to be sent to three types of persons: first, control group who had experienced neither phenomenon, but who nonetheless had a great interest in both; second, a group who had experienced NDEs; and third, a group that had experienced UFO abductions. He called his study *The Omega Project* and received detailed inputs from 264 persons.

Some of the questions asked in *The Omega Project* were designed to test for the following childhood traits in those who responded: tendency to be fantasy prone; responsiveness to paranormal experiences; sensitivity to alternate realities; tendency toward psychological dissociation; and incidence of childhood abuse and trauma.

Other questions sought to document the types of aftereffects as categorized in psychophysical changes and shifts in beliefs and personal values.

Every UFO researcher or interested reader should read Dr. Ring's book for the details of his study. His is the only exhaustive study that effectively deals with forming a personality profile of NDErs. That it also includes UFO abductees is a decided plus for UFO researchers. Such a study was long overdue. Its results produced what Dr. Ring has dubbed the "encounter-prone personality": a person who tends to more or less reflect the traits being tested for in *The Omega Project*.

I was especially impressed because my late father, who reported all kinds of psychic experiences, fit some aspects of this discovered profile like a glove. Orphaned early as a child, he was passed from relative to relative in very poor economic times. He suffered both physical and mental abuse. So much so, that the battered wife who took him in, brought him to a Catholic orphanage to save him from physical and mental harm. Later, another relative secured his release from the orphanage, and he was put in the care of a woman who ran a farm in the country. There he worked very hard without the benefit of a normal family situation.

I would assume that such childhood abuse could lead to the physical dissociation that Dr. Ring mentions in his study. However, to the best of my knowledge, his paranormal experiences did not begin until he was struck by lightning, as mentioned in *The Watchers.* Also, a study by NDE researcher Dr. Melvin Morse seems to indicate that child abuse may be an incidental, rather than a consistent, catalyst for producing Ring's typical NDE personality profile. As states Dr. Morse:

> Some researchers think that people with abuse in their childhood are more likely to have near-death experiences than those who do not. After interviewing more than 70 children and not finding any connection between child abuse and NDEs, I tend to disagree with this conclusion.[5]

In any event, Dr. Ring's study demonstrates quite convincingly that although NDE and UFO abduction experiences usually differ drastically in content, the percipients of both kinds of experiences tend to have the same kind of personality profile. Not only that, they tend to exhibit the same aftereffects.

These are persons, as Dr. Ring states, "who are especially likely to register and recall extraordinary encounters." However, he does go out of the way to state that:

> I do not intend to serve the interests of those who would "pathologize" these experiences or denigrate the individuals who report them.... I have only tried to answer some persisting questions about the psychological profile of those who relate them. The mystery and numinous power of NDEs and UFO encounters themselves remain intact.[6]

Thus, Dr. Ring's study does not reject the possible reality of NDE and UFO abductions. What it does conclude is that there are certain types of people who are more sensitive to experiences of this nature. They would also be more apt to remember and/or report such experiences more readily than others.

Does this mean that people who do not have these traits do not have these experiences? I think not. However, they might be less prone to remember or report such experiences. Only 10% of people who just sight an unusual object in the sky actually report it according to civilian and military statistics. According to Dr. Ring, only one of three persons who survives a near-death incident will later describe having an NDE of some kind.

---

5. Morse, 1992, pp. 34.
6. Ring, 1992, p. 149.

Why? Is it because not all people who survive near-death incidents have such experiences? Is it because some people forget or are fearful to report such experiences? Or, does it mean that all people who survive near-death incidents do have NDEs, but only remember and report them if they fall into the category of Dr. Ring's encounter-prone personality?

No one knows for sure, but Dr. Ring's study seems to indicate that his prototype is the most likely kind of person to experience, remember and report NDEs and UFO abduction experiences.

The commonality that most UFO abduction experiences show with the beautiful, awe-inspiring NDE appears to lie in the types of people that report them and their aftereffects.

According to Dr. Ring, a Gallop Poll taken in the early 1980s indicates that 8 million Americans have experienced an NDE. So, what is a near-death experience? We have talked much about it in abstract terms, but a description has been lacking. Dr. Ring summarizes the archetypal structure of an NDE as follows:

> What, then, is this classic NDE pattern that departs so radically from that associated with UFO encounters, especially of the abduction variety? To begin with, NDErs often report a tremendous feeling of peace, ease, and security at the onset of the experience. When perception becomes possible, they tend to find themselves "up above" their physical body, which they can plainly see below them, as a detached spectator would. Next (although typically in an NDE, there is no clear sense of time), they feel themselves to be moving through something like a tunnel or dark void toward a radiantly beautiful light. As they progress toward the light, they are engulfed by it and feel bathed in a pure, unconditionally accepting form of love. At this point, they may become aware of a presence (however, they won't necessarily see any figure as such) who may ask them to make a decision whether to continue further or return to their physical body, though occasionally the presence will enjoin them to "go back." Sometimes this aspect of the experience is accompanied by a rapid and full panoramic review of one's life. In other cases, NDErs will encounter the "spirits" of deceased relatives who may either beckon them to enter their realm or inform them it isn't their time, they must return. In any event, however, the experience is brought to a resolution. NDErs do, of course, eventually find themselves back in the physical world where they may feel either exhilarated over what they have experienced or depressed or angry about the fact that they are no

longer "there," but faced with the prospect of living in the ordinary world again.

Certainly, as I have said, such an encounter would seem to have little connection with the terrifying episodes of UFO abductions whose patterns we are now well familiar with. At the level of direct experience, this seems incontrovertibly obvious.[7]

Dr. Ring does acknowledge that some similarities in UFO abduction experiences exist on an archetypical level in that:

> Both NDEs and close encounters of the fourth kind...have the structure of initiatory journeys, even though their specific content and emotional charge are patently at variance.[8]

Therefore, in this context, Dr. Ring alludes to the fact that both experiences include an abrupt separation from one's normal physical environment to an unearthly environment, both experience some sort of ordeal, and both are returned to their normal environment.

But what relevance has this type of parallel between UFO abductees and NDE reporters have to do with the actual experiences themselves? If the NDE and UFO abduction experiences are almost totally dissimilar in content, why suggest that the two are intimately related, as I suggested in *The Watchers?* My reply is that it is because a residue of cases imply that such a connection *does* exist. Even Dr. Ring admits that he has cases on file that are hard to differentiate between the two types of experiences. Concerning a specific case of this nature, he states:

> What on earth—or in heaven—do we have here? Is this an NDE or some kind of UFO encounter? Clearly it has elements of both, and just as clearly it threatens to confound the dichotomy between these two types of experiences. In fact, it is what I have come to recognized as a "mixed motif" case, and as that phrase implies, it is not the only instance in my files. Among my respondents, I have found others who in describing what purports to be an NDE begin to talk about UFOs and aliens in the same context. Furthermore, there turns out to be a small but respectable number of persons in my sample who report having had (though, to be sure, at different times) both an NDE and one or more UFO encounters.[9]

Thanatologist Dr. John B. Alexander, an expert on the study of death, echoes Ring's findings in a paper delivered during the UFO Ab-

7. Ring, 1992, pp. 92.
8. Ring, 1992, pp. 92-93.
9. Ring, 1992, p. 110.

duction Study Conference held at the Massachusetts Institute of Technology between June 13-17, 1992. The paper is entitled *Comparative Phenomenology: Near-Death Experiences and UFO Abductions.*[10] He stated that recent studies have indeed revealed a striking commonality between NDEs and UFO abductions.

During a discussion period after his lecture, leading UFO researcher Jenny Randles acknowledged that British investigators have also noted this in some cases as early as 1982. She volunteered a striking example. It involved a near-death experience caused by a reaction to a drug administered by a dentist.

The patient underwent the typical OBE and tunnel experience. However, instead of entering a world of light, he entered a UFO! Alien entities warned that the Earth was in trouble and told him he had to return. They stated that he would have to fight off evil entities to get back into his body. After a struggle, he was able to return to the dentist's office where he saw the dentist attempting to revive him.

Thus, it could very well be that the content of the two experiences differs only because of the circumstances. If we take the Lucas' experiences at full face value, it is my opinion that NDEs and UFO abductions are controlled *by the same intelligences* but for totally different purposes, thus their difference in content. These proposed differences will be discussed in the next chapter.

Now let us reinforce the case for such a connection by reviewing and comparing the paraphysical components of the Lucas' experiences with those contained in the near-death experience.

Presence of OBEs

Since I dedicated a complete chapter to UFOs and out-of-body experience (OBEs) in *The Watchers,* I will simply define an OBE for those unfamiliar with the experience. An OBE involves a situation where someone finds their essence moving out of the body into a non-physical realm where they are no longer visible to those in the physical realm. Although the OBErs are able to see their physical body and the physical realm, they can no longer interact with it. Their body merely passes through physical objects as if they did not exist. NDEs begin with an OBE.

---

10. Alexander, 1994, pp. 342-347.

Excerpts from NDErs

Life After Life	Moody	
I saw my body in the water. I drifted up…floating right below the ceiling.[a]		

a. Moody, 1976, p. 85, 36.

Life After Life	Moody	
I was sort of floating…above the street. I could see myself on the bed below. I could see my own body…in the car[a]		

a. Moody, 1976, p. 37, 38, 40.

Excerpts from Betty's Experiences

In addition to physical abductions, Betty and others have experienced UFO abductions in a paranormal state of being—an OBE. Herein lies the paraphysical nature of some UFO abduction experiences. The following are excerpts from Betty's paraphysical UFO abduction experiences.

The Andreassson Affair Phase Two	Fowler	phase two
1950: And I'm standing there and I'm coming out of myself! 1950: There's two of me there. 1978: I see myself coming out of myself…. Bob…came out of his body, so that there were two of him!		

The Watchers	Fowler	phase three
1986: I see myself…laying on the couch…. I reach down to touch myself…my hand goes right through me. 1989: Oh! And I'm coming out of myself…. Oh-h-h, and I see myself just sitting there on the side of the bed, and yet I'm here! I'm going inside myself!		

Approaching the Light

NDErs report approaching a bright light in the OBE state, sometimes through a tunnel. Several typical descriptions follow: [italics mine]

Excerpts from NDErs

Transformed by the LIght	Morse	
I was floating and everything around me was dark.... And then there it was, a tunnel...with a very *bright light* at the end.[a]		

a. Morse, 1992, p. 52.

Life After Life	Moody	
I saw *light* going through this tunnel.[a]		

a. Moody, 1976, p. 55.

Coming Back to Life	Atwater	
I moved...out through the top of my head.... I noticed a *bright light* up ahead...with a brightness so brilliant it was beyond light.[a]		

a. Atwater, 1988, pp. 43..

Recollections of Death	Sabom	
I went through this period of darkness.... There was this *light*.... I started going towards that.... The light kept getting brighter and brighter...and the closer we got, the brighter it got.[a]		

a. Sabom, 1982, p. 43.

Excerpts from Betty's Experiences

The Andreasson Affair Phase Two	Fowler	phase two
1950: I went in the door and it's very bright.... I'm where there is light. 1967: It [The Great Door] is the entrance to the other world. The world where light is. 1967: We're going to enter the [Great Door].... Is this beautiful! [exhales loudly] Oh, we're running toward the light.... I'm just engulfed in light and blending into that light.		

Greetings by a Loving Being

When NDErs and Betty enter the light, they are confronted by a presence (seen or just sensed) that radiates and engulfs them with pure unconditional love that is indescribable. [italics mine]

Excerpts from NDErs

Life After Life	Moody	
I floated....into this pure crystal clear light.... I didn't actually see a person in this light, and yet it has a *special identity.* It is a light of perfect understanding and pure love. The light's what was talking to me. The *love* which came from it is just unimaginable, indescribable.[a]		

a. Moody, 1976, p. 68, 64.

Coming Back to Life	Atwater	
I noticed...a bright light ahead.... I was absorbed by it as if engulfed by a force field. I cannot describe how it felt, except to say it was "divine."...I was inside bliss.[a]		

a. Atwater, 1988, pp. 43.

Excerpts from Betty's Experiences

The Andreasson Affair Phase Two	Fowler	phase two
1950: I'm where there is light.... Words cannot explain it.... It's a greater love.		

The Watchers	Fowler	phase three
1989: Oh, the light is all over. It is wonderful. I cannot explain the wonder and beauty and love and peace. It is so joyous!		

Experiencing Oneness

In addition to feeling unconditional love, NDers and Betty receive a sense of knowing and understanding reality in its ultimate nature. Everything is part of a whole, fits together or is one.

Excerpts from NDErs

Closer to the Light	Morse	
I could see how everything...fits together.[a]		

a. Morse, 1990, p. 117.

Reflections on Life after Life	Moody	
This is a place where the place is knowledge—all knowledge.[a]		

a. Moody, 1977, p. 14.

Excerpts from Betty's Experiences

The Andreasson Affair Phase Two	Fowler	phase two
1950: I understand that everything is one. Everything fits together. It's beautiful.		

Meeting Robed Entities

NDErs meet tall robed entities that some take to be God, an angel or a religious personage. Betty also met with tall robed Biblical-like entities.

Excerpts from NDErs

The Omega Project	Ring	
The light came closer and closer at a high rate of speed. It then took on the shape of a man in a white robe.[a]		

a. Ring, 1992, p. 102.

Recollections of Death	Sabom	
It was all bright then.... He was tall.... He had a white robe on. He was standing with a very white robe.[a]		

a. Sabom, 1982, p. 49, 76.

Closer to the Light	Morse	
He was about seven feet tall and wore a long white gown.[a]		

a. Morse, 1990, p. 29.

Transformed by the Light	Morse	
We came to a place where there were many figures, some of them dressed in robes. I went to a place where I found a lot of people dressed in white robes.[a]		

a. Morse, 1992, p. 40, 121.

Excerpts from Betty's Experiences

The Andreassson Affair Phase Two	Fowler	phase two
1950: There is a tall white-haired man standing there, and he's got on a long nightgown.... His nightgown is glowing.... He's got bluish eyes.... I see two more of them over there.... They are real tall.... 1978: There is a very tall—looks like men in white robes with white hair that are escorting us to a door.		

The Watchers	Fowler	phase three
1989: I see someone coming now. There's someone—there's a tall person coming dressed in white...real tall and coming down those stairs.... It's a man....		

Encountering Beings of Light

NDErs describe human-shaped forms composed of light. Betty described the same type of entities during two of her OBE abduction experiences.

Excerpts from NDErs

Transformed by the Light	Morse	
A being was at my side, a being of light. There was someone else there, a Guardian Angel or something...made of light.[a]		

a. Morse, 1992, p. 142, 152.

Closer to the Light	Morse	
Beings of light on either side of him.... Beings of light told him that he could return to his body.[a]		

a. Morse, 1990, p. 113.

Recollections of Death	Sabom	
Like two people that were coming toward me...just outlines of light.[a]		

a. Sabom, 1982, p. 44.

Beyond Death's Door	Rawlings	
People were all around me.... They seemed to be in shiny clothes with a sort of glow.[a]		

a. Rawlings, 1979, p. 76.

Excerpts from Betty's Experiences

The Andreasson Affair	Fowler	phase one
1978: And there are other forms that look like people, but they're light.... They're just like human forms, but they're light! There's no features.		

The Watchers II	Fowler	phase four
1989: Oh-h-h, The Great Door has been opened. It's so bright! So bright in here. Oh, and...I see something coming. There's...such a bright light, and there's...beings coming, and they're all light—they're light beings and they're...moving with something.... Those...light beings are coming over, and they got this barrel that is moving, and it's revolving, and they're not even touching it.... That light being is going on the water and picking up that other shoe that flew over there.... There's...a light being that's pulling the opposite direction. Oh, I'm getting chills from this. [whispers] This is weird. Oh, it's so weird. It's like there's a tug of war going on for that old man.		

Turning into Light

NDErs report turning into a light being when they approached a loving presence in bright light. Betty reported changing into a light being on two occasions during abductions in an OBE state.

Excerpts from NDErs

The Omega Project	Ring	
Suddenly I was suspended in total light.... I was dressed in a flowing, glowing light and floating right beside me was somebody else.[a]		

a. Ring, 1992, p. 96.

Life After Life	Moody	
I left my body.... I took on the same form as the light.... The form I took had colors...orange, yellow, and a color that was indistinct to me. I took it to be indigo, a bluish color.[a]		

a. Moody, 1976, p. 102.

Excerpts from Betty's Experiences

The Andreasson Affair Phase Two	Fowler	phase two
1978: I don't see where Bob is...area is bluish color...starting to get a lavender color...[my] whole body looks like it's becoming light		

The Watchers II	Fowler	phase four
1989: Oh! *[breathless]* I can see the...Elder is changing to a white light being and...the grey is changing into a light blue one as we're running closer to the light and...I'm starting to change into a golden-colored light! This is beautiful.... I'm just engulfed in light and blending into that light.		

Communicating by Telepathy

Those who have NDEs report that they, like Betty, communicate with non-earthly entities in a non-verbal manner analogous to what we call mental telepathy.

Excerpts from NDErs

Life After Life	Moody	
I heard a voice...but like a hearing beyond the physical senses.[a]		

a. Moody, 1976, p. 57.

Recollections of Death	Sabom	
Without talking with our voices...it just registered in my brain.[a]		

a. Sabom, 1982, p. 47.

Transformed by the Light	Morse	
A Christ-like figure appeared to her and spoke without moving his lips. No words were exchanged, but I asked him maybe through telepathy.[a]		

a. Morse, 1992, p. 91, 97.

Excerpts from Betty's Experiences

The Andreasson Affair Phase Two	Fowler	phase two
1944: They're calling my name. It sounds as if somebody jumped into my head. 1949: I'm hearing it in my head.... He's talking to me, but I don't see any mouth moving. 1961: I think through his eyes or his head. I don't hear him talking.		

The Andreasson Affair	Fowler	phase one
1967: I'm talking with them, but they're not talking through their mouths.... I think it was a transformation of thought.		

The Watchers	Fowler	phase three
1989: The two of them think [exactly alike], you know? When the one is talking to me, it's like they're both talking to me, because they have the same thoughts.... He's talking to him and he's touching him on the shoulder, but he's not talking verbally. It's like he's talking somehow to him through the mind or eyes.		

Referring to "Home"

Excerpts from NDErs

Closer to the Light	Morse	
Suddenly he gained consciousness. He looked better and cheerful. He talked nicely to his relatives and requested them to go home. He also said, "I shall go to my home. Angels have come to take me away."[a]		

a. Morse, 1990, p. 49.

Recollections of Death	Sabom	
I could see my mother and Christ just saying, "Come on home, come on home." She…had a long sparkling silver gown on, and so did Christ.[a]		

a. Sabom, 1982, pp. 49-50.

Excerpts from Betty's Experiences

The Andreasson Affair Phase Two	Fowler	phase two
Betty: ...They said, "We're going to take you home.... Home is where the One is."		

Encountering Timelessness

Another significant similarity between NDErs and OBE abductees is that they sometimes describe the place where they have been brought as being a timeless environment. NDE researcher Phyllis Atwater writes that:

> Almost every single person returns knowing time does not exist. They come back knowing time is a matter of consciousness: past and future are really qualities of perception.[10]

Excerpts from NDErs

Coming Back to Life	Atwater	
What did I learn: Well, for one, I learned there are no limits, no time.... No past. No future. Only right now, this instant.[a]		

a. Atwater, 1988, p. 77.

Closer to the Light	Morse	
I think the difference in me was caused by the way I now saw time.... I realized that time as we see it on the clock isn't how time really is.[a]		

a. Morse, 1992, p. 75.

Excerpts from Betty and Bob's Experiences

The Andreasson Affair	Fowler	phase one
Alien to Betty: "Time with us is not your time. The place with you is localized. It is not with us."		
Betty: Time to them is not like our time, but they know about our time.		

10. Atwater, 1988, p. 82.

The Watchers II	Fowler	phase four
Bob: Time is nothing. There's no time up here. There is no time! And nothing changes. Fred: Do they [the aliens] age? Bob: No, they have been the same for years and years and years, they said—beyond my understanding.		

Wishing to Remain in the Light

Those NDErs who have encountered the loving personage in the light like Betty's encounter with the One in the light want to stay. Both are extremely reluctant to return.

Excerpts from NDErs

Transformed by the Light	Morse	
There it was—a tunnel of light with a very bright light at the end.... I was talking to this light.... I didn't want to go back. That was the last thing I wanted to do.... So I threw a tantrum.... "Why can't I stay?" I yelled. There was a beautiful light...so beautiful that I didn't want to leave.... I wanted to stay.[a]		

a. Morse, 1992, p. 53, 72.

The Omega Project	Ring	
I started to move rapidly toward something I knew was white light.... I knew I had a choice to go forever into the Light or stay. An enormous sadness filled me, like nothing before or since.[a]		

a. Ring, 1992, p. 95.

Excerpts from Betty's Experiences

The Watchers II	Fowler	phase four
Betty: I don't want to go. I don't want to go back. I want to stay! I want to stay!...Oh, this is everything, everything, everything.... Oh the light is all over. It is wonderful.... I cannot explain the wonder and beauty and love and peace. It is so joyous! Oh, glory, glory, glory.... I'm going to have to go back. *[almost crying]*		

Understanding Love

Both NDErs and Betty return from their experiences the a given realization that love, unconditional agape love, is the prime directive for humankind. Phyllis Atwater is just one of a number of researchers who have found this realization by those who have returned from a near-death experience. She writes that:

> Over and over again, I hear survivors tell of the love they experienced and how they want now to emulate that love, to develop and expand that love, so it will become a daily reality in their lives. They want to keep it alive and growing.[11]

Excerpts from NDErs

The following exclamation from a survivor of death, quoted by Dr. Kenneth Ring, expresses this realization quite graphically.

The Omega Project	Ring	
Love...is the main reason for our existence as human beings in our physical bodies. We must understand love in a holistic sense, altruistic love.... We cannot fully experience love unless we also know compassion...the ability to know pain and loss—not just our own pain and loss, but the ability to feel the pain and loss of others.[a]		

a. Ring, 1992, p. 178.

Excerpts from Betty's Experiences

The Andreasson Affair	Fowler	phase one
1967: He says...love is the greatest of all...because of great love, they cannot let man continue in the footsteps that he is going.		

11. Atwater, 1988, p. 65-66.

The Andreasson Affair Phase Two	Fowler	phase two
1944: *[After experience with ball of light]* I feel close to nature and love everything. 1950: Fred Max: Where are you now? Betty: I'm where there is light. Fred: Do you feel more love, the same love or any different degree than you have before? Betty: It's a greater love.		

The Watchers	Fowler	phase three
1989: Oh, this is wonderful, wonderful, wonderful. Oh, there is such love. *[Betty is in pure unadulterated ecstasy.]* Oh, there is such peace. *[long sigh.]* I'm just engulfed in light and blending into that light. It just permeates me.... It's wonderful. *[breathlessly]* It is just fantastically beautiful. It's just so much love, so much peace and so wonderful....		

Raising Environmental Awareness

UFO researchers have noted that abductees in many instances report that the aliens are greatly concerned about the ecological state of the earth. This concern was a primary component of the aliens' message to humankind through Betty. Thus, it is important to note that Dr. Ring's studies reveal that both UFO abductees and NDErs return from their experience with a great concern for the environmental state of planet Earth. Dr. Ring writes:

> ...From my background research on NDEs, it was impossible for me not to notice that today's ecological and planetary concerns were also matters to which many NDErs were at pains to stress that their own encounters with death had led them to become more sensitized. Indeed, a small subset of NDErs have even described to me (and other researchers have reported similar findings) that as a part of their experience or in its immediate aftermath, they have had a terrifying vision of global cataclysm.[12]

12. Ring, 1992, p. 180.

In the light of these similarities, Dr. Ring incorporated the subject of ecological concern into a segment of his Omega Project to statistically assess them in a scientific manner. His results indicated:

> ...Fully 85% of UFOers report an increase in their concern for planetary welfare following their UFO encounter, and of these, nearly 60% state that it has strongly increased. NDErs are similar, with almost 80% also indicating a positive shift on this item, and not quite half that number similarly saying that it represents a strong increase.... Thus, the heightened sensitivity to ecological matters and to the condition of our earth generally seems, statistically at least, to be among the most important value changes that follow extraordinary experiences.[13]

Excerpt from an NDEr

The Omega Project	Ring	
These experiences made me cherish all life as I had never done before. I really began to be aware of everything in my experience on a deeper level. I even began to "salute" animals I would meet, recognizing their individual worth.[a]		

a. Ring, 1992, p. 181.

Excerpts from Betty's Experiences

The Watchers	Fowler	phase three
And one of them is saying—"We have to because as time goes by, mankind will become sterile. They will not be able to produce because of the pollutions of the lands and the waters and the air and the bacteria and the terrible things that are on the earth.... Man is destroying much of nature."		

Based upon the preceding similarities and what is yet to be presented, there is little doubt, at least in my mind, that Betty's abductions in the OBE state and her visits to meet the One are synonymous with NDErs meeting the Presence in the light.

The primary difference being that NDErs are brought to this point because of temporary physical death and that Betty was brought to this point because she was chosen to show the world what lies behind so-called physical death.

---

13. Ring, 1992, p. 181.

This was hinted at during my first phase one investigation in 1977, but at that time it was not apparent to me. The farthest thing from my mind then would be any connection between life after death and the UFO phenomenon! Consider the following excerpts from Betty's hypnotic regression sessions in 1977. During the now meaningful holographic presentation of the death and rebirth of the Phoenix, Betty was addressed by a thundering voice.

The Andreasson Affair	Fowler	phase one
Voice: I have chosen you. Betty: For what have you chosen me? Voice: I have chosen you to show the world.... I shall show you as your time goes by. Betty: Why won't you tell me why and what for? Voice: The time is not yet. It shall come.		

True to form, Betty indeed was shown as her time went by. But I failed to understand it as *my* time went by! I thought, "What could a bizarre Phoenix possibly have to do with visitation by alien beings from another solar system?" Looking back, the message should have been clear. The Phoenix had been a symbol of immortality for ages past.

Unknown at the time, the Phoenix experience was setting the stage for all of the intricately interwoven revelations that would come through Betty during the course of my investigations. I was just too engrossed in my own interpretation of the UFO phenomenon to recognize it! Even the Great Door and the description of a world of light were briefly alluded to during this first investigation of Betty. But it, like the Phoenix, was completely disregarded.

The Andreasson Affair	Fowler	phase one
Investigator: What is the Great Door? Betty: It is the entrance to the other world. The world where light is. Investigator: Is that available to us as well as to you? Betty: No, not yet. *[Note: Normally it is entered at death.]*		

Betty's brief mention of a "Great Door" meant nothing to me then. The investigating team was more interested in the physical nuts-and-bolts side of Betty's 1967 experience. We knew nothing of the childhood experiences that lay buried within the recesses of her subconscious mind. Our only clue of a previous abduction was when Betty described an object being removed from her nose. We wondered how it got there, but were unable to break through a mental block at that time because of the distress it caused her.

During the phase two investigation, these childhood encounters surfaced. Puzzled, we recorded an escalating series of visitations that prepared her eventually for her OBE visit through the already mentioned Great Door to a world of light to meet the One.

The Andreasson Affair Phase Two	Fowler	phase two
Betty [1944]: They are taking me someplace, but not yet...something about five years or so.... It's coming to a time that I will know the One.... They're going to show me something...that everybody will be happy about...that everybody will learn something from. And they said people will understand...people that I tell...that I'm going to find the One. I will know the One...I will feel the One.		

Again, Betty's statements about the One meant nothing to me. It, like some other aspects of her experiences, were so bizarre and atypical that we tended to tune them out. We concentrated on aspects of her experience that were more representative of other abduction cases. Such seemingly offbeat references were suspected to be some kind of superimposed manifestation of her religious beliefs over her abduction experience.

But, references to the One continued to escalate as Betty relived her next two childhood encounters.

The Andreasson Affair Phase Two	Fowler	phase two
age 12: They said, "She's got another year."...They said I will learn about the One.		
age 13: Betty: They're just standing there looking at me with their fat brown eyes...and they said, "We're going to take you home.... Home is where the One is."		

Nonetheless, I continued to ignore this particular facet of Betty's abduction experience. When I wrote a sequel to the original book, *The Andreasson Affair,* that reflected the phase two investigation, I offered no comment upon it at all. I did, however, begin to address the psychic aftereffects of abductees and Betty's religious interpretation of her experiences. This represented my first few steps toward recognizing the paraphysical nature of the UFO phenomenon.

Then came the phase three investigation, when all of Betty's experiences seem to come together and reveal the alien entities' "Message to

Mankind." Again, however, I dealt mostly with the physical side of their message: the curious symbiotic connection between human and alien, the alien genetic engineering program, and alien concern about disastrous ecological problems that would cause the future sterility of humanity and other life-forms on earth.

Looking back in retrospect, I scarcely touched upon the other side of their message: that "Man is not made of just flesh and blood." This, even though the object lessons presented in Betty and Bob's UFO abduction experiences seemed perfectly designed to validate this truth. I simply noted the similarity between Betty's OBE abduction experience with the One and NDErs' experience with light beings and theorized that:

> The other side of the message concerns man's transition after physical death. His current existence in localized time is preparatory in nature. It may be just one of many steps behind and before him during his evolving being. The Watchers have already been allowed to experience these steps.[14]

Apparently I did not say enough, for here I am in the midst of a phase four investigation and another book that deals primarily with the paraphysical reality of UFOs and humankind. I did not expect this. I honestly believed that I had finally completed my investigation of Betty and Bob. However, the powers that be seem to be in control of the situation. I believe that the sobsequent experiences of the Lucas were meant to be probed at a later date in order for me to finish the rest of "The Message to Mankind," which I am attempting to articulate in this book. Betty's last visit to the One in particular again left her with a prime directive.

The Watchers II	Fowler	phase four
Betty: Oh the light is all over. It is wonderful.... I cannot explain the wonder and beauty and love and peace. It is so joyous! Oh, glory, glory, glory. Glory, glory. Oh, I'm going to have to go back. *[almost crying]* I have to go back for others, so that they too will see, will understand and know.		

I believe that this book may be one of the vehicles being used so that others will see, will understand and know.

However, the establishment of an explicit connection between Betty and Bob's OBE abduction experiences and near-death experienc-

14. Fowler, 1990, pp. 355

es is only initiatory to the shocking conclusion of "The Message" being developed in this book. The implications of such a connection coupled with other paranormal phenomena exhibited by UFOs lead us even deeper into the twilight zone of humankind's true nature and ultimate destination!

chapter fifteen

Implications

Swing low, sweet chariot, comin' for to carry me home. Swing low, sweet chariot, comin' for to carry me home. I looked over Jordan and what did I see? Comin' for to carry me home. A band of Angels comin after me. Comin' for to carry me home.

Spiritual

There is no doubt in my mind that an intimate connection exists between the UFO abduction experience and the near-death experience. Such a connection is supported by additional otherworldly components of the UFO phenomenon. Let us now examine these in detail before concluding this chapter with their mind-boggling implications.

The Paraphysical Nature of UFOs

First, the UFOs—the strange craft themselves—have long been known to manifest paraphysical properties beyond our ken. Those who have read *The Watchers* will recall my discovery of NASA and Air Force studies in 1968 that connected UFOs with extrasensory phenomena.

I also mentioned direct Pentagon interest in the paranormal aftereffects that followed in the wake of a CE-II by a helicopter crew. The helicopter crew's commander was asked by the Pentagon to monitor both himself and crew for any hint of OBEs, among other things. Interestingly enough, some members of the crew had OBEs after their encounter.

Recently, I found out what branch of the military has the task of investigating UFO reports that exhibit paranormal effects. This information is recorded on an August 22, 1974, Defense Intelligence Agency DD 1480 Form entitled *Defense Information Report Evaluation.* Armen Victorian acquired it through the Freedom of Information Act (FOIA).

The document originated from the US Defense Attache Office (US-DAO) at Madrid, Spain. It is addressed to an element of the Defense Intelligence Agency (DIA/DC4A1). It is apparent that a UFO event exhibiting paranormal phenomena had taken place and that DIA/DC4A1 was asking for help. The response by USDAO is enlightening.

1. The US Army Medical Intelligence and Information Agency (MI-IA) has the DOD tasking in areas of paranormal phenomenon of possible military significance. UFO activity has sometimes been suggested as a manifestation of this phenomenon. Your comments concerning the team of ESP specialists is especially appreciated. If possible, a follow-up would be useful to this Agency.

2. MIIA encourages reporting on UFO sightings, but has refrained from initiating official DIA collection requirements as this may open the proverbial Pandora's box.

3. MIIA appreciates your interest and open-minded approach.[1]

The document is signed by Captain John D. La Mothe, Deputy Director for MIIA. The value of the above information is noted as being *high* (unique, timely, and of major significance). It identifies the Defense Intelligence Agency as a collection agency for UFO reports. It reveals that the MIIA was responsible at that time for investigating the paranormal phenomena associated with UFOs. It demonstrates continuing interest by our government in the UFO problem after the alleged closure of its UFO Project in 1969. It also reveals our government's policy to keep official UFO investigations secret from lower echelon personnel by not "initiating official DIA collection requirements" for UFO reports. This is what was referred to in the document as opening pandora's box.

The MIIA is still alive and well today under a new name, but with the same mission. It is now called The Armed Forces Medical Intelligence Center (AFMIC) and is still under the purview of the Defense Intelligence Agency.

The paranormal nature of UFOs was recognized relatively early in modern UFO history. Renowned psychoanalyst and UFO researcher Dr. Carl Jung acknowledged this fact in his published book on UFOs. However, it is important to bear in mind that Jung did not possess the evidence we have obtained since his following perplexed statement.

> The impetus for the manifestation of the latent psychic contents was given by the UFO. The only thing we know with

1. Personal files.

> tolerable certainty about UFOs is that they possess a surface which can be seen by the eye and at the same time throws back a radar echo.... The simultaneous visual and radar sightings would in themselves be a satisfactory proof of their reality. Unfortunately, well-authenticated reports show that there are also cases where the eye sees something that does not appear on the radar screen, or where an object undoubtedly picked up by radar is not seen by the eye. I will not mention other, even more remarkable reports from authoritative sources.
>
> If these things are real—and by all human standards it hardly seems possible to doubt this any longer—then we are left with two hypotheses: that of their *weightlessness* on the one hand and of their *psychic nature* on the other. This is a question I for one cannot decide.... Of course, next to nothing has been gained as regards the *physical* explanation of the phenomenon. But the psychic aspect plays so great a role that it cannot be left out of account. The discussion of it...leads to psychological problems which involve just as fantastic possibilities or impossibilities as the approach from the physical side.... The alternative hypothesis that UFOs are something psychic that is equipped with certain physical properties seems even less probable, for where would such a thing come from? If weightlessness is a hard hypothesis to swallow, then the notion of a materialized psychism opens a bottomless void under our feet. Parapsychology is, of course, acquainted with the fact of materialization. But this phenomenon depends upon the presence of one or more mediums, who exude a weighable substance, and it occurs only in their immediate environment. The psyche can move the body, but only inside the living body. That something psychic, possessing material qualities and with a high charge of energy, could appear by itself high in the air at a great distance from any human medium—this surpasses our comprehension. Here our knowledge leaves us completely in the lurch, and it is therefore pointless to speculate any further in this direction.[2]

Perhaps, in Jung's time, it seemed pointless to speculate any further in such a direction. However, both UFO research and the field of parapsychology have progressed much since Jung penned these words.

There is no doubt, either to the military or civilian UFO researcher, that UFOs behave as if they had no mass, but paradoxically, they exhib-

---

2. Jung, 1959, pp. 116-117.

it mass at certain times. The reports, if taken at face value, describe both these properties.

On the one hand we have visible, seemingly physical, machine-like objects that perform right angle, turns at high speed without a curve radius; objects that move through the air at speeds well above sound, yet do not cause sonic booms; objects that hover, float and bob like a controlled helium-filled balloon rather then a heavy vehicle; objects that descend like lightweight falling leaves; and objects affected by air resistance causing them to move through the air in an up-and-down motion, like a boat skipping over the surface of water. On the other hand, the same objects display the attributes of *mass.* These include strong radar returns identical to those reflected off metallic aircraft, the deflection of bullets which ricochet off a solid surface, the causation of ground effects such as burns, broken branches, radiation and pod marks that indicate the landing of an object weighing tons. These characteristics in and of themselves present a great mystery, but the following ability is totally unearthly.

In Dr. Carl Jung's recently quoted statement about radar/visual sightings, the good professor alluded to some reports from authoritative sources that he dared not mention because "they are so bizarre that they tax our understanding and credulity to the limit."

Most likely, Jung was alluding to radar and/or visual sightings that reveal a displacement of UFOs from one point to another instantaneously *without benefit of a flight path.* The objects seem to disappear into another co-existing dimension and then pop back into ours at another location!

The Paraphysical Nature of UFO Entities

What about the entities that operate the craft that we call UFOs? Non-abductee witnesses observe the same types of craft and entities that are reported by persons abducted physically or in an OBE state. The reported entities, like their craft, exhibit the same dual physical/non-physical nature. Paradoxically, in either state they are able to pass through solid walls, doors, windows, etc. Again, they, like their craft, have the ability to appear within and disappear from Earth's space time continuum at will.

All of the above attributes have appeared in our study of Betty and Bob Luca, but they also are an integral part of hundreds of other reported UFO encounters. Coupled with these paraphysical properties is the fact that some UFO entities appear identical to those entities encountered by persons undergoing an NDE in an OBE state of being.

One could go on and on with examples that reflect the disparate, seemingly irreconcilable nature of the UFO phenomenon. In essence, UFOs and their operators present us with the same kind of paradox as light.

Light has proven to be both particle (material) and wave (non-material) in nature. UFOs and the entities that operate them are reported to be both physical and non-physical. Having made this point, let us now move on to some other odd paraphysical aspects of UFO reports. These also provide valuable clues to the relationship of UFOs to humankind's true nature and ultimate destination.

The Pre-death Knowledge of UFO Entities

One of the saddest events that took place during my long relationship with the Lucas was the death of two of her sons. It was also one of the more ominous occurrences because the UFO entities had told Betty ahead of time that it was going to happen.

Although I recorded this event in prior books about Betty, I mention it again, as it is applicable to the subject at hand.

After being told about her sons' impending death, the entity caused Betty not to remember until a later date. However, her subconscious mind still held the terrible secret. When she awoke on October 20, 1977, after the bedtime visitation, she found herself in a deep depression. Although she had no remembrance of her nocturnal visitor, she nevertheless had the strongest of premonitions that something terrible was about to happen.

During that day, Betty became so upset that she phoned and told me about it. I encouraged her to visit and chat about it on the following day. Betty brought her then new boyfriend, Bob Luca, with her, whom I had referred to MUFON investigators for an enquiry into his experiences. I had not met Bob up to that point, so their visit gave me a chance to get to know Bob personally.

When they arrived, Betty was an emotional wreck about the terrible sense of foreboding that hung over her like a sense of impending death. I comforted her as best as I could, and she returned home. Twenty-four hours later, both of her sons were killed in an automobile accident.

For over 25 years, I have kept some pages clipped out of a *Science & Mechanics* magazine. It is a wonder that I did. I usually discarded such cases as outlandish and products of a mentally ill mind. But, there it was waiting for me when I looked through my files doing research for this book: A report dealing with alien prediction of human death. It was thoroughly investigated by *Science & Mechanics* editor Lloyd Mallan. Now, after more than quarter of a century and my investigation of the Lucas, it no longer seemed so outlandish! The following reflects a good portion of Lloyd Mallan's report on the incident: [italics mine]

> One bleak evening last winter a lonely highway in upper New York State became the scene of what is probably the most terrifying flying saucer encounter that any human being has yet reported. It was the peak of...an unusually large number of sightings...that began in October and was still going on when I visited Ithaca, N.Y. .... More than 800 sightings of flying saucers were reported by the time I arrived there.
>
> The victim, or heroine, of the story is a slim attractive young blonde, the mother of two and a part-time beautician.... Her name is Rita Malley. She had reached her twenty-fifth birthday about three weeks before I met her. I was fully determined to study her every little gesture and facial expression as she talked. I wanted to be sure that she wasn't fabricating, exaggerating or being victimized by delusions that may derived from an hallucination. She spoke calmly, almost matter-of-factly, while sitting on a high stool in her pleasant kitchen, holding her five-year-old son, Dana, on her lap, throughout the nearly hour-long interview. I set up my tape-recorder on a work-counter, pointed the microphone at her and let it go. Here in her own words, is what was magnetically frozen on the tape.
>
> "My husband's name is John. He works at Morris Chain as a foreman. This is Dana on my lap. He's in kindergarten. I have a daughter, Renée, in the other room. She's six months old. We have a '62 red Ford convertible with a white top.
>
> "I was driving home late from a visit with a friend in North Lansing. I was going to be late making John's dinner. Dana was in the back seat, right directly behind me. He was running his mouth a mile a minute. You know how kids do at that age? It was on December 12th, in the evening, about seven o'clock. I was traveling on Route 34 going south, at a speed of about 60 miles an hour—or faster. This is the Auburn-Ithaca Road, where the speed-limit is 50.
>
> "It was a dreary night that night, with slight flurries of snow blowing away. There was no traffic at all. I didn't meet any car. Nobody passed me, and it was a dark night. The

clouds were real black, although the sky itself was kind of dark gray, so the clouds stood out against it. The wind was blowing, and the clouds were moving from east to west. The wind was so strong that when I had to make a turn, the car would kind of shift position. The wind was awful. It was coming from the left hand side and it whistled through the spaces between the convertible top and the body. The roof was flapping against the bars.

"I had on the high beams of my headlights. It was a straightaway part of the highway. There are no street lights in that area. It's kind of a barren stretch—fields and hills on both sides. And there are some homes, but they're back into the woods—a good distance away. The fields are wide-open spaces between the road and the woods.

"Just when I was midway between North Lansing, where my friend lives, and South Lansing—I was closer to Ithaca than I was to Auburn, in other words—I noticed this brilliant red glow, like, on the inside of my car, as though it were coming from the rear. 'Ah, oh!' I thought. 'It's a police car. I've been speeding.' I looked in the rear-view mirror and saw—nothing.

"There was nothing but this red light covering everything. And I thought, 'What is it?' And I just couldn't figure it out. And I was shaking like a leaf, you know, trying to figure a way out of this. I thought it was the cops, but I kept going, just waiting for the sound of their sirens to tell me to pull over off the road.

"I had just come around a bend in the highway and, as I said, was not on this straightaway. Well, anyway, I kept going, and just a little bit further up the road I was suddenly panicked. This object, whatever it was, suddenly appeared at my left. It came into sight over a telephone pole. And I glanced up.... I glanced out and saw brilliant red and green lights underneath an object that was airborne. It must have been 55 to 60 feet in diameter. It was round and had a little dome-like thing on the top. And it tilted once. I saw it once, tilted. You couldn't look right out and stare at it for long because the lights were so bright from it."

Rita Malley was almost in tears as she described the object. There was fear in her voice as she continued.

"It was, I realized, awfully quiet in the back seat and I looked back to see what Dana was doing. He was sitting straight up. His eyes were just bugging right out of his head.

And I yelled at him. I just screamed at him 'Dana, Dana! Are you all right?!' I think that's what I yelled anyway.

"His response was—nothing. He didn't say a word to me. He just sat there. He wasn't turning. His eyelids were not moving.

"The object was hovering at a height of probably three or four telephone-pole lengths. It extended a white beam of light from underneath—and it just completely took right over the controls of my car. My car stopped moving when it stopped.

"My first thought was to grab Dana and get out of the car and run. Then I thought, 'What good is it to run?' This object, this thing, had got complete control of me. I was shaking.

"I just didn't know what to do. What was happening? I became hysterical. I couldn't scream. My throat felt tight, and it was dry. The situation was weird. This was the first time I had ever been right-out scared. If you've ever been really scared, you'll know how I felt. My eyes started hurting, started burning. And I couldn't swallow. I think that was from being so scared—and shocked.

"And I turned away from the back seat because I just couldn't get any response at all out of Dana. My uppermost urge was to get him out there as fast as I could. But even if I picked him up and got out of the car and ran like mad, there just wasn't anybody to run to. I saw the small lights of a house way off in the woods, but to reach that house I would have to run more than a mile across a wide open field.

"While I was thinking these wild thoughts, I kept stamping on the accelerator—but the car wouldn't move forward. And the red and green lights on this object—it was disc-shaped—were going off in all different directions. Suddenly I realized that I was moving sideways. The thing was taking me off the road. I twisted and turned the steering wheel in the opposite direction, but no matter what I did—I even tried using the brakes—my car gradually moved sideways and took me right under the shoulder of the road. My front right wheel and my back right wheel were sitting in the alfalfa. The shoulder of the road must be 10 feet off the highway—and I must have been another five feet beyond that.

"On the other side of the road, my left side, the object was still hovering over the wires of the telephone pole. It was maybe 120 feet high and now about 180 feet away. The lights inside my car went right down to nothing. The headlights had slowly dimmed to where I could hardly see anything ahead of me. Only red and green flashes from the thing over the pole.

"I have an automatic gear-shift in my car. It was in drive. But the motor had stopped. It went down below an idle, which is hardly turning over. I was trying all the tricks I knew to get the car started. I even started pulling the light-switch back and forth—but I got nowhere.

"Meanwhile, I became aware of a strange noise from this thing.... It sounded almost exactly like a TV antenna vibrating in a wind. It was that same low humming noise. The hum at first sounded like a whole swarm of bees, a cluster of bees. Have you ever stumbled into a bees' nest? You know, they start coming at you? It sounded like a big fat swarm of bumblebees coming at me. And the suddenly the hum stopped when the *voices* began to talk.

"These voices came out of the thing, this hovering object. I want to explain: My car windows were rolled up tight, and, as I said, the wind was blowing. The voices sounded like a group of people, a *chorus* of voices. They were all talking at the same time, saying the same thing—only they spoke as if what they were saying was being translated into English. Because the words were broken. I mean, like when they said the word "Paul," they said "Paahl," like that. But the last name of the person they were talking about was very distinct. I knew what the last name was. "

She paused. Her face had lost some color. She was obviously upset. She shook her head before continuing.

"Every time I start telling this, I feel nervous. Right now I feel terrible, I have chills. In fact, I'm on the verge of crying right now. I cried after I got home following the incident. It's not easy to relive something like this. It's more than even unpleasant."

Rita Malley paused again. After about a minute, she went on:

"These voices...I couldn't tell whether they were male or female. I mean, there were so many of them all at once. They gave me a dreadful message: *Paul Donalds, Moravia, killed...near or in Massena in a tractor-trailer owned by Joe Etinger, Moravia.*

"I did not know Paul Donalds, except by name, because I knew his sister. Marian Donalds and I went to beauty school together.

"And then they said, these voices said, 'Your son will not remember the time stop the car from the time you left the highway.' [sic] I think that's what they said about Dana. Well, after about six or seven minutes of terror, my car gradually started to move back toward the road. I had no control over it at all. It moved itself right back onto the road. I was still holding onto the steering wheel and it actually turned like this... [She gestured as if she were turning a steering wheel to the left] like as if there was somebody sitting there instead of me.

"And I gradually came right up onto the highway, to my proper position in the right hand lane. My lights came back on. And this hovering object was staying directly opposite me, to my left, facing the car. I still had no control of the car as we moved along the highway.

"About three miles down the road, we came around a bend, like so [again she gestured to illustrate making a turn in her car] and we're coming into South Lansing, onto another stretch of road. The object was still off to my left, at the same distance and height. The white beam of light from underneath, it had gone off when it started to move. Just the blinking red and green lights all around the bottom rim of the thing were showing. They were so bright that it was hard to tell their shape, if they were round or square. The red was most predominant, but they were intermingled so brightly that they blended together.

"As I said, we're now on a straightaway. I was still under control of that thing in the air. Then I noticed some cars coming toward me. At this point the thing suddenly ascended toward the south. I didn't look to see where it went because I was immediately in control of my car again. I was too busy driving against traffic and trying to relax.

"But I was not too busy to be concerned about Dana. I had the feeling that there might be something seriously wrong with him, the way he had acted, as if he was hypnotized. So I called to the back seat, 'Dana?' And he answered, 'Yes.' I said, 'Did you see anything, Dana? Did you see what Mommy saw?' And he said, 'No.'

"He was all right. With that off my mind I scooted straight back home as fast as I could. We walked into the house. I was in a daze. John, my husband, asked me how come I had been away for so long. And I said, 'You wouldn't believe the reason. You wouldn't believe what I could tell you.' And I wasn't going to tell him.

"'Why can't you tell me what happened?' he asked. I thought his voice seemed irritable.

"Then I broke down. I was hysterical all over again. And my head was just—aah!—throbbing, throbbing! You can't imagine! Pain all the way down through the back of my neck. My eyes ached.

"Finally, I couldn't stand it any longer. John was trying to comfort me. And I blurted it out—the whole weird story. He didn't ask me any questions. We were just going to forget the whole thing. At the time, I didn't know anything about flying saucers.

"That night I woke up screaming from a sound sleep. I had somehow heard a low moaning, maybe quivering hum. I thought the thing was coming back after me again. And, of course, my husband, John, checked through the house to find out what was really causing that strange hum. He discovered it was the TV antenna vibrating because of the strong blowing wind. In my sleep it had sounded almost exactly like the humming from that hovering thing, before the voices began talking.

"The next day—it was late in the afternoon—I received a phone call from my sister who works at Cornell University. She said, 'What do you think of Paul Donalds' getting killed in Massena?' I was shocked. I didn't know what to think. And I said, 'You're kidding!' She said, very seriously, 'No, I'm not.'

"The details were exactly as the voices said. Paul Donalds had been killed in a tractor-trailer owned by Joel Etinger. That was the first I had heard of the actual tragedy. We'd just moved out this way and were not having any newspaper delivered yet."[3]

Such a report, coupled with the Lucas's experiences and Dr. Ring's finding of a UFO/NDE connection, seems to be telling us that whoever controls the UFO phenomenon is *intimately connected with the afterlife of human beings.* This is a deeply profound revelation with ever-escalating implications for humankind!

The next UFO encounter pertinent to our discussion has many similarities to both the Lucas' and Rita's experiences. Like Betty, the three witnesses were artists and devout Christians. Like, Rita, they too had the controls of their automobile taken over by a UFO. Important to our discussion is the fact that *one of the abductees believed that she was told by the entities of her impending death.* You will note other similarities as your read the following account that I have summarized below from

---

3. Mallan, July, 1968, pp. 31-33, 96.

the hypnotic regression session transcripts and reports prepared by supporting investigators.

This incident took place at Stanford, Kentucky, and involved the abduction of three women from their car on January 6, 1976. At the time, they were returning to their hometown of Liberty from a restaurant where they had celebrated Mona Stafford's 36th birthday. On the way home, the trio witnessed a bright red object in the sky, which they thought was a large aircraft on fire. A number of independent witness reported this same object in the area.

When the object approached, the driver lost control of the car. She could neither steer nor control its speed. The object was enormous, metallic and disc-shaped with a dome on top and a ring of red lights around it. A yellow light shone from its underside. Suddenly, a beam of bluish white light shot out from it and engulfed the car. Their last remembrance was the car somehow being moved into a roadside pasture. One hour and twenty minutes later, they found themselves intact in the car driving home to Liberty. They could not account for the missing time, the inflammation of their eyes and anomalous burns on the exposed flesh of their bodies.

Stranger things were yet to occur. Upon arriving home, the minute hand on the mechanical watch of one of the abductee's spun around the second hand. Her normally quiet and friendly parakeet went berserk. It would have nothing more to do with her and died a few months later. When she touched her mechanical bedroom clock, it stopped running and had to be discarded.

The following morning they reported the incident to the police and a Navy recruiting station. Someone at the station gave the story to a Lexington, Kentucky, TV station, which in turn brought their experience to the newspapers. Soon after, MUFON investigators contacted the trio and during an investigation they underwent hypnosis by Dr. Leo Sprinkle, a University of Wyoming professor who specializes in investigating UFO abduction reports.

Under hypnosis, the women relived being separated and taken to different locations for what seemed to be examinations or tests. One, whose eye were allowed to be open during the process, described her abductors as four-foot-tall humanoids with dark eyes and gray skin. Another was confronted with human-like entities both during and after the abduction. One was described as a "Biblical-like" entity.[4]

---

4. Bullard, 1987, p. 118.

It is beyond the scope of this chapter to record all of the amazing details that surfaced from the investigation of this report. As mentioned, some paralleled Betty's 1950 and 1967 experiences, including the removal of eyes, being taken through a tunnel chipped out of rock, OBEs, and continuing paranormal effects after the abduction experience. All three women also took and passed polygraph tests.

So far, like the initial segment of the Malley case, we seem to be dealing with the elements of a typical UFO encounter. But, like the Malley case, it contains *atypical* components of high strangeness.

One of the abductees, Mona Stafford, insisted that she had been treated differently from her friends, who had both undergone a terrifying physical examination with painful aftereffects. She made the following startling disclosure to the editor of her local newspaper. It was printed in the April 13, 1978, issue of the *Lexington Leader*. Pertinent excerpts follow:

> Dear Editor:
>
> I want to make a few statements on some errors that appeared in the *Lexington Leader*.
>
> They wrote that after we'd been taken aboard the craft I was examined by alien creatures about four feet tall with large slanted eyes.
>
> We were all three taken aboard the same space craft, but separated.
>
> I was transported to another craft. The people I remember were like of old times.... I wasn't examined, but tested. I believe for the future and for things that are going to take place in this world and the one to come.
>
> —Mona Stafford

It had been rumored that another of the three abductees, Elaine Thomas, had confided to investigators that the entities were going to come back for her at death. Still later, she allegedly told them that she had a strong premonition that she was going to die. I heard that she had died and wondered if the rumors leading to her death contained any substance. As part of the research for this book, I contacted Jerry Black, one of the chief investigators of the case. He confirmed what I had heard, but personally felt that Mona's beliefs might have been speculation coupled with a coincidental death. He seemed very reticent to accept the paranormal side of the case. Pertinent excerpts from my conversation with him are as follows:

Ray: I was looking through some of the material that you and others have sent me concerning the Kentucky abduction case.

Jerry: Right.

Ray: ...It seems that one of the women, I don't know if was Mona or Louise...[had] some kind of premonition of exactly when she was going to die?

Jerry: That was Elaine Thomas.

Ray: It was Elaine Thomas.

Jerry: She did pass away.

Ray: And...did she get this premonition during her abduction?

Jerry: No, it was something she told us...quite a few months afterwards.... She basically told ________ in a phone conversation that she was going to die, and it would look like some type of an accident and they [the entities] were coming back to get her, is what she said.... She said that actually less than three months of when she did pass away.... She started feeling bad. She had been to the hospital twice.... They couldn't find anything wrong.... I called Dr. _______, her doctor. He said that all he knows is that...she spit up some kind of oily stuff, and he didn't save it, and she died the next day. The EKG showed no sign of a heart attack or anything or any heart condition. And so I asked why he had put down heart conditions on the death certificate. He said, "Well, because I had no choice. What did you want me to put down?"...I don't have any way of knowing if there was anything wrong or not. They don't believe in autopsies down in that part of Kentucky. That's what happened. She did pass away, but it might have been a coincidence.

Ray: But she did equate it with what had happened to her?

Jerry: Well, *she* did. She did. She had told Mona, when she was visiting her in the hospital..."Please make them understand that all of this really happened to us. It really happened the way we said."...What was interesting was...that supposedly a ball of light appeared in her room the night she passed away.... She was in a semi-private room, and, according to Mona, the other patient [who saw it, too] obviously got upset. It wasn't anything big, just a small *ball of light*...just bouncing along off the walls and stuff very slowly, and the other patient called the nurse, and the nurse, according to

Mona, saw it and...then shortly afterwards, it just went out or disappeared, and Elaine explained to the nurse that "It's just them coming to get me."...I don't want to put anything into it, but this is what happened.... She was the one who always said that some aliens are good and there are some that are bad. She always said this ever since her experience.... There are a lot of mystifying things about this case that never came out.... She has always said that there was some kind of a religious connection with this phenomena.... I can't relate to it.... There's a lot of people in your studies that you've found, too....

Ray: Yeah, I [have come] across that with Betty.

Jerry: I don't understand. I can't relate to it.... I don't think there's any solid proof. I think that more or less these people are having...just really gut feelings.... The witnesses [the Kentucky abductees] I don't think were more religious....

Ray: All of them were fundamentalist Christians according to what I can gather.

Jerry: Yeah, that's right...they were church-goers, but they weren't fanatics about religion.... Sometimes, the way it goes back and forth, you sometimes wonder what all of this means.... What are we really dealing with?[5]

What *are* we dealing with? First, we have a woman who underwent a UFO abduction experience. Secondly, this same woman knew she was about to die and believed that the alien entities would come for her at death. Thirdly, on the night of her death, her room was visited by a ball of light. All three of these components have striking commonalties with the near-death experience. Pre-death warnings and balls of light are also common elements in UFO and NDE reports.

NDE researcher Dr. Melvin Morse writes:

> These pre-death visions are intensely real experiences that a dying person has while still conscious.... The dying patient often sees God, angels, dead relatives or visions of heaven superimposed upon reality or actually present at the deathbed.[6]

Dr. Morse relates an account about a boy named Cory who was dying of leukemia who fell asleep in his mother's car on the way back from the children's Hospital. When they arrived home, Cory said to his mother: "Don't worry about my leukemia. I have been to the crystal

5. Names, report and transcripts in author's files.
6. Morse, 1990, p. 48.

castle and have talked with God." Cory described God as an old man with a beard and a halo. This being engulfed Cory in a loving light and told him not to worry because he wouldn't be dying yet.

Those of you who are familiar with Betty Luca's experiences will be most interested in reading Cory's description of where he had gone to meet the being in the light. Dr. Morse states that: [italics mine]

> Cory said that while asleep in the car he had traveled up a *beam of light* to heaven, where he crossed a moat on a rainbow bridge and visited the crystal castle.[7]

Procurement of the abductee via a beam of light is common to many abduction cases. However, what Cory describes next is a near replica of Betty's theophany when she encountered the Phoenix and the thundering voice she took to be God. If you will recall, Betty was taken into an area and over a high roller-coaster-like bridge over water into a crystal structure radiating the colors of the rainbow where she too was engulfed in a loving light and given a message. Pertinent summarized excerpts follow.

The Andreasson Affair	Fowler	phase one
Its just on this thing we're standing on as we're going along…seemed like bridges in the air…the sea was off to the side…and I'm coming to a bright light—crystals that have rainbows all in it. It is crystal all around.… They are taking me through those crystals.… Oh-h-h, that bright light.… And I'm just there before that bright light.… I hear somebody speaking in a loud voice…"I have chosen you to show the world."		

Later, Cory was visited by the same entity that he had talked with in the Crystal Palace. The entity told him the exact week that he would die. Dr. Morse later confessed that: [italics mine]

> Things happened that convinced me that Cory was right in trusting his visions. For one, he far outlived my predictions for a treated patient who'd had four relapses. For another, *Cory died the same week that God told him he would.*[8]

Another account reported by Dr. Morse was related to him by relatives gathered at the bedside of a dying person. As they conversed with him, he gazed excitedly at a stairway on the other side of the room.

---

7. Morse, 1990, p. 53.
8. Morse, 1990, p. 55.

Closer to the Light	Morse	
Suddenly he exclaimed: "See, the angels are coming down the stairs. The glass has fallen and broken." All of us in the room looked toward the staircase where a drinking glass had been placed on one of the steps. As we looked, we saw the glass break into a thousand pieces without any apparent cause. It did not fall: it simply exploded. The angels, of course, we did not see. A happy and peaceful expression came over the patient's face and the next moment he expired. Even after his death, the serene peaceful expression remained on his face.[a]		

a. Morse, 1990, p. 49.

Significantly, balls of light are a typical component of many UFO abductee reports. During the Lucas' shared OBE abduction in 1978, the entities demonstrated they could change to light beings and balls of light. Bob was terrified when he observed one of the small gray entities suddenly turn into a being of light.

NDErs have also described intelligent balls of light visiting and communicating by telepathy with them on their death bed. Are we dealing with the same phenomenon? Consider the following NDE that involves such a phenomenon. The account again comes from Dr. Melvin Morse who had been told of it by a fellow physician while lecturing in Germany. [italics mine]

> When I met Schroeter while lecturing in Germany, he told me of a patient who had a near-death experience and floated out of her body. She saw a *ball of light* approach her body and listened as her body and the ball of light carried on a conversation. Finally the ball of light said: "You won't join us for another thirty years." She then returned to her body.
>
> This and the many cases like it have led Schroeter, myself and others to believe that the temporal lobe is a receiving system, one that allows us to hear voices from a source outside our bodies and perceive the light that comes to us at the point of death.[9]

Coincidental or Correlative UFO/Death Cases?

I would be remiss not to mention the following two incidents that appear to be connected with the UFO phenomenon and its paranormal knowledge concerning the human death experience.

---

9. Morse, 1992, p. 196.

The first concerns a phone call in the night that I had received many years ago. I remember it well because of its bizarre nature. At the time, I didn't know what to make of it. I neither recorded the date nor made a paraphrased record of the conversation. The following is my best recollection of the phone conversation.

The phone call was allegedly from one very upset nurse. She was familiar with *The Andreasson Affair* and Betty's sketches of the small gray aliens. She said that she responded to a call from an elderly patient who was deathly ill. The old woman described a terrifying experience to her. The patient said that she had awakened to see a group of small gray creatures with big heads standing around her bed. They seemed to be examining her. When she awoke and looked at them in terror, they just disappeared.

The patient did not equate the creatures with UFOs, but was in a panic as she simply described what she had seen. The nurse told me that she felt compelled to call and tell me. She tracked down my phone number through information. I thanked her very much, the conversation ended and I went back to sleep.

If we take this nurse's report at face value, we have a situation where a person near death suddenly awakes to see the typical group of gray UFO entities around her. Was this an hallucination? If so, why did she describe the exact replica of UFO entities under such a circumstance? Had the elderly person unknowingly begun an NDE and seen these entities during a fleeting OBE? Does this account provide another clue to a UFO/afterlife connection?

The above experience reminds me of yet another case involving UFOs and the death of a witness. The story is recorded on a tattered old news clip that I had filed with the Rita Malley case. It involved an apparently reliable woman who sighted a UFO at very close range while waiting for a bus at North Amherst, Massachusetts, on January 16, 1976. There are two intriguing things about this case that may be connected with our current discussion. Of course, if someone back then told me that I would be equating it with a UFO/afterlife connection in the future, I would never have believed it! The following are pertinent excerpts from the newspaper accounts. [italics mine]

> Woman Saw UFO for 30 Minutes
>
> Ambulances and fire trucks may no longer have a local monopoly on blinking red lights.
>
> A gray vehicle that preferred tree-top level to the more down-to-earth traffic routes was reportedly sighted Tuesday night by a voter returning from the polls in North Amherst.

And although it apparently was not an emergency vehicle, the truck-sized interloper was carrying a flashing red light. Terry Cunningim, 29, says she believes in UFOs (Unidentified Flying Objects) now, after spending 30 minutes in the vicinity of this one. *She may have been taken aboard, she believes, with her memory nearly completely blanked out afterwards.*

She was standing at a bus stop on busy North Pleasant Street, and *said she was apparently the only one to see the object,* which hovered shyly behind a tree beyond the reach of street lights.... She said the thing was photographing her because she saw a number of flashes of light that she thought must be flashbulbs going off.

Ms. Cunningim, a Colonial Village resident who moved here from St. Louis in August because of a sister in Northampton, is attending "SKILLS," a secretarial training school. She was seeing a friend off on the bus in North Amherst after voting there—she lived in North Amherst when she registered to vote in August.

She turned to walk toward Amherst, she said, and happened to look up. *The object appeared rather suddenly,* she said, perhaps 50 feet away from her, and hovered there behind a treetop.

It was shaped rather like a bullet, pointed at both ends, and was hard to see in the dark, she said. A red light on the top flashed like an ambulance's. She thought she saw mirrors or windows in the sides, because of reflections. The flashing white lights came out of these windows, she said.

Although she didn't have a watch, she estimates the encounter to have lasted 30 minutes because of the buses that went by. The object, she said, moved—when she moved. If she stepped a few feet to one side, it moved a few feet. It appeared to be watching her.

Despite the fact that North Pleasant Street is heavily trafficked, there were *no pedestrians who appeared to see it, and no cars stopped.* The object hung over the yard of a house of 1184 North Pleasant Street, she said.

The reason she thinks that she may have been taken aboard the [craft] is that a number sticks in her mind for no apparent reason: 00:30. There have been reports from others, in particular Barney and Betty Hill of Portsmouth, N.H., who spoke at UMASS recently, who said they encountered a UFO and were taken aboard. Although the Hills said they did not remember being taken aboard, they said hypnosis revealed they were examined by humanoid creatures in the supposed spacecraft.

> When questioned by the *Gazette,* Ms. Cunningim said she was unaware of the Hills and their reported experiences, but she said she may seek hypnosis herself to see what could have gone on.
>
> The craft, she said, vanished as swiftly as it had come. Someone came up to Ms. Cunningim to ask about the next bus, and she turned her head to answer. When she looked back, it had left.
>
> William A. Dent, a University of Massachusetts professor of physics, felt that he would take more stock of Ms. Cunningim's account if there had been more witnesses. Ms. Cunningim, he pointed out, concluded that the object was both very large and very close. "I don't know what she saw," he said.[10]

Thus far, if taken at face value, we have a reliable witness who claims to have watched a large UFO at close range for a half hour. It flashed a bright light at her. It moved when she moved. She stood on a busy street gazing at it, while no one else seems to have observed it. Thus, it was visible to her, but invisible to others. It disappeared when someone interrupted her gaze with a question about a bus schedule. After the object disappeared, she was left with a strong feeling that she had somehow been brought aboard the object although she could not explain how this could be.

This case reminds me of Betty and Bob's shared OBE abduction from their home in 1978 and of Betty's OBE abduction from her trailer in 1986. If someone had peeked into the Lucas' home, they would have seen them standing together in front of the bathroom door. If someone had looked into their trailer, they would have seen Betty lying on a couch reading the Bible. No one would ever have thought in their wildest dreams that they had been abducted via an OBE. This would also apply to other reports of OBE abductions covered earlier in this book.

Is it possible that the bright light that flashed at Terry beamed her into the object in an OBE state of being? If so, her physical body would have remained standing inanimate near the bus stop gazing at the object. Is it possible that the UFO could only be seen by a person in this altered state of being? This would surely explain why Terry did not attempt to point the object out to others, which would have been a normal thing to do. It would also explain her confusion about somehow being aboard, yet still standing on the sidewalk.

---

10. Hough, November 18, 1976, p. 1.

Thus, passing drivers and pedestrians would just have seen Terry waiting near a bus stop staring idly into space. Only when someone came up and asked about a bus schedule would Terry be returned to her physical body. Once in this state, she could no longer see the object. To Terry, it seemed that the UFO just vanished. Compare this scenario to what Bob Luca had been told by the aliens about this very kind of thing during his OBE abduction with Betty in 1978.

Fred: OK, but, what I want some help with is hypothetically, I could pop in your home at Meriden at any moment, and you have to have some measure of time that you were not present. Is that true?

Bob: I was present, and Betty was present in Meriden, but Betty was present and I was present in that plane also.

Fred: OK, so if I were to have hypothetically walked in and jostled you about or shaken you, whatever, you would have been primarily returned to this plane?

Bob: That's true. It would be done in an instant—a flash of an eye.

I entitled this chapter "Implications." Thus far, we have seen some extremely strong connections between the UFO phenomenon and the afterlife. Now it is time to start to think about what such a connection implies. Let us summarize what we have discovered thus far.

1. Leading NDE researcher Dr. Kenneth Ring has provided documentation for a definitive commonality between the types of people who report NDEs and those who experience UFO abductions. Both tend to exhibit the same personality profile, and both report the same kind of aftereffects.

2. Dr. Ring reports that he has a number of cases on file that he alludes to as mixed motifs. These cases involve persons who experience what seems to be a UFO abduction during their NDE.

3. Dr. Ring acknowledges cases where persons have had NDEs and UFO encounters at different times in their lives.

4. In the last chapter, I documented a great number of similarities between Betty and Bob Luca's experiences and NDEs. Both involved:

    a. being in an OBE state
    b. traveling toward a bright light
    c. being greeted by a loving being
    d. experiencing oneness

e. seeing beings of light
f. being transformed into light
g. communicating by telepathy
h. being brought "home"
i. having a feeling of timelessness
j. exhibiting extreme reluctance to leave the place of light
k. returning with a sense that love is fundamental
l. showing extreme concern for earth's ecological state

5. In this chapter, I documented that:
   a. Both UFOs (alien craft) and their entities are paraphysical in nature. Both reportedly have the ability to enter and exit our world seemingly from another space-time continuum.
   b. UFO and NDE entities know in advance when certain human beings are going to die.

The above similarities seem to be way beyond the chance of being coincidental. There is no doubt in my mind that they are reinforcing in the most powerful way what the aliens have told and shown Betty—that humans, like the UFO entities and their craft, have a dual nature. In our case, we are indeed, as the entities insist, more than flesh and blood.

Betty, and Bob to a lesser extent, have been used by the aliens as a living audio/visual presentation to show humankind this first basic truth about the reality of humanity's nature.

The Watchers II	Fowler	phase four
Betty: And he says that I will have to disrobe. Oh. Oh! And I'm coming out of myself [an out-of-body state]. I'm coming out of myself. My body is like a robe!		

It is also overwhelmingly apparent to me that Betty's UFO abduction experiences are meant to reveal to us that the UFO phenomenon and the near-death experience are rooted in a common source. This is especially apparent during her OBE abduction experiences. Betty's meeting with the One in a world of light differs from an NDE only in that she was taken there from a physical body in perfect health rather than from a traumatic situation. I believe that Betty's experiences were created purposely by the source behind the UFO phenomenon to show that this very UFO/NDE connection exists.

Critics may charge, and rightly so, that Betty Luca's pleasant abduction experiences appear to be an aberration when compared to that of most abductees. Why should she be treated so differently? Most other abductees report an *unpleasant* experience comparable to being treated like laboratory animals.

Based upon all that has been revealed through Betty, I can only surmise the answer to this question. First, this is just what should be expected if indeed Betty has been especially chosen to show the world these truths. Secondly, the different emotional responses on the part of typical NDErs and UFO abductees could be attributed to two completely different purposes behind their experiences.

NDErs, like Betty, are each a living message both to themselves and to humankind that so-called physical death is not annihilation. Their ecstatic experiences are aborted welcomes to the next stage of our existence. Upon return, they are vibrant witnesses to what lies beyond through their accounts and changed lives.

Most abductees represent the physical side of the connection between the UFO phenomenon and the human death experience. On the one hand, the typical abduction experience appears undeniably linked to a genetic engineering program to produce greys who serve as workers or caretakers for the Elder-type entities.

If you will recall from *The Watchers,* Betty's grey captors used her to comfort a human surrogate mother. They told Betty that they themselves are mature human fetuses grown outside a human womb. They demonstrated this by taking a fetus taken from the surrogate mother that Betty comforted and placing it in an artificial womb.

In *The Watchers* it was pointed out that such a process is analogous to neoteny. This is the natural phenomenon of a fetal or a larval form of species that bypasses normal physical development and becomes sexually mature. Also, it would appear from the identical appearances of some greys that they may also be the product of cloning.

On the other hand, typical UFO abductees themselves appear to be going through some sort of grooming process for what lies beyond. They are visited, checked and operated on periodically, just as humans would do to a herd of animals being raised for a specific purpose. In addition to collecting sperm and ova for their genetics program, the Watchers appear to be somehow improving the stock of the human herd through means known only to them.

Human Health Concerns of Entities

Such articles as implanting monitoring devices, using punch biopsies, taking scrapings from fingernails, tongues and skin, obtaining urine and feces samples, and performing body and mind scans, seem to be related to our physical health as part of a selective breeding process.

The UFO phenomenon's concern with human health sometimes shows up unexpectedly in other ways. For example, abductee Whitley Strieber was exhorted by his abductors not to eat candy and other sugar-based food.[11] When he asked why, they told him that he would be shown the reason. Circumstances soon brought news of an abductee who had been visited by alien entities as she lay in her deathbed dying from uncontrollable sugar diabetes. It is interesting to note that sometimes this same concern for the health of abductees appears as a seeming off-key, nonsensical element of an otherwise typical UFO encounter. The following example is illustrative of this.

This case involved one of four women in an automobile who had a very close encounter with a UFO. She was interviewed by Dr. J. Allen Hynek, Director of the Center for UFO Studies (CUFOS). Later, the report appeared in the January/February 1983 issue of the *International UFO Reporter* published by CUFOS. The story initially made the front page of the *Atlantic News & Advertiser*, Hampton, New Hampshire. Excerpts follow:

> It is approximately 10:15 P.M. on the night of Thursday, September 30, 1982. Four local women are driving west on Exeter Road. A short distance past Hampton Machine Company, the driver of the car, Mary Ann Poland, 44, of Allson Drive in Seabrook, notices what she takes to be an airplane coming in low over the trees. "That airplane is flying very low," she remarks casually to her fellow companions.
>
> The other three women do not at first pay too much attention to Poland's remark until, that is, Poland shouts, "That's not an airplane! Look at it!"
>
> The four women then stare in amazement at the strange craft gliding in the sky above them at treetop level. The huge craft (later described as "big as a house") could be clearly seen in the night sky.... Its oval shape is easily discernible, as the entire craft is ringed with flashing red and white lights. "Stop the car!" Mary LaMontagne, 29, of P Street, Hampton Beach, yells from her limited vantage point in the back seat.

11. Strieber, 1988, pp. 148-149, 177.

> Poland begins to apply the brakes, but before she can come to a full stop, LaMontagne and Rose Messina, 25, also of P Street, hop out of the car, seemingly oblivious to the dangers of jumping from a moving vehicle. Poland and Nicky LeClair, 53, of Park Avenue in Hampton, watch in disbelief as their two friends vanish into the darkness up a nearby driveway. La Montagne and Messina, feeling totally without fear or apprehension, dash the length of the driveway.... They reach the edge of a patch of woods and then stare in awe as the inexplicable object of their attentions comes to a stop almost directly above them. Both women stand completely still, enthralled with the massive craft, its flashing lights, and a larger ray of light, which beams down "like a path to the sky."
>
> For a few brief seconds, LaMontagne and Messina watch the object, which hovers soundlessly so close above them, the only noise being the soft rustle of leaves in the wind. Then the craft begins to move again, sliding quietly away from them to the protective cover of the woods. In an instant it is gone, and the two awe-struck women suddenly realize that a porch light has been snapped on at the nearby house. They turn and run back to their anxious companions in the car.[12]

On the surface, this UFO sighting seems to be a typical Close Encounter of the First Kind (CE-I), but the story did not end there. Mary LaMontagne told the reporter, a personal friend and Dr. Hynek that while standing under the object she had received a telepathic message. (italics mine)

> *They want me to be healthy....* I sensed that it was OK and that they are not here to hurt us...that there are evil people down here, and they were going to do something about that problem.... I just know there is more, but I don't know when.[13]

The telepathic message seemed to be transmitted via the green beam of light that shone down upon them. As a result of her experience, Mary quit smoking after indulging in two and a half packs a day for the past fourteen years. The reporter added that "LaMontagne claims she had no desire to smoke, and her three friends are all equally amazed at her uncanny ability to quit cold turkey."[14]

Who would ever have suspected the reason for such a UFO sighting? If this woman wasn't completely open about her experience, it, like

---

12. Jenkins, November 23, 1982, p. 1.
13. Jenkins, November 23, 1982, p. 1.
14. Jenkins, November 23, 1982, p. 1.

probably others, would go unnoticed. Most people would hesitate to even relate a UFO close encounter. Few would be willing to confess that they had received a telepathic message about their health!

Why would UFO entities go so far out of the way to tell one woman to stop smoking because of health reasons? This question is just as puzzling as to why some people are sent back from death's door and told it is because they have a specific job to finish. Perhaps Mary has been selected out of the human herd for some special purpose that requires good health on her part. Perhaps Mary's health has a paraphysical/symbiotic effect upon the entities? Whatever the reason, which may be beyond our comprehension, it seems to be part of a constant interplay between life here and life in the hereafter. For if we take and integrate the total characteristics of the UFO and NDE phenomenon at full face value, the bottom line implication is that death may be the ultimate UFO abduction experience!

chapter sixteen

The Ultimate Abduction

> *When the long awaited solution to the UFO problem comes, I believe that it will prove to be not merely the next small step in the march of science, but a mighty and totally unexpected quantum jump.*[1]
>
> *J. Allen Hynek [1972]*

In the closing paragraphs of *The Watchers,* I posed a number of unanswered questions. Among them were the following:

> Several mysteries...still remain unexplained. Who are the mysterious tall, robed, human-appearing figures that are involved in UFO and near-death experiences? Are they our original ancestors from somewhere else in this vast universe? What is the complete meaning behind the Great Door being opened and available to all humankind? When will all abductees meet with each other?[2]

Little did I know when I penned the above words that I would be writing yet another book on the Lucas' experiences that would provide probable answers to these provocative questions. Let us first consider in some detail the possibilities for the origin of the robed humanoid entities, as well as the human race, because their source may possibly have common roots.

---

1. Hynek, 1972, p. 234.
2. Fowler, 1990, p. 349

Who Are They?

Are They Imagined?

This hypothesis suggests that both the UFO phenomenon and NDEs with their reports of humanoid entities are simply products of the human's mind. The suggested explanations for the UFO phenomena include hoaxes, misinterpretation of natural phenomena, misidentification of mundane objects and hallucinations caused by electrical effects on the brain generated by tectonic strains in the earths crust.

I personally cannot accept such explanations in the light of the evidence thus far collected for both UFO and NDE phenomena. There are just too many facets of either phenomenon that do not fit these valiant attempts to provide an "anything but" answer!

UFO reports are consistent regarding typical configurations, flight characteristics and generated effects upon living and inorganic matter. They have been recorded on film, radar and magnetic-detection devices, sometimes simultaneously with visual sightings. They have been sighted all over the world, in and out of the Earth's airspace and on or near the ground.

Official documents reveal conclusively that major governments have shown a great interest in UFOs on the grounds of national security and scientific inquiry. Although perhaps 80% may be explained away in terms of the above explanations, 20% still remain in the unknown category.

Interestingly enough, hoaxes and hallucinations caused by an electrical stimulation of the brain's temporal lobe at death are theories advanced for the origin of NDEs. Although I am not considered to be an expert in the field of NDEs, I nevertheless am very well read on the subject and have interviewed persons who have had such an experience.

It is significant to note that purely anecdotal studies at the grassroots level have now evolved into scientific studies conducted by members of the medical community. Many are convinced, based upon such studies, that the NDE is not a product of the imagination. Many reports indicate strongly that the person's essence actually leaves the body and is able to observe and describe activities both near and at a distance from the body during the initial phase of the experience.

The NDE accounts are remarkably consistent in both adults and children. Dr. Ring's studies reveal the existence of similar aftereffects in the lives of NDErs. I am personally convinced that NDEs are exactly what the experiencers believe them to be—an existence apart from the body that involves temporarily entering a dimension different from, but possibly co-existent with, our own plane of existence.

In conclusion, humanoid entities are an integral component of both the UFO and NDE experience. If UFO and NDE experiences cannot be successfully explained away as imaginative, neither can the humanoid entities that appear to control them.

Are They Extraterrestrial?

In order to properly address the possibility of humanoid extraterrestrials (ETs) visiting Earth, it is necessary to briefly describe how scientists believe the humanoid form of humans developed on Earth. What is the general consensus among scientists concerning the origin of *Homo sapiens?* The following will serve as an overview of their findings.

During my detailed studies of the evolution of the human species in preparation for a course that I teach on origins, I found that the family tree of all humans based upon fossil evidence has undergone drastic changes over the past few decades.

One of the more recent stabs at a family tree traces our lineage back to a small long-snouted bewhiskered mammal called *Plesiadapis.* It took to the trees about 70 million years ago and may have been the rootstock for primates.

A primate belongs to an order of mammals that includes lemurs, lorises, bushbabies, monkeys, apes and *Homo sapiens.* Primates have large brains, prehensile hands and five digits. The first primate to evolve from *Plesiadapis* about 18 million years ago was *Dryopithecus Africanus,* dubbed "Proconsul" by Mary Leakey.

Some theorize that the next evolutionary step upward was *Ramapithecus* about 9 million years ago. Its place as the missing link in our family tree is now in dispute between biologists and paleontologists. However, it may have been the first small ape to walk upright. Apes are thought to have split from the human line between 5 and 7 million years ago.

Next came small-brained hominids, dubbed *Australopithecines* (Southern Apes). An African fossil specimen of this type of hominid, named *Australopithecus afarensis* (dubbed Lucy), appears next in the conjectured family tree about 3.5 million years ago. This line then moves to *Homo Habilis* (2 million years ago) to *Homo Erectus* (between 1-1.5 million years ago) and to *Homo Sapiens Archaic* (about 500,000 years ago). There is a dispute whether the line continues directly to *Homo Sapiens Sapiens,* Cro-Magnon/Modern Human (35,000 years ago) or indirectly through *Homo Sapiens,* Neanderthal (40,000 years ago). Some believe that the Neanderthal evolved separately and was an evolutionary dead end.

Now, what does this discussion about the origin of our species have to do with humanoids observed during UFO and NDEs? It basically narrows down to whether the humanoid form could have evolved on a planet other than the Earth. Let us briefly discuss such a possibility.

When CE-III first were reported, scientists scoffed at the reports of humanoid creatures. Carl Sagan voiced the opinion of most scientists:

> It would be most remarkable if four and a half billion years of independent biological evolution on...two planets had produced identical end results, even if their environments were not so dissimilar.[3]

Of course, it is always a possibility that some universal law (for want of a better word) may govern the course of evolution everywhere and that humanoid life forms are the ultimate result. If so, such a fact would short-circuit all that I am about to say. But, for the sake of argument, let us take the above statement made by Sagan to be true.

Interestingly enough, Sagan made the above statement at the criminal trial of one Helmut Winckler, who, among alleged criminal activities, claimed to meet a very human-appearing man from another planet. Believe it or not, Sagan was called into the courtroom as a surprise witness to disclaim Winckler's remarks on the basis of the same type of scientific findings we have just discussed that relate to the origin of human life on Earth.[4]

The point of this whole discussion is that we do have some fossil evidence that provides a rough picture of human evolution from primates over millions of years. Based upon fossil evidence, our ancestral home appears to have been Africa rather than some extra-solar planet. Nowhere do we find evidence that our ancestors were brought here intact from some extraterrestrial source. However, there are hints that our evolution may have been aided and abetted by an ET source.

It is at least possible that the very origin of life itself on our planet could have originated from humanoid ET entities. If that were the case, evolution may have eventually produced creatures in the own image of those ETs either by the natural course of evolution or by aided interfer-

---

3. Sagan, 1966, p. 16.
4. Sagan, 1966, p. 13.

ence on their part from time to time. How could one possibly come to such a seemingly way-out hypothesis?

In *The Watchers* I pointed out that Drs. Francis Crick and James Watson, who had uncovered the structure of DNA, had come to a startling conclusion. They proposed that life on Earth may have sprung from tiny organisms from a distant planet—sent here by a spaceship as part of a deliberate act of seeding. They based this premise on the fact that DNA is too complex for it to have developed naturally on Earth and on the fact that there exists only one genetic code for all of Earth's living organisms. The force of their argument is that if living things sprang to life in some great primeval soup, as biologists theorize, it is incredible that living things with a number of different genetic codes do not exist. In brief, a single genetic code seems to be entirely compatible with the notion that all life evolved from an unearthly source.

If we accept Crick's conclusion that all of Earth's life forms came about from seeding by ET intelligences, then it is much easier to believe that these same intelligences continued to have an interest in their handiwork. But, what about the human family tree?

First, it would be only fair to point out that proposed family trees are just that—*proposed.* One of the main problems encountered in forming such a tree is the scarcity and incompleteness of the historical hominid specimens.

Another problem is the missing fossil record for apes. Apes appeared in the fossil record more than 25 million years ago and a progression in evolution took place until about 8-9 million years ago. At this juncture, the fossil record for apes disappears into nothingness. Incredibly, modern orangutans, chimpanzees and gorillas simply appear on the modern scene! Their fossil record for the past 5-7 million years has yet to be discovered.

Other important discoveries continue to be made that challenge a simplistic inevitable and inviolate upward route from specific primates to *Homo sapiens.* A recent problem deals with a conflict between fossil and genetic evidence relating to human origins. Such genetic evidence may be pertinent to our discussion.

As we have seen, paleontologists have proposed a human family tree on the basis of limited fossil evidence. Such evidence has suggested that *Homo sapiens* evolved from archaic forebears around the world over the past million or so years. It indicated that the evolutionary split between humans and apes occurred as long ago as 18-25 million years, depending upon which family tree you accept. But, on the other hand, genetic studies indicate that human and ape genes are too similar for this split to have taken place more than several million years ago! Genetic studies also appear to lead to the startling conclusion that our species can be traced along maternal lines of descent to an African woman who lived about 200,000 years ago! Some nicknamed this postulated woman Eve!

In addition to these recent shattering discoveries, we are still left with the Neanderthal/Cro-Magnon problem. As we noted in a recent family tree, paleontologists are still at a loss regarding how to link the Neanderthals and Cro-Magnons. Some believe that there is no apparent link between the two. Neanderthal's development was too far below the fully human Cro-Magnon who seemed to have appeared relatively suddenly. The gap between them seemed to be too wide and the jump too quick in the fossil record. Is this yet another hint of ET interference with our evolution?

One can see that the road leading to *Homo sapiens* is rougher than some older textbooks would have had us believe. Such theories and problems as described above may indicate that humanoids may have indeed developed elsewhere than Earth, and that we in some fashion are their progeny. In line with this reasoning, we will close this particular discussion by observing in another way the evolution of life on Earth.

It is difficult for us to think of time in terms of billions or even of millions of years. Therefore, let's compress time into units that we use on a daily basis. We will start with the very first appearance of life on Earth in the form of blue algae about 3 billion years ago.

If we superimposed 3 billion years of development between algae and Homo sapiens onto a 24-hour clock, the entire history of mammals would occupy just one hour. Humans would appear just a few seconds before midnight! We are literally the new kid on the block on planet Earth.

Now, let us draw our attention to the period that the ever-evolving human line of development has dwelled on the Earth. This amounts to less than 2.5 million years. Let us compress this amount of time into a period of just one year. Having done so, we would have to move from January 1 to December 28 before reaching the beginning of our own historical era. This era, a brief 6-10,000 years, is nestled in the last two days of the year.

It is now December 31. Babylon, China, Egypt and Rome rose and fell in the early morning hours. Socrates, Plato and Aristotle lived around 9:30 A.M. At 8:57 P.M., Columbus discovered America. At 9:16 P.M., Copernicus proved that the Earth orbited the sun. At 10:27 P.M.,

Watts perfected the steam engine. At 11:09 P.M., Darwin formulated the theory of evolution. At 11:21 P.M., Fermi split the atom. At 11:41 P.M., the first computer was built. Between 11:43 and 11:48 P.M., humans developed the airplane, the liquid fuel rocket, the satellite and the manned spacecraft. At 11:49 P.M., a man landed on the moon. It is now about 11:50 P.M., the science and technology curve is climbing almost straight up. Where is it leading us? To the planets? To the stars?

Think a bit about the above scenario. For over 11 1/2 months, humans slowly grope upward along their evolutionary path. Agriculture does not even begin until December 28th! Then, relatively speaking, civilization suddenly appears in Sumer. Is this evidence of ET influence?

In *The Watchers,* I noted that Carl Sagan suggested that Sumer's abrupt appearance as an advanced civilization may have been attributed to contact with an ET race. Sagan stated:

> We do not know where the Sumerians came from. Their language was strange; it had no cognates with any known Indo-European, Semitic, or other language, and is understood only because a later people, the Akkadians, compiled extensive Sumerian-Akkadian dictionaries.[5]

Sagan then went on to quote from Sumerian legends that told of being contacted and civilized by unearthly entities. Mentioned earlier in this book is the fact that this hypothesis has been developed and published in a number of previously mentioned books by Zechariah Sitchin.

Are the humanoid entities under discussion related to ETs that influenced life on our planet in the distant past and continue to do so today in the guise of the UFO phenomenon? How would such entities relate to the NDE phenomenon? These are questions that must be addressed if a true connection exists between UFOs and NDEs. This will be a matter of further discussion later, but for now, let us move on to the next possibility for the possible origin of these humanoid entities.

Are They Human Time Travelers?

The notion of the future possibility of traveling through time has been entertained since H.G. Wells wrote *The Time Machine: An Invention* in 1895. One of the more recent tales about time travel was the popular movie *Back to the Future* and its sequels.

---

5. Sagan, 1966, p. 456.

Compared to books and papers espousing the ET hypothesis for UFOs, very little has been written on the possibility that UFOs represent Earth-born human beings coming from the future to visit us.

In *The Watchers* I mentioned and quoted a paper on time travel published in the *MUFON UFO Journal* by Dr. Michael Swords.[6] Dr. Swords is MUFON's consultant on the history of science and technology. By profession, he is a professor of natural science at Western Michigan University. He used the concept of neoteny to explain a sudden leap in structural difference between the human and his nearest genetic cousin, the chimpanzee. I used the same concept to support the greys' claim to Betty that they were human fetuses grown in an artificial womb. Neoteny is that natural phenomenon where a fetal or larval form of species bypasses its normal physical development and becomes sexually mature. Therefore, the greys, I concluded, were in actuality mature human fetuses.

Dr. Swords originally used the same argument to support his theory that the greys are a future form of *Homo sapiens* who have traveled back in time to visit our present civilization. In building his hypothesis, he proposed that human origin and the phenomenon of neoteny might be intimately linked.

Swords theorized that neoteny could explain why humans and chimpanzees have nearly the same structural genes, yet have quite large structural differences in their body makeup. He pointed out that such differences between human and apes are much closer when a comparison is made between human forms and embryonic ape forms. Thus, he concluded, *Homo sapiens* might very well be in a physical sense, a fetal ape which has become sexually mature.

Dr. Swords then went on to postulate that in the distant future, due to technical complexity increases in the world, the pressure for selecting greater intelligence in our offspring might become inescapable. The genetic switch to the next neotenous jump in human evolution might be artificially produced through a genetics engineering program.

He proposed that human fetuses removed and grown in artificial wombs might look very much like the greys reported today. Such a future program would dramatically narrow the genetic diversity of the human species, just as it does today in agriculture. Thus, the greys might be future humans coming back in time to harvest the cells of their subjects.

---

6. Swords, February 1985.

Swords concludes that such a need to revitalize and expand a future gene bank would explain the extreme interest of the greys in harvesting of sperm and ova during the examination of human abductees.

Dr. Swords admits, however, at the conclusion of his paper that his hypothesis is based primarily upon the appearance of the aliens and their abilities. He states that:

> In sum, the idea has within it potential answers for all the (most) common objections to UFO-anecdotal descriptions. But it brings up a pair of very large objections in their place, namely:
>
> 1. How in the world do you travel in time, and is it even imaginable in a rational universe?
> 2. This theory is essentially *post hoc*, and those few things which it might predict are things which are likely never to be testable. This unfortunately concerns the theory scientifically, and consigns it ever to be a speculation—except for some lucky person with personal experience and internal knowledge of what may be going on.
>
> Who knows? Perhaps as the UFO phenomenon goes on, some bits and pieces of concrete evidence may piece together to unexpectedly support one of the several leading theories, including this one.[7]

The only book recently published which goes into great detail in developing a hypothesis for the time-travel origin of the UFO phenomenon is entitled *Visitors From Time* by UFO researcher Marc Davenport.[8] Marc does an excellent job in collecting and correlating data from all over the world to undergird the proposition that UFO entities are able to manipulate and travel through time. I would recommend purchasing this book for those interested in the further studying of the time travel theory.

Estimate of the Situation

Betty and Bob came back from their abductions with detailed accounts of their experiences with humanoid entities that carried them away. It is now time to record the accounts of what NDErs claim to

---

7. Swords, February 1985, p. 13.
8. Davenport, 1994.

have observed beyond encountering a radiant being of light that meets and sends them back to their bodies.

How do NDErs describe where they were taken? Who else do they report seeing? What do they say? These questions must be answered to obtain an overview of the UFO/NDE connection for final analysis.

Description of Death's Foyer

The Omega Project	Ring	
I felt as if I had been in another dimension, maybe spiritually many, many light years away from this planet and felt like an alien back here. After this experience...it seemed as if I was a stranger living on another planet. I felt so different...have never truly felt the same since this incident happened.... No longer is this Earth my home.[a]		

a. Ring, 1992, pp. 106, 107.

Life After Life	Moody	
I could...see something which one could take to be buildings. The whole thing was permeated with the most gorgeous light. I suddenly found myself in a rolling field. It was beautiful, and everything was an intense green—a color unlike anything on Earth. There was light—beautiful, uplifting light—all around me. The next thing I knew it seemed as if I were on a ship or a small vessel sailing to the other side of a large body of water.[a]		

a. Moody, 1976, p.76, 73, 74.

Reflections on Life After Life	Moody	
All of a sudden I was somewhere else. There was a gold-looking light, everywhere. Beautiful, I couldn't find a source anywhere. It was just all around, coming from everywhere.... I seemed to be in a countryside with streams, grass, and trees, mountains. Off in the distance...I could see a city. There were buildings—separate buildings. They were gleaming bright...sparkling water, fountains...a city of light I guess would be the way to say it. Well, it's a place.... It's really beautiful, but you just can't describe it.... There is a river...flowers and everything.[a]		

a. Moody, 1977, p. 16, 17.

The Omega Project	Ring	
I...was looking out of a round window and seeing the blackest, blackest with tiny white sparkles. I later realized I was experiencing deep space.... I turned my gaze from the window to my left. There was a bright white light directly above me with...seven thin tall figures around me. I later realized I was on some kind of operating table.... All of a sudden, I was tumbling head over heels (figuratively—as I was out of my body) and saw the Earth...land masses, changing, getting closer and closer, not unlike an airplane crashing, [traveling at] unbelievable speed, and finally falling from the couch to the floor.[a]		

a. Ring, 1992, p. 109.

Taking these descriptions at face value, NDErs are brought to a place similar to Earth, but in another dimension. Although in an out-of-body state, the NDEr is just as *physical* in this realm or dimension as the trees, flowers, grass and buildings around them. The last description noted might as well have been a description by Betty gazing out of the cylindrical space ship's windows at the star-studded sky! Even Dr. Ring admits that this particular experience would be hard to differentiate from a UFO OBE abduction experience. He has a number of cases on file similar to this particular one which, as mentioned earlier, he calls NDEs with a mixed motif because of their similarity to UFO encounters.

Greeters at Death's Foyer

Another common thread running through hundreds of recorded NDEs is an encounter with family members or friends who have previously died. They, like the Elders that Betty and Bob have encountered, often are wearing white robes!

The Omega Project	Ring	
I see this guy with a long robe.... I do not know him, but have the feeling he is one of my grandfathers. They have both died before I was born.[a]		

a. Ring, 1992, p. 101.

Life After Life	Moody	
I recognized my grandmother and a girl I had known when I was in school, and many other relatives and friends.... I felt that they had come to protect or guide me. It was almost as if I were coming home, and they were there to greet or to welcome me. I had the feeling of everything light and beautiful.[a]		

a. Moody, 1976, p.55-56.

Life After Life	Moody	
Bob had been killed.... Bob was standing there...not in the physical form, yet just as clearly, his looks, everything.... It was kind of a clear body. Instantly from the other side appeared my Uncle Carl, who had died many years earlier.[a]		

a. Moody, 1976, p.55-56, 76.

Recollections of Death	Sabom	
"How can this be?"...My mind was saying, "But I can't be seeing Daddy and talking to him—he's dead." ...Yet I could see him perfectly. I could hardly wait to get conscious so that I could tell my mother that I had seen my father. My particular company lost 42 dead. All 42 of those guys were there.... They didn't want to go back. That was the basic tone of our communication...that we were all happy right where we were. My older brother, who had been dead since I was a young fellow...patting me on the shoulder, saying, "It's entirely up to you.... If you want to stay and you don't want to be back in your body, and you see how bad shape it's in, you can stay, and I'll be right by your side and everything is going to be fine." There were all my relatives, my grandmother, my grandfather, my father, my uncle who had recently committed suicide. They all came towards me and greeted me.... My grandparents were dressed...all in white and they had a hood over their heads. Two men met me.... They said, "We're here to show you the way...." They were both dressed the same, like a khaki uniform, but that's kind of hazy.[a]		

a. Sabom, 1982, pp. 22, 23, 47, 48, 48, 49.

Transformed by the Light	Morse	
I remember seeing a light.... Suddenly hands were reaching to me, and I saw my grandparents. The hands and my grandparents weren't just part of the light, they were the light...my grandparents who had been dead for several years.[a]		

a. Morse, 1992, p. 4.

Greeters' Message to NDErs

Those who greet NDErs, whether relatives, strangers or the loving being or beings of light typically give them the same basic message. Either they are given the choice to stay or they are arbitrarily commanded to go back to their body because it is not their time. The reasons given for sending them back are intriguing. Let us examine some typical examples.

The Omega Project	Ring	
It is not time yet.... You have work to do.[a]		

a. Ring., 1992, p. 101.

Life After Life	Moody	
Go back. Your work on Earth has not been completed. Go back now.[a]		

a. Moody, 1976, p. 76.

Recollections of Death	Sabom	
We'll see you later, but not this time. We're here to show you the way.... If you do not wish to go, we've got to get. Don't be concerned. We'll be back for you. And a voice, a clear voice, said, "You can't go yet. You have unfinished business." And I hear a voice say, "Go back!"...and whoever spoke said my work on Earth wasn't over yet, that I had to go back to complete it.... All I hear was his voice; it was loud, thundering, just like a clap of thunder coming out of nowhere.[a]		

a. Sabom, 1982, p. 54.

Transformed by the Light	Morse	
They said I had solved most of my problems and could now go either way. That meant I could either stay with them in the light or go back to my body. It was up to me, and it wasn't absolutely necessary to stay with them.[a]		

a. Morse, 1992, p. 4.

It is most intriguing that many NDErs are told to return to their bodies because either they have not yet finished their task or they have not yet solved their problems. In either case, it implies that the persons being addressed have unfinished business to attend to before entering the world of light.

In other instances, NDErs are simply told to return because it is not time for them to come. In others, they are simply given the choice to stay or go. All of the above scenarios imply that the greeters at death's door are fully aware of the identity, given task and death date of the NDEr.

Let us now consider what we have learned from the experiences of the Lucas and near-death survivors. If indeed, an intimate connection exists between UFOs and NDEs as the evidence suggests, how does it correlate with the possibilities of ETs and time travelers?

It is quite apparent, if we pool all the evidence together relating to the similarities between the Lucas' reported experiences and the reports brought back by NDErs, that the white-robed entities reported by both parties bear a striking resemblance to one another. This similarity not only involves their physical appearance, but as we have seen in the preceding chapter, many other facets of their nature as well.

No longer do we have to take into consideration a parallel development of humanoid life forms on an extra-solar planet. It may very well be that they coexist with us, but in another plane of existence where time as we know it does not exist.

Is it possible that they are us? Is what we call physical death just another step in human evolution? Have our ancestors gone on ahead of us and continued their existence and evolution in a world beyond our physical senses?

The entities encountered by NDErs are human in appearance and, like humans, wear clothes. Their environment is similar to that of the Earth's except everything is bathed in light and appears more real than real. Our Earth's environment is but a shadow of what the NDErs report.

That clothes, buildings and even space craft are reported by some NDErs indicates that they are describing what appears to be another physical-like civilization rather than some wispy spirit world.

The mind-boggling ability of both UFO and NDE entities to know so much about us indicates that there is an on-going interface between our worlds usually unseen by human eyes. It makes one think, "Who am I? What am I? What is humanity?" The entities may have hinted at our initial nature when they told Betty:

> They keep seed from man and woman so the human form will not be lost.
>
> They are the caretakers of nature and natural forms.... They have been caring for it since man's beginning. They watch the spirit in all things.
>
> They are the caretakers and are responsible. And this is why they have been taking the form from man.

What is meant by a form? Isn't it the physical shape of a thing or person—a body design? Have they created workers from human and earthly other-life forms to carry out specific tasks on our plane of existence? Are the reports of reptilian and insect-like humanoids actually genetically related to insects and reptiles here on Earth? Such a product of super-advanced genetic engineering is possible as "nearly identical molecular mechanisms define body shapes in all animals."[9]

The gray Watchers (mature human fetuses) told Betty that they are being used to assure that the human and natural forms will not be lost. They also appear to be responsible for monitoring the spirit or life-essence of the living forms that dwell on Earth. This raises some very mind-boggling questions in the light of all that we have discussed about the striking UFO/NDE connection.

Could it be that the UFO phenomenon and NDEs are controlled by an advanced civilization existing in another dimension peopled in part by human beings who have entered that dimension through the death process? Could it be that the human-like Elders are what we will evolve to be in a future existence?

Are human beings in this plane of existence a larval form for this civilization? Is this civilization peopled by what we are to become? Do

---

9. McGinnis, February 1994, p. 58.

we return again and repeat the process as part of a constant inter-balanced exchange between matter and energy?

Are UFO abductions and animal mutilations the visible tip of environmental monitoring and breeding programs? Are such programs being carried out by intelligences who are dependent upon us for their survival in a humanoid form in another dimension—a paraphysical symbiosis?

Are other kinds of earthly life forms translated into their dimension upon so-called physical death? If so, it is no wonder that the UFO entities encountered by abductees and NDErs are concerned about the environmental problems humankind have created on Earth. We may be poisoning and destroying their very source of existence. Remember the greys' reason for harvesting ova, sperm and human fetuses?

Betty: And they're telling me that they're doing this because the human race will become sterile by the pollution and the bacteria and the terrible things that are on the Earth.... And, they are taking the seeds so that the human form will not be lost—that they, too, are made of the same substance.... The fetuses become them—like them. They said they're Watchers...and they keep seed from man and woman so the human form won't be lost.

The above hypothesis of course cannot be proved. It will sound outrageous to those who see the UFO phenomenon as strictly a nuts-and-bolts phenomenon. It will seem equally outrageous to those who consider the NDE phenomenon strictly psychological or physical in nature.

I am sure that many of my peers and readers will think that many years with the subject have adversely affected me mentally! Nonetheless, this hypothesis certainly goes a long way in explaining the paraphysical reality of the UFO phenomenon and humankind, which is supported by an overwhelming amount of anecdotal testimony.

It also could explain the dissimilar emotional reactions on the part of the typical UFO abductee and NDE—frightful and joyful reactions respectively.

On the one hand, UFO abductions and animal mutilations may represent house calls by breeders and/or veterinarians checking up on the health of future forms that will be the progenitors of their civilization. Some entities may have good bedside manners and some may not be quite so nice to their patients. Different human beings may be singled out and treated differently from one another just as we raise lower life forms for different purposes.

NDErs, on the other hand, are the finished product and are welcomed wholeheartedly (although prematurely) as newborn babes to their home. They are welcomed not by the greys, but by the same types of beings that the Lucas encountered during their shared OBE abduction—Elders, light beings and of course, in Betty's case, the One.

It would also explain abductee reports of being trained by alien entities during their abduction experience. (Who knows, perhaps while some of us sleep at night, our essence goes to school!) Why would they be subliminally trained on foreign instruments for seemingly nonearthly applications, except for some future responsibility in the world to come? This is perhaps why some NDErs are sent back to finish a specific task that will in some way benefit them and their own future progression in the reported world of light.

Indeed, such a world may, like our current plane, just be another step in our paraphysical evolution. The size and nature of the universe that we sense as physical creatures of time seems beyond our comprehension. We may be seeing only a small part of it.

The Light-Beings' Treatise on Life & Death

One would think that if the above hypothesis is correct or near the mark, then the entities might specifically say more about human death and afterlife to the Lucas other than by the object lessons shown them and others. They have. The problem is that in the past I had no reason to ask the Lucas if they had.

However, the subject did come up inadvertently when Fred Max was questioning Bob Luca about his shared OBE abduction with Betty in 1978. During this segment of Bob's experience, he was with one of the white-robed Elders waiting for Betty to be returned to him. The following is a transcript of this portion of the hypnotic regression session:

Bob: ...This is a privilege, you know, for someone that hasn't advanced this much to be here. To be here and observe this is a privilege. Normally people that are at my stage of development would [not be here].

Fred: How do you know that?

Bob: Because the...two big guys told me.

Fred: Do they tell you together or separately?

Bob: *[pause]* It's hard to tell, they're...almost like twins.... It's almost like what one thinks, the other one thinks at the same time.

...I'm not sure of who says what.... I don't think they're talking. I think...it's just thought.... I'm not sure.

Fred: What *form* is Betty in? Is she a light form or a solid form?

Bob: No, he said that...she was one of those people, one of those...ghosts or...light people.

Fred: Light people. Did you ask this or was it offered?

Bob: No, they told me when they were explaining to me that...I'm not that advanced.

Fred: OK, but, what I want some help with is hypothetically, I could pop in your home at Meriden at any moment and you have to have some measure of time that you were not present. Is that true?

Bob: I was present and Betty was present in Meriden, but Betty was present and I was present in that plane, also.

Fred: OK, so if I were to have hypothetically walked in and jostled you about or shaken you, whatever, you would have been primarily returned to this plane?

Bob: That's true. It would be done in an instant—a flash of an eye. You see, the body...is the shell...the real you is the light person inside—the motivation, the light force, the part that does not die, the part that goes on and on. That's the light person. That's the real you! Not the body, not...the part that you see. I guess I'm getting a little education here.

Fred: The spirit?

Bob: Oh-h-h, *[sighs]* I feel better knowing that. And, you know...that part doesn't die.

Bob's shocking answer was not what any of us had expected. Later he would tell me that he was utterly amazed to hear what he had said when he listened to a tape of the session.

Fred: Where does that part go from here?

Bob: That part...advances through stages. Our existence here...that we know of now, is only one step of many in a long, learning process. This process, the human mind is unable to comprehend just as it is unable to comprehend the endlessness of the universe in space. It is a never-ending process. It will always be and has always been.

Fred: OK. Can you look back over your existences, as if you could see more, so much more? Can you look back and see where you've been? See another existence?

Bob: The spirit can, because it has existed in different bodies at different times.

Fred: OK. Can we go to another time or existence for a few moments?

Bob: *[sighs]* I...don't think that's a good thing to do.

Fred: Why?

Bob: Because to go back to another time, another existence, means to go through the death process. And that process sometimes can be very traumatic depending upon where you were and what happened before. And it's not that you can't go back, it's that I don't think that I would like to, because I have an idea that I would not like what I would see.

Fred: Can you go into the future?

Bob: The future is not to be known by us, as it is something that can be given at times, when it's deemed proper, but it is not our decision to determine when that time will be. It is the decision of the Elders, those who watch over, make that decision and...help us if necessary. An example would be...to give a personal warning that would enable them to avoid a bad situation. On occasions like that, people are given a glimpse into a future event...on the scale of an earthquake or a volcanic eruption. The person that is given this information may make it known, and often they are not believed. But people miss the point. Oftentimes, these people are given that information because at that time, there may be thousands of people involved. The message may be to only one or two people—to listen, to believe—and for that reason, all through the course of their life, by not being in that place at that time or whatever...they may complete their life cycle in the manner that they are supposed to.... Accidents...do happen, but yet those who have a destiny to fulfill, if they're not to leave this plane before this destiny is fulfilled—they will be given a way out, a way to avoid a bad situation such as not getting on an airplane that they think may crash, not being in a town where an earthquake is about to happen, not being on a boat that will sink. In these cases, a glimpse of the future is given for a specific person, not for all. But, those who are to respond are made aware.

This was getting to be a bit much. We wondered where on earth Bob was suddenly getting such erudite information. It seemed to be beyond his own world view of things. So, Fred suddenly blurted out the question we all had on our minds. The answer was more than we had bargained for and raised even more difficult philosophical and theological questions.

Fred: How do you have this information?

Bob: This is my teaching from these tall light beings. It's imparted to me, and I don't even know—it's just given. I don't know how it was. I didn't have to read anything. They didn't really physically say anything. It's just an understanding that I've been given.

Fred: How often do they talk to you when you are home? Do they know where you are or see you?

Bob: *[sighs]* They know and can find anyone at any given time, anywhere. This is determined through the spirit, not through technology, and certainly not through road maps.

Fred: Are you constantly being monitored?

Bob: We are all constantly being monitored. Nothing that you do in your life escapes them. It's just like...a recorder. Your life, your existence on the Earth plane, is all recorded from the time you are born until the time you die; everything is there. How you react, what you do during your life. Even your innermost thoughts, feelings and emotions. They're all recorded. It's all part of the process. This process determines how rapidly you will advance and what your next step or phase will be, what teaching you need to receive, what hardship you must undergo to deepen your understanding. It's all recorded.

Fred: Are you saying that some level of life is fair?

Bob: Life is wonderfully fair. Those of us in this plane just don't understand it. When you see a small child that becomes ill and dies, people weep, they cry, they grieve. They grieve for themselves. The child does not need to be here any longer. The child has already advanced, much as you would skip a grade in school. It is not a bad thing. People that are sick or injured...their faith is being tested. The reactions are recorded. This determines whether or not they need more teaching. They need to advance spiritually. Can they go to the next step? Is there more they must learn? When the physical body leaves, you do not die, people need understanding. The ones that grieve for the ones...who pass on are grieving for themselves cause they will miss that person. The person has not died. The essence of the person has not died. The physical body has died, and that is not the person. *[sigh]* Life is stages, like a never-ending school.

Fred: If they can, say, have you come visit them, and they can have you see more, do they take people...like some of the world leaders who aren't as friendly, like Hussein? And do they give him the greater view so that he that he can say then, "Oh, my goodness, if I saw more, what better could I do."

Bob: People like Hussein?

Bob frowned. He obviously did not recognize the relevance of Hussein's name as he was reliving a 1978 experience. But, he assumed Hussein must be an evil leader if Fred said so.

Bob: The...understanding is needed. Without those who are detrimental to society, those who are advanced cannot be tested. Hussein serves a necessary purpose. Evil serves a necessary purpose. Without all evil to overcome, the righteous could not advance and triumph. It's all...part of the system—I guess you could say—the order of things, just as the planet must rotate about the sun. There must be a degree of evil. There must be sorrow. There must be suffering, because without these things, there is no advancement and nothing to overcome. *[speaks emphatically]*

Fred had been slowly losing his professional non-emotional detachment with his subject. It was obvious that Bob's discourse was getting more disturbing to him by the moment. It would get no better.

Fred: Are you saying that evil is *positive?*

Bob: Evil on an earthly plane is the negative aspect. Evil on the larger plane is part of the overall plan that gives us all a chance to advance and rise above it. Everyone in the earthly plane has the ability to do evil. Those that don't—those that fight evil, those that learn and overcome evil, those who have advanced—have gained tremendously in [the] next realm. Everything in nature...has a plus and a minus, a light and dark, a negative and positive, a good and bad. It must be, for without some content of evil, there can be no good. There can be no growth.

At this point, Fred completely lost his composure. His voice was now filled with emotion.

Fred: We *need* evil for good? *[sounds incredulous]*

Bob: We do not need evil for good. We need choice. The creator gave us choice. We cannot use that choice unless we have two choices to make. Evil or good. It is so simple. It's beautiful. But there must be evil to be the choice. It's simple. I don't know how to explain it. Evil on this plane must exist. *[with emphasis]*

Fred: *[taken aback by all of this]* I guess I need more understanding though. I'm feeling that as we evolve as a civilization—won't there be more good, more kindness?

Bob: That would only be due to those who are advancing. And, yes, eventually there will be. But, there will be some very distressing times before that happens.

Fred: What do you mean—distressing times?

Bob: As the population of this planet increases, there will be those that *have.* There will be those who are greedy. There will be those that have not and are starving or will starve. There will be much dissension. There will more conflict. The world, this plane, is not perfect. There will be evil.

Fred: Always?

Bob: There will come a time when evil will be wiped away. That time is not close at hand.

Fred: When that time comes, will our growth cease?

Bob: When that time comes, our growth will not cease. Rather, we will advance into further planes of existence. Right now, the...type of society that you speak of is not possible.

Fred: Because?

Bob: Because the people of this plane as a whole are not very advanced spiritually. Technology is advancing. Spirituality, unfortunately, is not keeping pace. Man is developing many things which are harmful to him, which he does not understand. Man needs spiritual growth badly.

Fred: Where do animals fit in?

Bob: Man will be very surprised to find where animals fit in. I told you: All that is done is recorded, and many foolish people think the harm they've done to animals will not count. It will. All that the Creator's made is not to be taken lightly. And the most lowly to the most magnificent, much is to be learned.

Fred: Do animals evolve?

Bob: Animals exist on more than one plane for a reason. They do not evolve as human beings. The human spirit, or the spirit, is the ultimate creation.... There is nothing above that in all the things that have been created. This is the Creator's masterpiece. The...spirit goes on and on. The spirit can evolve.

It can overcome evil. The spirit...gets closer and closer. The whole idea of advancing is to get closer and closer to the Creator. That is the ultimate goal. The spirit can neither be harmed nor improved. The only thing it can do is advance and grow. *[Pause]* It's a very beautiful thing.

Fred, completely taken aback by Bob's simultaneous answers to such far-reaching questions, decided to go for broke and ask the ultimate question.

Fred: Define the Creator.

Bob: That is like asking a person to define to you the length and breadth and depth of space, or the universe. It is not within this mind to comprehend all that the Creator is.

What Bob was reportedly told by the Elders during subliminal education is directly applicable to the discussion that immediately preceded it. It confirms what religions have been teaching about the immortality of the soul for centuries gone by. Indeed, aerial phenomena and the entities associated with religion may be yet another manifestation of the intelligences behind the UFO and NDE phenomena.

The UFO/NDE phenomena, especially in the light of the Lucas' astounding revelatory experiences, indicate that these intelligences are telling us that they come from where we are going. Death, in essence, is the *ultimate* abduction experience!

chapter seventeen

Repercussions!

I...regard the UFO phenomenon as a physical manifestation of a form of consciousness...alien to humans but...able to coexist with us on the Earth. When...a UFO is visible to us in the reality of everyday life, I think it constitutes both a physical entity with mass, inertia, volume and energy, and a window toward another mode of reality.[1]

Jacques Vallée

What on earth have I written? That was my reaction as I sat back and pondered both the contents of this book and the extensive evidence that supports its shocking conclusion. What will my family and church friends think? How would I accommodate such a revelation into my already overworked expanding Christian worldview?

How will my peers in ufology react? Will they think that I am a theologian in a UFO researcher's clothing, propagating the faith? I trust not. I am doing my utmost to present an unbiased approach to the paraphysical and theological components of UFO experiences.

As a saving grace, however, I would remind my readers that this book, like *The Watchers,* has been based upon a "what if" premise. Its conclusion is based upon taking the evidence within its covers at full face value.

In addition to providing a summary of this evidence, I will use this chapter to discuss societal reactions to UFOs and an afterlife. This will provide both the reader and myself with an idea of how the hypothesis presented in this book might be received. Lastly, I will then present

1. Vallée, 1990, p. 144.

some final closing thoughts concerning my long-time involvement with the Andreasson case.

Recapitulation

In Part I, "Paraphysical Paradigms," we encountered the dual nature of the UFO phenomenon and entities head-on. As Jacques Vallée stated in the opening quote to this chapter, we are faced with a physical manifestation of a form of consciousness that travels to and fro from another mode of reality. The entities can instantly transfer this inter-dimensional ability to human beings at will through an OBE.

Part II and its pertinent parallels provided a number of discussions relating to the experiences of the Lucas. We traced belief in paraphysical beings called the Watchers back to the beginning of civilization. Alternative explanations for segments of Betty's experiences were explored, but not proven, in "Memories or Mirages." "Plausible Precedents" and "Correlations" provided strong circumstantial evidence for the reality of their experiences.

Part III provided evidence linking the UFO phenomenon and the near-death experience (NDE) together. This evidence included: A detailed comparison of the content and psychological aftereffects of the OBE abduction and NDE; statistics from Dr. Ring's *Omega Project;* and documentation of the UFO entities' relationship with the time of human death. This data, coupled with the uncanny similarity between UFO entities and NDE's entities provided evidence for phenomenon prognosis: The UFO abduction experience and the NDE are different sides of the same paraphysical coin! As they often say: If it walks like a duck, quacks like a duck and looks like a duck—it's a duck, folks! Thus, I am convinced that there is no other explanation (barring alien deception) that UFOs and their entities come from behind death's Great Door.

Reactions

General Public

Because of the fantastic suggestion that UFOs are related to human afterlife, it behooves us to examine society's reaction to such a bizarre hypothesis. Since such an astounding assertion as this has never been made, we are forced to make an assessment based upon public reaction to UFOs and an afterlife in general.

To UFOs

In March 1987, a Gallup poll indicated that "Only one-third of the public deny existence of UFOs, extraterrestrial life."[2] UFO research Robert Durant notes that:

> Another way of putting this is that there are three adult Americans who believe that "UFOs are real" for every two skeptics. With only one out of three citizens saying "nonsense" and the rest either believers or fence-sitters, one wonders about the reason for the contempt with which the subject is treated by...politicians and media executives.[3]

To an Afterlife

What does the general public believe about life after death? Again, we turn to Gallup for statistics published in 1982.[4] The results of the poll are summarized below.

> In his national poll, 53% of the general population of the United States said they believe in Hell...66%...said they believe in "a heaven where people who have led good lives are eternally rewarded."[5]

As mentioned earlier in this book, a Gallup poll conducted in 1982 indicated that eight million Americans believed that they had experienced an NDE. George Gallup admitted that this was a conservative estimate, with perhaps 23 million being a more accurate figure. Although this poll involved only Americans, studies have shown the NDE to be a universal experience.

Speculated Reaction?

I believe that only a small segment of the general public would even consider the possibility of a UFO/afterlife connection. UFOs to the popular mind are occupied by ETs from another solar system, not by humans who have further evolved in a paraphysical civilization entered via death. Such a crazy idea would appear to be the product of a misguided mind!

---

2. Durant, p. 9.
3. Durant, p. 20.
4. Gallup, 1982, pp. 185-190.
5. Graham, 1987, pp. 34-35.

The Theological Community

The subject of life after death is most closely associated with the teachings of religion. How would theologians react to the conclusion that we have drawn from the UFO experiences of Betty and others?

Circumstances of country of birth and cultural exposure make my scope limited in this area. I can only speak from the viewpoint of Christian theology. I trust that others from different religious backgrounds will study the possible effects of UFO experiences and those of others upon their own belief systems. Such studies, of course, would have to be purely hypothetical, but they nevertheless may prove to be valuable in the future if more evidence is forthcoming to substantiate the UFO/afterlife hypothesis.

To UFOs

Unfortunately, within some segments of Christendom, UFOs are just as unwelcome to the halls of theology as theology is to the UFO research community! I have been very much immersed in both communities and have often tested the theological waters for reactions to UFOs. This has been accomplished by study, correspondence, questionnaires after UFO presentations and one-on-one conversations with ministers, priests and lay persons.

I have found that the theology of the fundamentalist and evangelical wings of the church would be most adversely affected by UFOs bearing non-earthly entities. These two branches of Protestantism represent what is called Conservative Theology. Fundamentalists are Biblical literalists. Evangelicals approach the Bible with only a slightly more scholarly approach.

Fundamentalists believe in a six-day creation and that man is the crown of God's creation. The idea that super intelligent life from another solar system or dimension would be anathema to them.

Those few fundamentalist professionals that have studied the UFO problem have concluded that UFOs and their paranormal effects are Satanic in nature. UFO entities are considered to be demons or fallen angels.

Interestingly enough, some have equated them with the fallen Watchers mentioned in the book of Enoch. According to Enoch, the spirits of the evil Watchers who raped human females and created hybrid progeny, still dwell on Earth and deceive humankind.... This tradition was incorporated into Christian tradition and theology. The evil spirits of the Watchers became the demons and fallen angels mentioned in Biblical and extra-Biblical writings.

A typical fundamentalist position statement on the subject of UFOs follows:

> Man is being manipulated by outside forces. This manipulation is not by beings from outer planets, but by extraterrestrial beings with the ability to fly through the heavens, not with machines, but with spiritual power. These demons are deceiving humankind.[6]

I would comment here that I do not dismiss the premise that *evil* paraphysical entities exist. Although not investigated as extensively as UFOs and NDEs, professional studies of demonology present anecdotal evidence for the reality of such malevolent beings.

It is significant to mention in this context that some UFO abductees describe their abductors as being very much like the traditional demons. Some abductees described good entities coming to their rescue from such malevolent entities. Their experiences are similar to Betty and Bob's account of being rescued by an Elder. Dr. Thomas E. Bullard records only a few cases of this nature in his detailed study of abduction reports.

UFO Abductions	Bullard	Case 188b
...Reported...shadowy figures who wanted her to follow them.... They [entities] ridiculed her profession of Christian faith, though higher beings were able to overcome these presences.[a]		

a. Bullard, 1987, p. 76.

However, for most of Western culture, the very thought of demons elicits scoffing or laughter. Demons, like many other aspects of the paranormal, are tuned out by a society conditioned by rationalistic materialism.

The best work that I have read on this subject is a book entitled *Hostage to the Devil,* written by Dr. Malachi Martin.[7] Dr. Martin, a former Jesuit professor at the Pontifical Biblical Institute in Rome, was trained in theology at Louvain, specializing in the Dead Sea Scrolls and inter–testamentary studies. He received his doctorate in Semitic languages, archeology and oriental history. He subsequently studied at Oxford and at the Hebrew University.

---

6. Segraves, 1975, p. 184.
7. Martin, 1977.

Dr. Martin is also author of a number of scholarly books including the national best sellers, *Vatican, The Final Conclave, The Jesuits* and *Hostage to the Devil.* From 1958 to 1964 he served in Rome, where he was a close associate of the renowned Jesuit cardinal Augustin Bean and Pope John XXIII. At the time he researched and wrote *Hostage to the Devil,* he was the religion editor of the *National Review.*

I record Dr. Martin's background so the reader will realize that the aforementioned research into demonology was done by a person of academic stature—a person who was given access to unpublished official documents of the Roman Catholic Church.

These documents contained case studies of alleged demon-possessed individuals who received the rites of exorcism by specialists within the Church. Prior to this, the subjects were carefully psychoanalyzed by professionals to ascertain if their symptoms could be related to some known mental disorder.

Dr. Martin presents each case study in some detail. Many of the possessed were those who had become engrossed in occult practices. Their real stories make the fictionalized film version, *The Exorcist,* look tame in comparison. Dr. Harvey Cox, Chairman of Applied Theology at Harvard Divinity school, called Malachi's study "An amazing book...stunning and vivid. From my own perspective, it is the only book that I have ever read that caused deep consternation on my part."

Dr. Martin's studies immediately came to mind during a segment of Betty's OBE tour with one the Elders to a hospital room. There she described what certainly appeared to be evil entities attempting to possess a bed-ridden man. Parts of Betty's experience are pertinent here and thus bear repeating in a summary fashion. [brackets mine]

Betty: He [an Elder] touches my shoulder again and whew! Just bright white light.... We're in another place.... It's like a hospital room.... There's an elderly man lying in the bed and.... Is that weird!

Fred: What's weird?

Betty: There's some, there's some black things that are trying to pull that person [the man in bed] out.

Fred: What do you mean, black thing?

Betty: Oh-h-h! *[Betty is so excited she can hardly get her words out.]* Wait a minute, there's...a light being that's pulling the opposite direction.... It's like there's a tug of war going on for that old man.... It seems like they're pulling something out of him or trying to pull him [his essence, his spiritual body] out of him. Like...I came out of my body—it was like something was trying to be pulled out of his body and there...was a tug of war going on.

Fred: Are they [black things] symbolic of being evil...two forces, like good and evil?

Betty: Yes, it seems like that. It seems like...the black that was at the head. Two black thin things with no features or anything, just like long arms and skinny bodies and a head and some legs...were like hovering in the air pulling...at something. And there was a light being that was at the bottom by the chest and it's pulling at something, pulling back.... And the tall...Elder with me threw two...tiny marble-like balls of light at those two black things, and they took off.

If we take Betty's account at face value, she seems to be observing the typical light being described by NDErs at a dying person's bedside. In the accounts that we have read, often such entities accompany a dead person down a tunnel to the world of light. But, who are the dark entities? Are they the demons of Dr. Malachi's studies—the demons that are mentioned in the religion and cultural beliefs from antiquity?

Evangelicals, although less literal in their interpretation of the Bible, still maintain a rigid but conditional belief in its inerrancy. Some still believe in a six-day creation, others have developed theories of theistic evolution and progressive creationism in an effort to harmonize the Bible with science.

Thus, most still believe that humans are God's crown of creation in the universe. They would view UFOs and their entities as a threat to their belief system. Some have shown some curiosity about UFOs and extraterrestrial life and have speculated how they might fit into their system of theology.

World famous clergyman and evangelical Billy Graham recently discussed his belief in the possibility of extraterrestrial life with David Frost on national television. After the broadcast, I was told that his statement created quite a stir at a leading Evangelical school in my hometown of Wenham. Students at Gordon-Conwell Theological Seminary were shocked by his statement that extraterrestrial life was possible!

Dr. Graham is also probably the only leading evangelical to discuss UFOs and their possible relation to Christian theology in a best-selling book. He writes:

> Some Christian writers have speculated that UFOs could very well be a part of God's angelic host who preside over the physical affairs of universal creation. While we cannot assert

> such a view with certainty, many people are now seeking some type of supernatural explanation for these phenomena. Nothing can hide the fact, however, that these unexplained events are occurring with greater frequency around the entire world and in unexpected places....
>
> Some sincere Christians, whose views are anchored in a strong commitment to Scriptures contend that these UFOs are angels. But are they? These people point to certain passages.... Any attempt to connect such passages with the visits of angels may, at best, be speculation. What is interesting, however, is that such theories are now being given serious attention even by people who make no claim to believe in the God of the Bible.[8]

From my own experience within the evangelical community, most Christians of this persuasion would not be as free-thinking as Dr. Graham on the subject of UFOs.

During my past research into the study of extraterrestrial life and theology (exotheology), I was able to obtain a copy of an official study prepared for NASA by the Brookings Institution. Its results were to be used to help formulate this country's policy relating to the discovery of extraterrestrial life and its subsequent impact on various facets of society, including the scientific community. Pertinent excerpts from this study are quoted below.

> The fundamentalist (and anti-science) sects are growing apace around the world and as missionary enterprises, may have schools and a good deal of literature attached to them. One of the important things is that, where they are active, they appeal to the illiterate and semi-illiterate (including as missions, the preachers as well as the congregation) and can pile up a very influential following in terms of numbers. For them, the discovery of other life, rather than any other space product, would be electrifying. Since the main ones among these sects are broadly international in their scope and are, in some important source of value interpretation, a central social institution, an educational institution, and so on, some scattered studies need to be made both in their home centers and churches and their missions, in relation to attitudes about space activities and extraterrestrial.... It has been speculated that, of all groups, scientists and engineers might be the most devastated by the discovery of relatively superior creatures, since these professions are most clearly associated with the

8. Graham, 1975, pp. 11-12.

> mastery of nature, rather than with the understanding and expression of man. Advanced understanding of nature might vitiate all our theories at the very least, if not also require a culture and perhaps a brain inaccessible to Earth scientists.[9]

Based upon my own study and observations, the above report's conclusions, although penned in 1961, would still be highly relevant today concerning both fundamentalists and evangelicals.

Lastly, we have the liberal wing of the Christian Church, who often embrace the findings of higher criticism both in their interpretation and opinion of the Bible. Their theology would be more humanistic and less dogmatic than conservatives. Thus, some constituents would adversely react to the subject of UFOs for rationalistic reasons rather than for a strictly theological bias. Others would be more apt to accommodate rather than reject the reality of UFOs.

To Near-Death Experiences

NDEs represent a threat to both fundamentalists and evangelicals. They seem to infer a *universalistic* view of life after death rather than judgment and eternal punishment for those outside their faith. Indeed, NDE researcher Raymond Moody reports the following sentiments of those who have had NDEs.

> In most cases, the reward-punishment model of the afterlife is abandoned and disavowed, even by many who had been accustomed to thinking in those terms. They found, much to their amazement, that even when their most apparently awful and sinful deeds were made manifest before the being of light, the being responded not with anger and rage, but rather with understanding.... According to these new views, development of the soul, especially in the spiritual faculties of love and knowledge, does not stop at death. Rather, it continues on the other side, perhaps eternally, but certainly for a period of time and to a depth which can only be glimpsed, while we are still in physical bodies, "through a glass darkly."[10]

Because of publishing reports made by NDErs, Dr. Moody writes that he received caustic criticism from the fundamentalist and evangelical wings of the Christian church.

---

9. House Report No. 242, 1961, pp. 215, 225.
10. Moody, 1976, pp. 97-98.

> The...group of ministers who have voiced criticism of near-death experiences speak from a theological perspective which lies on the conservative side of the spectrum. I am referring to those who say that near-death experiences are directed by satanic forces or evil demons.... For my part, I must confess that it was unsettling to be accused—even if only by implication—of being in league with the devil. My religious belief is very important to me, and one hardly knows how to defend oneself against such an accusation as satanism.[11]

The following statement by Billy Graham is a comparatively soft-spoken summary of a leading evangelical leader's view on NDEs, but differs little in content from fundamentalist theological thought.

> Today the dying experience is more openly discussed; however, many of the accounts I've heard or read of those last moments tend to confuse the biblical doctrines and raise more questions than they answer. A good example is the popularity of accounts of "near-death" experiences, in which a person claims to have approached death (or even died) and then come back to life.
>
> It is not my purpose to doubt the sincerity of those people who have recounted their "out-of-body" experiences.... I have heard many such stories offered in vivid detail, and, without exception, these life-after-death experiences seem to reduce the fear of dying....
>
> But these experiences are not the bases for eternal truths, nor are they a solid foundation for our confidence in life after death. They may be dangerously deceptive. They must be examined in the context of God's Word.... Each man dies once, and there are two possible results and destinations. "Just as man is destined to die once, and after that to face judgment" (Hebrews 9:27). What bothers me about the life-after-death stories is that regardless of whether the person is a believer or not, seldom in these experiences does death appear to have any negative consequences—which is a direct contradiction of the Bible's teaching.... If all death experiences are the same, there is no judgment or hell, and the Word of God is a lie. We do not presently know for certain what the source is for those "out of body" experiences. Some have even suggested they are sometimes satanic in origin, since they can deceive people about the true nature of death and salvation, and (in this view)

11. Moody, 1977, pp. 58-59.

are a satanic counterfeit of the Christian's assurance of heavenly rest.[12]

Many liberal theologians would not consider Christianity to be an exclusive religion. Their emphasis would also be more on social reformation rather than Biblically-based evangelism. They would not necessarily have the same concept of heaven and hell as their conservative counterparts. Dr. Raymond Moody stated the following concerning the reaction of liberal Christian ministers to his research and books.

> One kind of objection has come from some theologically liberal ministers who see the function of the church as essentially an ethical task, having to do with advancing social reform and helping to establish social justice for all. From this theological perspective, they seem to have come to the conclusion that concern with survival of bodily death is old fashioned. I have heard several such ministers remark that they feel that the concern with life after death is vanishing, or at least that it should be...in keeping with this viewpoint, an elderly...minister's...antagonism toward the study of near-death phenomena seemed to be based on the concept that doctrines of afterlife have sometimes represented disguised attempts at social suppression.... I have found ministers who will not discuss near-death experiences because they feel that they represent medical phenomena. On the other hand, several physicians have told me that they would not discuss such experiences with their patients because they feel that they are within the realm of the patient's religious life. In short, it appears that to some people, this phenomenon is one of those areas lying between two worlds which is predestined to be unpopular.[13]

Other ministers theologically somewhere between liberal and conservative persuasions were more amicable to Dr. Moody's work.

> Numerous ministers have told me that they have had parishioners who told them of near-death experiences; they seemed pleased to get the insight of someone whose professional background lies outside the ministry. Quite a few ministers have told me that they feel these experiences confirm things which are said about life after death in The Bible.[14]

---

12. Graham, 1987, p. 40.
13. Moody, R. A., 1977, pp. 556, 61.
14. Moody, R. A., 1976, p. 53.

And, I would be remiss to mention in passing that what used to be the Unitarian-Universalist wing of the Christian Church has regularly embraced UFOs, NDEs and other paranormal into a eclectic theology similar to that of the "New Age" movement. I write "used to be" because this denomination voluntarily removed itself from the Christian Church.

Speculated Reaction

Based upon what we have just read and my overall contact with both conservative and liberal elements of the Christian church, the idea that the UFO phenomenon and the afterlife are intimately related would be utterly rejected. Conservatives would label it as the devil's propaganda, and most liberals would think the whole idea preposterous!

The Ufological Community

Mainstream Researchers

I have been a member of the UFO research community for more years than I would like to remember. UFO research has taken up a large portion of my life. Thus, I am cognizant of the prevailing attitudes and theories relating to the nature and origin of UFOs.

The vast majority of researchers interpret the UFO phenomenon in terms of a physical nuts-and-bolts civilization visiting Earth from another solar system. The paranormal aspects of the UFO phenomenon are either summarily dismissed or explained as the paranormal effects of advanced technology.

What about the closely related theological components found in UFO experiences such as those reported by Betty? This aspect was discussed by leading UFO researchers at the MIT abduction conference. Budd Hopkins, John Carpenter and Richard Hall are on the leading edge of abduction research, and their comments probably sum up the three positions held by most of the ufological community. Their judgments, if you recall, were quoted in the introduction to this book. In summary they are as follows:

Hopkins: The biggest cloud on the horizon...is a kind of theological argument which...is essentially a waste of time.

Carpenter: Perhaps that's their method of coping with it.

Hall: That's the way the experiencers, certain ones, seem to be taking it. To them it's...beginning to be a profound philosophical, religious issue.

An elaboration of these comments is reflected in the three major positions below.

1. Any attempt to deal with the nature of the phenomenon, especially when related to a theological interpretation, is "a waste of time.... We've got to get people away from those judgments." Thus, Hopkins and others would insist that researchers just concentrate their attention on what is happening to human beings and help them explore their own personal experiences. They would place reports containing theological elements as a manifestation of "paranoia or rationalizations...a certain kind of a denial."

2. The second position suggests that abductees interpreting their experiences within a theological context are superimposing their belief system over them. Some believe that Betty Luca has done this very thing in order to cope and preserve her Christian belief system.

3. The third position acknowledges that the theological component is cropping up in a number of abduction reports as an integral part of the abduction experience. The abductee, not the investigator, is reporting this seeming aberration. The idea is coming from the abductees themselves, who thoroughly believe it to be the very quintessence of their experience.

Please realize that I am not being critical of any of these positions. They are being presented only to compare the current mindset of mainstream ufology as opposed to the hypothesis presented in this book. I do not expect an enthusiastic response!

Borderland Researchers

I have selected two researchers on the outer fringe of mainstream research. I believe that their hypotheses best accommodate the concepts presented in this book. They are Jacques Vallée, who advocates alternate hypotheses for the physical ET origin of UFOs, and Dr. Barry Downing, who equates UFOs with phenomena recorded in the Bible. First, let us discuss Dr. Vallée and his findings.

Formerly, as I was a strong advocate for the nuts-and-bolts nature and physical ET origin of UFOS, I was dismayed to see Dr. Vallée and Dr. Hynek move toward a paraphysical hypothesis for the nature and origin for UFOS. However, the Andreasson case and subsequent studies of other cases slowly but surely had me join their ranks!

It is not my intention to present Vallée's thoughts in detail within this short chapter. A few quotations will suffice to gauge the reaction of those who support Vallée's paraphysical postulate for the nature and origin of UFOs. The lead-in quote for this chapter clearly demonstrates Vallée's point of view in a nutshell.

Vallée is clearly stating that from our perspective, UFOs and their entities have the ability to be physical in our plane of existence. At the same time, he states that they are a non-physical form of consciousness from another plane of existence. In essence, when we observe the UFO phenomenon, we are looking through the window of another mode of reality.

It is also significant that Vallée is the only veteran UFO researcher that exhorts UFO researchers to come to terms with the similarity between the UFO and NDE phenomenon.

> It is time to accept the fact that the UFO phenomenon is able to act upon the minds of human beings, to induce thoughts and images that are similar to those described by people who have had near-death or out-of-body experiences and even to medieval witnesses of demons and elves.[15]

The contents and conclusion of this book are certainly in harmony with Vallée's above exhortation to the UFO research community. Vallée also may be right about OBE and NDEs being mental images *induced* by the UFO phenomenon. However, I believe that the evidence more strongly points to their being real objective events. My examination of the evidence being collected by UFO and NDE researchers indicate that UFOs and NDEs are different manifestations of the same phenomenon.

Vallée, far from being a theologian, nonetheless has recognized the possibility that religion may also be yet another manifestation of the UFO phenomenon. He writes that:

> It is in the literature of religion that flying objects from celestial countries are most commonly encountered.... The fundamental texts of every religion refer to the contact of the human community with a "superior race" of being from the sky. This terminology is used, in particular, in the Bible.[16]

---

15. Vallée, 1990, p. 144.

What is interesting and somewhat paradoxical is the fact that scientists like Vallée, rather than theologians, are making a UFO/Bible connection! This is also true of scientists outside of UFO research altogether, as can be easily illustrated in the following paragraphs.

Leading radio astronomer/SETI researcher, Dr. Frank Drake, theorizes that the account of Ezekiel, which I discussed in detail earlier, may be related to extraterrestrial visitation.[17]

Carl Sagan mentions the Soviet ethnologist M. M. Agrest's hypothesis that "events described in the Bible were in reality based on the visit of extraterrestrial astronauts to the Earth" and states that "such hypotheses are entirely reasonable and worthy of analysis."[18] "As had Agrest, the Soviet astronomer Kazantsev also suggested that angels could be men from space."[19]

It is no wonder that Billy Graham is amazed that such ideas are being entertained by non believers. Dr. Graham's statement provides an excellent lead-in to the introduction of Dr. Barry Downing. Downing is the other person selected to gauge the reaction of borderland researchers to the hypothesis posed by this book. Downing, like Vallée and others, also recognizes a UFO/Bible connection. The difference, however, is that Downing is a member of the cloth.

Downing currently serves as a member of MUFON's Advisory Board of Consultants in the field of theology. However, since he is not as well known as Vallée, a brief resumé of his credentials is in order.

Dr. Downing pastors Northminster Presbyterian Church in Endwell, New York. His undergraduate work was in physics. He received a Divinity degree from Princeton and a Ph. D. degree from the University of Edinburgh, where he specialized in the relation between science and religion. His hypothesis can be best summarized from the publisher's remarks on the cover of his book, *The Bible and Flying Saucers:*

> The author presents his revolutionary concepts by placing the world of the Bible and the world of space travel, flying saucers, and relativity theory side by side to explore the possible relationships between the two worlds. Beings from "another world" are reported in both the Old and New Testaments. These beings, angels or messengers from another world, often seem to be associated with some sort of space vehicle ("the pillar of cloud and of fire," "the clouds of heaven,"

---

16. Vallée, 1969, p. 3.
17. Sullivan, 1964, p. 241.
18. Sagan, 1966, p. 241.
19. Vallée, 1965, p. 166.

> "the wheel in the sky," "the chariot of fire") which could correspond to today's flying saucer and UFO reports....
> Far from destroying the Biblical concept of God, Dr. Downing's interpretation strongly supports it—the invisible God who makes himself known through mediators. His exposition bridges the Jewish and Christian faiths by comparing beings from, or in, the "other world" (God, Jesus, angels and Elijah, who was reportedly taken away in a UFO) significant to both groups of believers.[20]

Based upon Biblical accounts and the new physics, Downing, like Vallée, proposes that UFOs originate in "a universe coexisting in the same space with our own universe."[21] Downing's hypothesis comes the closest to Betty's belief in a divine origin for the UFO phenomenon.

If we strip away the religious connotation of Biblical reports of aerial phenomena and heavenly entities, Vallée and Downing are not too far apart in their hypotheses. Both propose that UFOs and their entities have a paraphysical nature. Both propose they originate from an "invisible world" or "other mode of reality."

Speculated Reaction?

Based upon the statements and attitudes of the UFO research community, I believe that only those on the fringe of mainstream ufology will consider the hypothesis proposed in this book worthy of further consideration. This conclusion notwithstanding, I would exhort both UFO and NDE investigators to begin to examine the results of each other's research for the purpose of comparative analysis. Particular attention should be given to those reports dubbed "mixed motif" by Dr. Kenneth Ring. If this book provides the catalyst for such a cooperative study, its publication will have been well worthwhile.

The Author

I am sure that many by now believe that I have completely abandoned my earlier physical ET/space traveler hypothesis. No, I have not. If we take abductee's reports at face value, we are dealing with entities from another plane of existence that can travel through the far reaches of outer space with ease. What I have changed my mind about is the nature of such beings and their craft. I do not believe that they are physical in the sense of what we believe this word to mean.

---

20. Downing, 1968.
21. Downing, 1968.

The entities' nature and their world of light are not impeded by the physical laws that govern our plane of existence. They can appear physical in our space-time, but that is only because of their ability to manipulate matter and energy. Betty was also told that their technology, like themselves, was paraphysical in nature.

> They have technology that man could use.... It is through the spirit, but man will not search out that portion.

The entities revealed to Betty that their mode of travel is through the manipulation of space and time. In essence, they are not bound by the space-time constraints that restrict interstellar space travel by humans.

> The future and the past are the same as today to them. Time to them is not like our time, but they know about our time. They can reverse time. Time with us is not your time. The place with you is localized. It is not with us. Cannot you see it?

Many CE-III and CE-IV reports contain references to time by UFO entities. Some of these reports regarding time reflect the capabilities revealed to Betty by the entities.

It is not in the scope of this book or the capability of the author to scientifically discuss the existence of theorized time warps, worm holes and the probable existence of multiple dimensions of reality proposed by the so-called new physics. The NDErs travel through a tunnel to another world may be analogous to the methodology of space travel via a technology that weds matter with spirit, a technology that can instantly move in space from one point to another without physically traversing the distance between them.

The late Dr. Hynek illustrated this concept to me during a visit. Holding up a piece of white paper horizontally, he drew points A and B in the middle of the paper on each sides respectively. He then proceeded to show how human technology would travel from A to B. He drew a line along the top of the paper from A to the edge of the paper. He proceeded to go over the edge and backtracked the line along the lower portion of the paper until it reached point B. Then, he took the point of the pencil and punched it through the thin paper from A to B. He smiled and said, "That's how *they* may do it!" A simple illustration, but a capability far removed from us in our world of localized time.

Where are other dimensions? They certainly are not going to be discovered by optical and radio telescopes. They may coexist with us here on Earth, in the solar system or anywhere in the universe. Their essence may be just as physical in their realm as ours is on our Earth. Perhaps the life forms of light who dwell in such realms are the rule in the universe. Their use of matter to evolve forms for pure consciousness to dwell in may be more of an exception than the rule.

It all boils down to a chicken and egg-like paradox. Which came first in the universe: consciousness or matter? Matter as we know it may just be an expression or creation of consciousness that has always existed. All religions and philosophical discussions about origins boil down to just two possibilities. Either matter itself is eternal or it is created by an eternal consciousness (God?). And, what is matter? The answer to this question brings us right back to the nature of UFO/NDErs and their timeless world of light.

Not too long ago, Newtonian physics described the makeup of the universe in terms of molecules composed of atoms made up of electrons, neutrons and protons. NDE researcher Dr. Melvin Morse comments:

> That has been the accepted view of matter—until about fifty years ago. Then science discovered an even smaller world than the atom. They call this tiny world wave/particle duality.... Physicists have split the atom into smaller and smaller particles, they have discovered to their surprise that there is no final tiniest part of nature. Rather, here are forces best described as wavelengths of electromagnetism, or light. These pieces of light serve as the fundamental building blocks for everything. What this theory tells us is that everything we consider to be real actually breaks down into simple light, in all of its various wavelengths. This is the same message that came from many NDErs in the study. As one patient said, "I could see the light in all my own cells and in the universe. I could see that light was God."[22]

Our physical bodies, perhaps even consciousness itself, are in their final essence composed of light. We may appear to be but animate star dust to the materialists of this world. The old adage, dust to dust, may still apply for all outward appearances. But, it was light from which we came and light to which we shall return.

The world of light is our home. What we do there, and where we go from this place in forms that are uninhibited by time, is something to ponder during our short time here on Earth. It brings to my mind

---

22. Morse, 1992, p. 135.

once again what abductee Patrolman Herbert Schirmer was told by one of his captors who pointed to the starry sky: "You yourself will see the universe as as I have seen it!"

Appendix A

List of Hypnosis Sessions

SESSION #	DATE	HYPNOTIZED	HYPNOTIST
1	11/06/92	Betty	Fred Max
2	11/21/92	Bob	Fred Max
3	2/26/93	Betty	Fred Max
4	3/21/93	Betty, Bob	Fred Max
5	5/02/93	Betty	Fred Max
6	5/08/93	Betty, Bob	Fred Max
7	10/17/93	Bob	Fred Max
8	11/13/93	Betty	Fred Max
9	4/06/94	Betty	Bob Luca

Appendix B

Credentials of Fred Max (Hypnotherapist)

Fred Max has a B.A. in Psychology and an M.S. in Research and Quantitative Analysis. He is a member of the International Society for Professional Hypnosis. For nearly two decades, Fred has taught hypnosis to area physicians, psychologists, nurses and dentists. He has lectured on hypnosis and behavioral medicine at Boston College Graduate School of Behavioral Medicine, Southern Connecticut State University, University of Massachusetts, Westchester Community College, American Cancer Society, and many other area Universities and organizations. Fred has appeared on television many times in conjunction with the UFO abduction phenomenon. His work has been published in leading books on this subject including *The Andreasson Affair Phase II, The Watchers* and most recently in *The Watchers II.* He has also prepared a demo tape on hypnosis for interested parties.

Fred uses his hypnosis and counseling skills in the areas of weight regulation, smoking cessation, regressions, stress reduction, pain management and sports motivation. Fred may be reached at the following address and phone number.

Fred Max
425 Juniper Lane
Cheshire, CT 06410
(203) 272-6346

Raymond E. Fowler

Biography

Raymond E. Fowler was born in Salem, Massachusetts, and received a B.A. degree (magna cum laude) from Gordon College of Liberal Arts. His career includes service with the USAF Security Service and with GTE Strategic Systems Division. He retired early as a task manager and senior planner involved with major weapons systems development.

Ray's contributions to ufology are respected by UFO researchers throughout the world. His investigative reports have been published in congressional hearings, military publications, newspapers, magazines and professional journals in the USA and abroad. The former USAF UFO projects' chief scientific consultant, Dr. J. Allen Hynek, called Raymond Fowler, an "outstanding UFO investigator.... I know of none who is more dedicated, trustworthy or persevering." Ray currently serves as national director of investigations on the board of directors of MUFON, the Mutual UFO Network, an international group that investigates UFOs.

He constructed and operates Woodside Planetarium and Observatory and offers star shows, telescope viewing and beginners' courses for children and adults on the subjects of astronomy, origins, vegetable gardening, freshwater fishing and UFOs.

Ray has presented thought-provoking slide shows on both UFOs and astronomy to hundreds of adult and children's groups throughout and beyond New England. These include programs for colleges, public schools, professional engineering societies, lodges, church groups, social clubs, Boy Scouts and Girl Scouts.

Bibliography

Alexander, John B. "Comparative Phenomenology: Near-Death Experiences and UFO Abductions," *Alien Discussions: The Unabridged Proceedings of the Abductions Study Conference.* Ed. Andrea Pritchard, David E. Pritchard, John E. Mack, Pam Kasey, Claudia Yapp. Cambridge, MA: North Cambridge Press, 1994, 342-347.

Atwater, P. M. H. *Coming Back to Life.* New York: Dodd, Mead & Co., Inc., 1988.

Binder, Otto O. "Flying Saucer Mother Ships," *Saga,* (December 1967), 36.

Boston Globe Magazine, (October 11, 1992), 20-27.

Boylan, Richard J. *Close Extraterrestrial Encounters.* Newberg, Oregon: Wild Flower Press, 1993.

Bullard, Thomas E. *UFO Abductions: The Measure of a Mystery.* Mount Ranier, MD: The Fund for UFO Research, 1987.

___. "Abductions in Life and Lore," *International UFO Reporter,* vol. 12, no. 4 (1987), 17.

Companion Bible. London, England: The Lamp Press.

Carroll, Lewis. *Through the Looking Glass.* New York: Random House, 1946, 30-31.

Charles, R. H., Ed. *The Book of the Secrets of Enoch.* Oxford, England: Clarendon Press, 1896, ch. 1-3.

Connor, Steve. "Scientists Note Dramatic Decline in Sperm Count," *San Francisco Chronicle,* (March 8, 1992), A-1.

Coxe, Cleveland A., Ed. *The Ante-Nicene Fathers: The Testaments of the Twelve Patriarchs.* Michigan: William B. Eerdmans Publishing Co., 1951.

Crane, Frank, Ed. "The Protevangelion, Chapters III and XIV," *The Lost Books of the Bible,* New York: Bell Publishing Co., 1879.

Davenport, Marc. *Visitors From Time.* Murfreesboro, TN: Greenleaf Publications, 1994 2nd ed.

Davies, Paul. *Other Worlds.* New York: Simon & Schuster, 1980, 185.

Downing, Barry H. *The Bible and Flying Saucers.* New York: J. B. Lippincott Co., 1968.

Durant, Robert J. "Evolution of Public Opinion on UFOs," *International UFO Reporter*, vol. 18, no. 6, 9.

Evans, Craig A. *Noncanonical Writings and New Testament Interpretation.* Peabody, MA: Hendrickson Publishers, 1992, 23, 31.

Fatima Crusader (brochure). Servants of Jesus and Mary, Fatima House, RD #1, Box 281, Constable, NY 12926.

Fell, Barry. *America B.C.* New York: Pocket Books, Division of Simon and Schuster, 1979, 1989, 265-266.

Fiore, Edith. *Encounters.* New York: Doubleday, 1989.

Fowler, Raymond E. The Andreasson Affair. Newberg, Oregon: Wild Flower Press, 1994 Reprint.

___. *The Andreasson Affair—Phase Two.* Newberg, Oregon: Wild Flower Press, 1994 Reprint.

___. *The Allagash Abductions.* Newberg, Oregon: Wild Flower Press, 1993.

___. *The Watchers.* New York: Bantam, 1990.

Gallup, George, Jr. with William Proctor. *Adventures in Immortality.* New York: McGraw-Hill, 1982, 185-190.

Gaster, Theodor H., Ed. *The Dead Sea Scriptures in English Translation.* New York: Doubleday Anchor Books, 1956, 63.

Graham, Billy. *Angels.* New York: Doubleday & Co., Inc., 1975.

___. *Facing Death and the Life Hereafter.* Minneapolis: Grason, 1987.

Hall, Richard H., Ed. "Satellite Objects," *The UFO Evidence,* (1964), 25, 27.

Harvard Magazine, (March-April, 1992), 6.

Hopkins, Budd, David M. Jacobs, John E. Mack, and Ron Westrum. *Unusual Personal Experiences: An Analysis of the Data fromThree National Surveys Conducted by the Roper Organization.* Las Vegas, NV: Bigelow Holding Corporation, 1992.

Hough, Phyllis. "Woman Saw UFO for 30 Minutes," *Daily Hampshire Gazette,* (November 18, 1976), 1.

Jacobs, David M. *Secret Life: Firsthand Accounts of UFO Abductions.* New York: Simon & Schuster, 1992.

Jenkins, Tom. "The Hampton Encounter," *Atlantic News & Advertiser,* vol. 7, no. 8 (November 23, 1982), 1.

Joseph Smith's Testimony (brochure). The Sacred Grove, Smith Farm, Palmyra, NY.

Jung, Carl G. *Flying Saucers.* New York: The New American Library, A Signet Book, 1959.

Kahn, Fritz. *Design of the Universe.* New York: Crown Publishers, Inc., 1954.

Keyhoe, Donald E.. *The Flying Saucer Conspiracy.* New York: Henry Holt and Co., 1955.

Lawson, Alvin H. "Position Statement," *Encyclopedia of UFOs,* New York: Double Day & Co., 1980.

Love, Scott. "20th SPSS Cuts Down on Mystery Tracks," *AFSPACECOM Publish Affairs,* (August 1992), 5.

Mallan, Lloyd. "Ithaca's Terrifying Flying Saucer Epidemic!" *Science & Mechanics,* July, 1968, 31-33, 96.

Martin, Malachi. *Hostage to the Devil.* New York: Bantam Books, 1977.

McGinnis, William and Michael Kusiora. "The Molecular Architects of Body Design," *Scientific American,* (February 1994), 58.

McKusick, Marshall. *The Davenport Conspiracy.* Iowa: The University of Iowa, 1970.

McLaughlin, Robert B. "How Scientists Tracked a Flying Saucer," *True,* (March 1950), 26.

Medina, John. *The Outer Limits of Life.* Nashville, TN: Thomas Nelson Publishers, 1991.

Moody, Raymond A. *Life After Life.* New York: Bantam Books, 1976.

——. *Reflections on Life after Life.* New York: Bantam/Mockingbird Book, 1977.

Morse, Melvin, with Paul Perry. *Closer to the Light.* New York: Villard Books, 1990.

——. *Transformed by the Light.* New York: Villard Books, Random House, 1992.

Moulton Howe, Linda. *A Strange Harvest.* Video (1980, 1988).

——. "Moving Lights, Disks and Animal Mutilations in Alabama," *MUFON 1993 International UFO Symposium Proceedings,* 1993, 39.

Abduction Roundtable Video. Narr. Fred Whiting, Mt. Rainier, MD: Fund for UFO Research, 1992.

Pratt, Rutherford H., Jr. *The Forgotten Books of Eden.* New York: Bell Publishing Co., 1953.

Prophet, Elizabeth C. "Jubilees," *Forbidden Mysteries of Enoch,* Montana: Summit University Press, 1983.

"Proposed Studies on the Implications of Peaceful Space Activities for Human Affairs," House Report No. 242, (1961), 215, 225.

Rampa, T. Lobsang. *The Hermit.* London, England: Corgi Books-Transworld Publishers, Ltd., 1971.

Randles, Jenny. *Alien Abductions.* New Brunswick, NJ: Inner Light Publications, 1988, 22, 57.

Randles, Jenny and Peter Warrington. *UFOs: A British Viewpoint.* London, England: Book Club Associates, 1979.

Rawlings, Maurice. *Beyond Death's Door.* New York: Bantam Books, 1979.

Ring, Kenneth. *The Omega Project.* New York: William Morrow and Co., 1992.

Rogo, D. Scott, and Ann Druffel. *The Tujunga Canyon Contracts.* Englewood Cliffs, NJ: Prentice-Hall, 1980.

Sabom, Michael B. *Recollections of Death: A Medical Investigation.* New York: Harper & Row Publishers, Inc., 1982.

Sagan, Carl, and I. S. Shklovskii. *Intelligent Life in the Universe.* San Francisco, CA: Holden-Day, Inc., 1966.

Segraves, Kelly L. *The Sons of God Return.* New York: Pyramid Communications, Inc., 1975.

Sitchin, Zecharia. *The 12th Planet.* New York: Avon Books, 1976.

___. *The Stairway to Heaven.* New York: Avon Books, 1980.

___. *The Wars of Gods and Men.* New York: Avon Books, 1985.

___. *Genisis Revisited.* New York: Avon Books, 1990.

___. *The Lost Realms.* New York: Avon Books, 1990.

Shrine of Our Lady of La Salette (brochure). The National Shrine of Our Lady of La Salette, Ipswich, MA 01938.

Smith, Marcia S. *The UFO Enigma.* Library of Congress: Congressional Research Service, March 9, 1976, CRS-37.

"Sperm Counts Are Way Down," *Daily Courier,* (September 11, 1992), 10B.

Strieber, Whitley. *Transformation.* New York: Beech Tree Books, William Morrow, 1988.

Sullivan, Walter. *We Are Not Alone.* New York: McGraw-Hill Book Co., 1964.

Swindoll, Charles. *Living on the Ragged Edge.* Waco, TX: Word Books, 1985.

Swords, Michael D. "Ufonauts: Homo Sapiens of the Future?," *MUFON UFO Journal,* No. 202 (February 1985).

Vallée, Jacques. *Passport to Magonia.* Chicago: Henry Regnery Co., 1969.

___. "Anatomy of a Phenomenon: Unidentified Objects in Space?" *Scientific Appraisal,* (1965), 1a.

___. *Confrontations.* New York: Ballantine Books, 1990, 144.

Vanderkam, James C. "Implications for Judiasm and Christianity," *Symposium at the Smithsonian Institution: The Dead Sea Scrolls After Forty Years.* Washington, D. C.: Biblical Archaeology Society, 1991, 1992.

Wall Street Journal, (May 14, 1992), A1.

Whiting, Fred, narrator. "Abduction Roundtable" video. Mt. Ranier, MD: Fund For UFO Research, Inc. 1992.

Wilson, G. L. "Section 2: Deep Space UCT Processing: 2.0, UCT Acquisition," *Uncorrelated Target Precessing Book,* (February 16, 1993), Par. 2.0.1, p. 8.

Va[illegible] Jacques [illegible] Chicago [illegible]

[illegible] Theatre [illegible] Order [illegible]

[illegible] Press [illegible] the Beach [illegible]

[illegible] James [illegible] 1960 [illegible] Salt [illegible] Wash. [illegible]

[illegible] Federal [illegible] 1976 [illegible]

[illegible] Rogers [illegible]

[illegible]

List of Figures

Index

A

O

P

Q

R

S

T

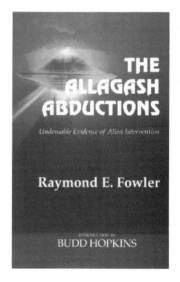

Raymond E. Fowler's

THE ANDREASSON AFFAIR

The Documented Investigation of a Woman's Abduction Aboard a UFO

If you have not read the intriguing Volume I of the Andreasson series, it's a must read! It will give solid background to an astonishing case of ET abduction, recounting gripping tales of genetic experiments and actual contact with ETs.

> *"This book,...if true, must rank with the great classics of scientific revelation."*
>
> *New York Times*

ISBN 0-926524-25-9 Trade Paper: $13.95

And...

THE ANDREASSON AFFAIR—PHASE TWO

The Continuing Investigation of a Woman's Abduction by Extraterrestrials

The harrowing tale of a Massachusetts housewife and her discovery of lifelong contact with ETs continues! The Andreasson case continues with Betty's discovery of ET visitations throughout her life, starting at age 5! This fascinating sequel both answers many of the questions raised by the first Andreasson Affair and presents some extraordinary new facts.

ISBN 0-926524-28-3 Trade Paper: $15.95

S & H is $3.00 for each book and $.75 for each additional book.

The WATCHERS

The Secret Design Behind UFO Abduction

RAYMOND E. FOWLER

The third book in the Andreasson case, which dares to ask the question:

"Why are they here?"

$5.99

ALL BOOKS AVAILABLE THROUGH WILD FLOWER PRESS.

CALL 1-800-366-0264 TO ORDER TODAY!